KT-117-616

WHO'S THAT GIRL?
WHO'S THAT BOY?

CLINICAL PRACTICE
MEETS POSTMODERN
GENDER THEORY

Lynne Layton

THE ANALYTIC PRESS
2004 Hillsdale, NJ London

© 2004 by The Analytic Press, Inc., Publishers

All rights reserved. No part of this book may be reproduced in any form:
by photostat, microform, electronic retrieval system, or any other means,
without the prior written permission of the publisher.

Published by The Analytic Press, Inc.
101 West Street, Hillsdale, NJ 07642
www.analyticpress.com

Tyepset in 11 pt. Goudy Old Style

Library of Congress Control Number: 2004103400

ISBN: 0-88163-422-0

Printed in the United States of America
10 9 8 7 6 5 4 3 2 1

WHO'S THAT GIRL?
~HO'S THAT ~OY~

CLINICAL PRACTICE MEETS POSTMODERN GENDER THEORY

Worcester College of Technology

0129628

Bending Psychoanalysis Book Series
Volume 2

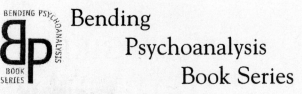

Bending Psychoanalysis Book Series

Jack Drescher, M.D., Series Editor

Contents

To my many families

Foreword—Who's That Analyst?

Gender beliefs. They are in the air we breathe. They are almost as invisible as air. In fact, because gender beliefs are often taken for granted, their component parts can be difficult to examine. For this and other reasons, the Bending Psychoanalysis Book Series is proud to re-present Lynne Layton's *Who's That Girl? Who's That Boy?* For by inviting us to ponder embedded beliefs about masculinity and femininity, Layton ably shows how gender is socially constructed.

The subject is a timely one—and relevant not just to the clinicians and academicians for whom this book is written. There is a growing tension in today's culture between competing groups that are trying either to reinforce or to eliminate "traditional" categories of masculinity and femininity. On the conservative side of the issue, gender categories are treated as normative, god given (or evolutionarily given, in some cases), and necessary and vital to maintain social stability. The deconstructive side, on the other hand, regards rigid gender categories as oppressive, man made, and an unnecessary obstacle to a social inclusivity where one's gender (or sexual identity) is not prescriptive of one's life choices.

The deconstructive project relies on "gender bending," an activity in which stereotypical notions of masculinity and femininity are turned on their head. Often this is done playfully (although irony has a role as well). In fact, the playfulness of gender-bending can be quite dramatic—as in the stage performances of drag queens or beginning New York's gay pride parade with hundreds of "dykes on bikes." But playfulness is also evident in the work of serious contemporary scholars like Layton. Winnicott (1971), an early devotee of psychoanalytic paradox, noted that "serious" and "playful" are not necessarily contradictory:

Playing facilitates growth and therefore health; playing leads into group relationships; playing can be a form of communication in psychotherapy; and, lastly, psychoanalysis has been developed as a highly specialized form of playing in the service of communication with oneself and others. The natural thing is playing, and the highly sophisticated twentieth-century phenomenon is psychoanalysis [p. 41].

It is with "serious playfulness" in mind that the Bending Psychoanalysis Book Series was originally conceived. Among other things, we intend to further a growing dialogue between psychoanalysis and the playful deconstructive approaches of gender studies, gay and lesbian studies, and queer theory. *Who's That Girl? Who's That Boy?* is just such a project. Layton, at heart, is a clinician doing seriously playful work.

There are many questions to ponder in Layton's work. For example, she asks how gender beliefs—what we believe about our own genders and what we believe about those of others—are transmitted from outside the self to inside. Traditional psychoanalytic approaches appear to have sidestepped the question. For example, Robert Stoller (1985), an innovative—one might even say gender-bending—analyst of his time, drew on the early work of John Money (Money, Hampson, and Hampson, 1957). Following a psychoanalytic tradition that concretizes mental processes and functions, Stoller, defining them as psychic "structures, posited the existence of a "core gender identity" (CGI) that "tells" people whether they belong to one gender or the other. It remains uncertain, however, what these structures are made of.

Relational analysts like Layton, on the other hand, do not believe in psychic structures. Instead, they argue that gender identities are forged in a relational matrix, an ongoing dialogue/performance with the culture regarding the meanings of masculinity and femininity. Cultures, of course, do change with time and so do cultural beliefs about gender. Freud's notions of masculinity and femininity are no longer ours. But how would one describe psychoanalysis' core gender beliefs today? What immediately comes to mind is Justice

Potter Stewart struggling to define pornography: he said he knew it when he saw it! Many analysts seem to hold similar views about masculinity and femininity: they know it when they hear about it.

Gender beliefs are an important clinical issue, regardless of a patient's reason for entering treatment. To be clinically useful, psychoanalysis must also be self-conscious about the social matrix in which its assumptions are embedded. We take on the irrational beliefs of patients, but what if our assumptions are equally irrational, or at least unquestioned? Furthermore, the cultural tensions between gender conformity and gender bending can be found in the narratives of many patients—but only if one knows how to listen for them. Layton certainly does. In addition to showing us how she listens to her patients, she also invites us to consider contemporary expressions of gender beliefs through her original analyses of pop star personas (Madonna), films (*Blue Velvet*), psychoanalytic theory (Kohut), and postmodern theory (Judith Butler and others).

Reading *Who's That Girl? Who's That Boy?* one is left wondering why some life stories unfold in the language of gender. Why, to paraphrase Susan Coates (personal communication), are some people "more gendery" than others? I am not certain that anyone really knows. But I am certainly glad that Lynne Layton is more gendery than most analysts and that she is willing to share her insights with the rest of us.

References

Money, J., Hampson, J. G. & Hampson, J. L. (1957), Imprinting and the establishment of gender roles. *Arch. Neurol. & Psychiat.*, 77:333-336.

Stoller, R. (1985), *Presentations of Gender*. New Haven, CT: Yale University Press.

Winnicott, D. W. (1971), *Playing and Reality*. New York: Routledge.

Jack Drescher, M.D.
February, 2004

Preface

A male client of mine, who is married to a female, recently pointed to his heart and passionately told me, "I am bisexual, and bisexuality is my core." An alcoholic in recovery, he added that just as he felt that being an alcoholic is core to who he is, whether he is drinking or not, so, too, is being a bisexual. Although he has not had a drink in two years, he acknowledges frequent cravings to taste alcohol and to be high; it is this that makes him identify himself as alcoholic. Although he is married and loves his wife, he recognizes frequent desires to be with men sexually and he has erotic feelings for men that are different from his erotic feelings for women.

Since I am a clinician who is interested in postmodern theory, this particular moment in our session had great resonance for me and evoked what I shall describe in the rest of this book as a struggle—both a struggle in how I understood what he was saying and a struggle with what to do clinically. I was not sure what I made of his description of a core sexual identity or a core alcoholic identity. Postmodern theory has made me suspicious of words such as *core*, words that evoke a fixed identity, one that is natural, outside of social construction, not subject to change. And yet I very well understood why what he was describing felt core to him—I even think I understand what a core feeling feels like. So what do clinicians trained in object relations and relational analytic theories do with such a moment? Certainly we try to understand as best we can what the client means when he says he is alcoholic and bisexual at his core, what he understands by the categories *alcoholic* and *bisexual*. In questioning this, we are postmodernists; that is, we do not assume that these categories have a fixed meaning, transparent and

intelligible to all. But do we question what he means by *core*, or do
those of us schooled in Winnicottian notions of the true self just
assume we know what he means? Do we question, as a postmodernist
would, the very way that he conceives of selfhood? If his bisexuality
is core, then what does it mean to be married? And to be married
to a woman? Do we assume, as most postmodernists would, that any
notion of core or self is not only imaginary but inherently oppressive because it reduces heterogeneity to homogeneity, or do we, as
some postmodernists might, applaud the fact that the client takes
for granted that he can be married to a woman and also be bisexual,
that he has acknowledged the multiplicity of identity?

   With regard to sexual desire, do we normalize bisexuality as the
logical result of what postmodernists see as the fluidity of sexuality?
Or do we wonder whether, in fact, the client is gay and using his
marriage as a way not to act on forbidden homosexual desire (in
which case the clinician might want to ask whether he recognizes
frequent desires to be with other women)? If we think he might be
gay, aren't we then subscribing to yet another version of essentialism, another kind of core (he thinks he's bisexual, but he's really
gay)? And with regard to gender, do we assume that, just because
he looks like what we call a man, he *feels* like a man with men and
with women? What does it do to our ideas of gender identity if he
tells us he feels like a certain kind of man with some men/women
and a different kind of man with other men/women—or that he feels
like a certain kind of woman with some men/women? Do we call
such fluidity pathological, assuming that people ought to have a
unified gender identity? Or do we act on the postmodern assumption that all gender identity is fluid, that the definition of masculinity presumes that of femininity as its other, that the two are never
found in isolation?

   As is the case with many clients such as this one, we discovered that his gender and sexual fluidity are but two of many parts
of his identity that shift between two values, one of which has cultural and familial approval and the other of which does not: for
example, businessman and artist. Many of these situations are experienced as either/or states; he is pained by the feeling that he has to

choose one and deny himself the experience of the other. Is what we are seeing in the sex/gender realm, then, real fluidity or a kind of splitting? Is there anything in the postmodern conceptual arsenal that can help us distinguish between a fluidity that reflects the capacity flexibly to try on identities and a fluidity born of trauma, in which a person oscillates between polarized and split-off parts of the self?

These questions, the ones asked and the ones unasked, continuously vex me as a clinician sensitive to the way that sexism, heterosexism, racism, and class inequality have historically found their way into psychoanalytic theory and practice. While I still am not sure that I agree with the poststructuralist assertion that our very grammar, which marks the "I" as separate from its attributes and deeds, is oppressive, a view that complicates discussions of "agency," I am certain that I want to understand more about such assertions.[1] And I want to know what the implications of that assertion might be for clinical work, which is highly individualistic and often devoted to helping the client feel more agentic. When I first began work on this book, I could not imagine questioning the certainty of a client who called him/herself heterosexual and who had not found that designation problematic, had not seemed to suffer from it. After years of engaging with postmodern theories, particularly those that claim that these clear designations always involve pernicious exclusions that

---

[1]My sources for the postmodern theories that inform this book are almost exclusively in postmodern feminist culture criticism. Sarup's (1993) introduction to postmodernism and poststructuralism distinguishes poststructuralism from structuralism as follows: poststructuralism is focused on the critique of structures, which always presume a center, a fixed principle, a hierarchy of meaning, and a solid foundation/origin. Bertens (1995) produces a history of uses of the idea "postmodernism," and I follow his decision to include poststructuralism as a particular version of postmodernism. Bertens's book suggests that there are really only a few things that the dizzying number of postmodernisms have in common: a respect for and elaboration of heterogeneity in self and other, and a breaking down of boundaries between entities perceived to be in opposition, such as high and low art. In this text, I distinguish among several variants of postmodernism and poststructuralism.

affect not only one's experience of self but also how one treats others, I begin to imagine asking such questions.

For those clinicians who know little about postmodern theory, this book provides an introduction to its multiple incarnations. In each chapter, I struggle with the value and difficulty postmodern views of gender and sexuality offer clinicians. Having been trained in the relational analytic paradigm, I seek compatibilities and incompatibilities between relational and postmodern theories. More specifically, each chapter of the book approaches the connection between postmodern feminist theories and relational analytic feminist theories from a different angle.

Postmodern theories have perhaps been most positively received among clinicians critical of mainstream psychoanalytic discussions of gender and sexuality. Many of those clinicians who have adopted precepts of postmodern theory, however (see, for example, most of the essays in Glassgold and Iasenza 1995), unproblematically combine a poststructuralist critique of, for example, heterosexism, with Winnicottian notions of a true (for example, lesbian) self or Kohutian notions of a cohesive self. This is done without recognizing that such constructs are anathema to poststructuralists, that poststructuralism is critical of anything core, essential, unified, or coherent. If we want to be poststructuralist clinicians, does that mean abandoning such constructs? Is it possible to *be* a poststructuralist clinician? While I most certainly do not give a clear answer to these questions, I do raise the issues of compatibility and incompatibility, and so I hope that this book will also be useful for those clinicians who are already engaging postmodern theories.

Finally, I hope that this book will be useful to academic psychoanalytic feminists of all schools. For those few who are already familiar with relational psychoanalytic theory, the book represents a clinician's attempt to integrate postmodern views with the views of relational analytic feminism. For those who exclusively use Freudian and Lacanian psychoanalytic models, I offer the book as an introduction to the valuable contributions of relational analytic theory and clinical work. The various chapters were written at different times and for different occasions, some for clinical presentations, some for academic journals of cultural theory, some for psychoanalytic journals, and some for presentations on popular culture. The introduction, however, begins with neither clinical work nor postmodern theory but with a discussion of social movements. I begin here because the social movements of the '50s, '60s, and early '70s raised the issues about identity and subjectivity, about the effects of oppression on identity and subjectivity, that made me want to become a clinician. Indeed, those movements raised the questions about culture, identity, agency, and freedom that relational feminist analytic theory and postmodern feminist theory seek to answer, and that is why the two schools of inquiry are important to me as clinician, feminist, academic, and seeker of a just society.

Acknowledgments

The essays in this book are the product of years of conversations with clients, with friends and colleagues, with students, with texts, and with editors. My greatest debt of gratitude goes to my clients, who have given me a rich appreciation of the complexities of negotiating a gender identity. I want also to thank the members of my postmodernism and clinical practice study group: Susan Fairfield, who has put almost as much time into this book as I have and whose insights and readings have been enormously challenging and helpful; Carolyn Stack; Joel Greifinger; Richard Nasser; and Jill Bloom. I have been in a feminist theory study group since about 1984, and I want to thank those friends in it who have nurtured a feminist spirit: Nadia Medina, Ann Murphy, Katy Conboy, and Sarah Stanbury. Barbara Schapiro and Jean Wyatt were wonderful readers of several chapters and great conversation companions. I want also to thank Wini Breines, Doreen Drury, Seyla Benhabib, Peter Kassel, and Claudia Tate for stimulating readings and conversations. My students at Harvard University, Beth Israel-Deaconess Hospital, and the Massachusetts Institute for Psychoanalysis have all contributed greatly to the ideas in this book; special notice goes to the students in my courses on popular culture for keeping me situated in the '90s. Thanks are due to those who have provided me with rich and collegial academic homes: the Psychiatry Department of Harvard Medical School and Harvard University's Committee on Degrees in Women's Studies. For their inspiring texts, I especially want to thank Jessica Benjamin, Judith Butler, Nancy Chodorow, Virginia Goldner, and Tania Modleski. For their editorial expertise and support, I want to thank Catherine Monk and Cindy Hyden. And for their love, I want to thank my parents, Shirley Goldberg and the late Marvin Goldberg; my brother and sister-in-law, Jeffrey Goldberg and Anne Koterba, who, among many other things, gave me a getaway house in which I could think my thoughts; my favorite analyst, Roberta Isberg; my significant other, Oliver Buckley, who really gets it; and my unbelievably large and wonderful circle of family and friends.

1

Introduction

The social movements of the '50s and '60s—civil rights, the student movement, the women's movement, and gay liberation—made visible a plethora of identities and experiences heretofore rendered invisible by the power of postwar dominant culture not only to appear homogeneous and democratic, but seemingly to secure consensus on this appearance from its citizenry. Once in motion, each of the social movements played a major role in spawning the next one, for each time a liberation movement formed around one identity element—race, for example—consciousness was raised about oppression toward other identity elements, such as gender or sexual preference. As people in coalitions such as the pre-1965 mixed race and gender Student Non-Violent Coordinating Committee rubbed up against differences with "others," both group and individual identities were revealed time and again to be multiple and contradictory. White women in SNCC, for example, wanted to join black women in a protest against the organization's sexism, but for black women race proved a more politically crucial identity element than gender at that time. When whites were expelled from SNCC, two of the white women—Casey Hayden and Mary King—joined the student movement, where sexism was also rampant, and they became cofounders of the predominantly white "women's liberation movement" (see Evans 1979).

These social movements harbored a multiplicity of identities and interests, but they tended to operate within an essentialist paradigm that we now refer to as *identity politics*. White feminism assumed that there was some identity that all women shared and argued for rights on that basis; gay and lesbian liberation assumed that sexuality defined an identity; when SNCC expelled white people, the assumption was that black liberation was for black people. But as the history of these movements reveals, the definitions of identity that were formulated reflected the interests of those who formulated them. Though these definitions claimed to cover all the members of the group, they tended both to include and to exclude. From the beginning, women of color did not feel that feminism spoke for them; NOW's early history of homophobia certainly played a role in the movement for lesbian separatism. Each new movement defined identity in a way that would accommodate those excluded by earlier definitions, but still they excluded.

While activists in the nineties continue to struggle for the rights and visibility of people of color, of women, of gays and lesbians, theorists have turned their attention to the nature of the multiple and contradictory identities and experiences that the movements made public and to the way that dominant groups exercise the power to silence heterogeneity both within the self and within the population. Cynics might say that social activism has given way today to an apolitical preoccupation with identity and the psyche. But the writings of white academic feminists, people of color, queer theorists, and others in fact carry on the left political work of the earlier movements, revealing that the ways the movements conceived identity tended to replicate structures of domination and weaken the movements. In the later 1970s and 1980s, for instance, those women of color who never felt a part of "women's liberation" elaborated striking theoretical critiques of that movement's assumed white middle-class female subject. In so doing, they not only presented different models of raced and classed gender identities and agencies, but importantly revealed the way that the "white female subject" is constructed in relation to, and in a power differential from, the "non-white female subject" (see, for example, Alarcon 1990, Collins 1990, hooks 1990, 1992, Moraga and Anzaldúa 1983, Sandoval 1991, Smith 1984). While challenging identity politics, theorists give identity its due as they explore the histories of particular groups constituted around identity elements: the history of gay men, of black middle-class women, of working-class lesbians. This theoretical work is quite political, not least of all because it counters a dominant mood in the country today to return to the fifties fantasy of homogeneity, a mood reflected in backlash legislation against affirmative action, welfare, and abortion rights; in the racist, sexist, and homophobic behaviors of the "angry white male"; in the hysteria over legalizing gay marriages and in the Supreme Court ruling that invokes free speech to bar Irish gays and lesbians from marching in St. Patrick's Day parades.

Some of the theoretical work on identity has occurred in the languages of Anglo-American psychoanalytic theory (object relations, intersubjective theory, self psychology, relational-conflict theory). I will refer to this work broadly as "relational." Some has occurred in the several languages of postmodernism/poststructuralism (by which I mean those that draw on the work of Derrida, Foucault, Lacan, Lyotard, Baudrillard, or Deleuze and Guattari).[1] And some occurs in a genre of proliferating autobiographical writings in which, for example, white women and women of color locate themselves psychically and socially in relation to dominant and marginalized sub-cultures (Pratt 1984, Anzaldúa 1987). The legacy of social movements is a tension that structures these current debates on identity: identities are multiple, contradictory, fluid, constructed in relation to other identities, and constantly changing—they have no essence; yet, at the same time, people in groups identify or are identified as like,

---

[1]In this text, I work with Lacanian feminist culture criticism. For an introduction to Lacanian clinical work, see Dor 1997a,b. A good introductory text on Lacan is D. Evans 1996. A good introductory text on Derrida is Norris 1987. See Kellner 1989 on Baudrillard, and McNay 1992 on Foucault and gender. Key primary texts are Deleuze and Guattari 1983, Derrida 1976, Foucault 1980, Lacan 1977, Lyotard 1984.

and they produce histories that lend their identities coherence over time. Are identities then fluid, or cohesive, or both? This question preoccupies academic and clinical theorists alike.

The impetus for writing this book is my attraction to postmodern deconstructions of identity and my struggle to make sense of postmodern theories in relation to Anglo-American clinical theory and clinical work. I first engaged with postmodern theory in Lacanian feminist film criticism, then in Lacanian and Derridean feminist discussions of identity fluidity, and finally in Foucaultian feminist work on the discourses and institutions that produce subjectivity, gender identity, sexuality. There are many versions of postmodernism, but the one that is important for clinicians to engage with is the one that challenges the metanarratives of Western culture (see Lyotard 1984). This version critiques particular tenets of the Enlightenment: the rational, unified subject at the center of bourgeois discourses (law, psychology, medicine, science), the belief that history has a teleology and always moves in a progressive direction toward its end, and the belief in essences and "universal truths" that hide their own social constructedness—and do so to guarantee privileges to some subjects and not to others. This postmodernism makes us aware that categories such as *woman* are used to constrict the multitude of ways that women can be; that heterosexuality and homosexuality, masculinity and femininity have been produced as discrete identities to ensure the continuance of compulsory heterosexuality and male dominance, whereas they in fact co-construct one another; and that the historically shifting white-establishment definitions of what constitutes a black identity reveal that the construct *race* is not an essence but a socially constructed fictive category.

As a clinician drawn to postmodern theories, I find that my growing awareness of the fictional status of gender, sexual, and racial categories keeps bumping up against my awareness of how these categories are experienced psychologically. The tension is well captured in Gates's (1996) discussion of the life and work of Anatole Broyard, literary critic and writer. Broyard, a "black" man, passed as a "white" man for all of his adult life. Broyard accurately felt that were he to "come out" as black he would be expected to write as a black: to write about black writers, about race. His interests, on the other hand, lay elsewhere, in European high modernism for example. The postmodernist Gates wonders: If Broyard successfully passed, was he black or was he white? Black and white are revealed as culturally constructed fictions.

But Gates shows us another side to this story. To pass as white, Broyard repudiated his family, particularly its darkest members. Some of Broyard's racist remarks suggest that he not only passed, he repudiated blackness. When we look at the psychic and other career effects of Broyard's disassociation from "blackness," we get a sense of why clinicians might be loath to regard racial (or gender) categories as fictions. For Gates and those he interviews imply that Broyard's choice to repudiate blackness made him unable to do the very thing he most wanted to do: write good fiction. His always autobiographical fiction had a hollow ring; it was psychologically unconvincing. On the cultural level, then, Broyard's life reveals that race is a fiction. On the individual level, the one immediately present in clinical work, we find that Broyard could not so simply choose his race and that he did not escape the psychological effects of race assignment. In a racist culture, race is a fiction that is deeply lived. And often it is in part lived as traumatic.

Until the past few years postmodern and psychoanalytic relational languages have appeared mutually exclusive, and postmodern feminists, particularly Lacanians, have actually been quite dismissive of the object relations tradition. Recent work suggests, however, that some of the seeming differences between postmodern and relational discourses on identity may be "false antitheses" (Fraser 1995). For example, relational work on the multiplicity of identity (Bromberg 1996, Mitchell 1993), the effect on the patient of the subjectivity of the analyst (Aron 1991, 1992, Hoffman 1983), and the recognition of uncertainty and paradox in the analytic situation (Ghent 1992, Hoffman 1987, Pizer 1992) is clearly compatible with a postmodern paradigm.

This book focuses on the gender theories of postmodern and relational analytic feminists, and there are similarities among them as well. For example, postmodern feminism's attack on "humanism" is in part an attack on the way that the propertied, upper-middle-class white Western male successfully arrogated subjectivity to himself for centuries and denied it to others. This was accomplished via a proliferation of laws, literatures, and medical discourses that presumed that the interests of this dominant group of property owners were coincident with the interests of everyone else in the society, that their interests were "human" interests. As Barthes (1972) and many others in the postmodern tradition have shown, the process involves generating narratives and images that make what is historically class-, race-, and gender-specific look universal, natural, timeless, and mythic. Feminist theorists in the object relations tradition have articulated a similar critique of the autonomous male Enlightenment subject. Their work focuses on the psychology of this subject and how it is culturally reproduced. Clinically, their concern is with the narcissism of this subject, the way the inability to see the other as a separate subject with his/her own interests is structured into this subject's gender identity, agency, and modes of relating.

If the problem is narcissism, then we might ask whether postmodernism actually offers a new way of figuring identity or whether, like relational analytic feminism, postmodernism is more accurately described as a critique that unmasks the narcissism of the Enlightenment subject—a critique that reveals what a politically motivated modernism hopes to conceal about identity. Stuart Hall (1987), a black Jamaican British academic, reflects on this question by examining his own experience. After many years of being consigned to the margins, he notes the irony that his experience of himself as dispersed and fragmented has become normative, even celebrated, in the postmodern world. He finds himself centered by claims that "identity" is by nature de-centered, claims made by his white British colleagues in Lacanian, Derridean, and Foucaultian traditions. Hall wonders whether "this centering of marginality [is] really *the* representative postmodern experience" and he concludes that it is not, that there is a continuity between the modern and the postmodern: "what the discourse of postmodernism has produced is not something new but a kind of recognition of where identity always was at" (p. 115).

My interest in postmodernism as critique comes from this same sense that it describes "where identity always was at"—but in very new ways. Foucaultian critiques of identity begin with the force of institutions; Derridean and Lacanian critiques begin with the force of language. I started my history of contemporary discussions of identity with social movements, because the narcissism of the universal subject first began to be unmasked when nonwhites, feminists, gays, and lesbians made their own subjectivities and interests public. Postmodern theories have helped me understand some of the ruses of the narcissistic subject and how a variety of cultural discourses, including the discourse of psychoanalysis, function in tandem to sustain myths of universality and naturalness. At the same time, I have found Anglo-American psychoanalytic theory necessary to understand the psychological workings of narcissism (Fairbairn 1954, Guntrip 1971, Kernberg 1975, 1976, 1980, Kohut 1971, 1977, 1984).

In the following pages, I bring postmodern, feminist, and psychoanalytic discourses on gender, agency, and relationship together in what I hope will be a fruitful conversation/confrontation (see Flax 1990). Despite Flax's (1990) work on the topic, most Anglo-American clinicians have not yet come into contact with the difficult ideas and even more difficult languages of postmodern theories. In Anglo-American psychoanalytic feminist circles, a tradition has evolved over the past twenty years that interweaves a focus on gender with the insights of object relations theory, self psychology, infant research, and relational or intersubjective theory. While, as I suggested above, there are points of intersection between these discussions of gender and those of postmodernists, the different languages and different presuppositions about subjectivity have made it difficult for the two camps to meet in meaningful discussion. In the rest of the Introduction, I explore tensions between the two sets of languages that are generated by the different assumptions about self, other, culture, and identity that structure the theories. I will look at the following interrelated points of tension: (1) the place of culture in the construction of the subject; (2) subjectivity, culture, and the practice of psychoanalysis; (3) the use of the terms *self, individual, ego, subject*; (4) the account of agency; (5) the account of the other and the relation between self and other; (6) the functioning of categories; (7) fluidity and coherence. Differences in the way these are conceived reveal the possibilities and difficulties of incorporating postmodern ideas into clinical work. In describing and critiquing some of the differences between postmodern and relational theories, I define the working assumptions of self, other, and agency that inform the rest of the book.

SOURCES OF TENSION BETWEEN RELATIONAL AND POSTMODERN IDENTITIES

The Place of Culture in the Construction of the Subject

When postmodern academics use the word "psychoanalysis," they usually mean the theory of Lacan or Freud. Indices to postmodern psychoanalytic texts rarely contain references to Benjamin, Fairbairn, Guntrip, Kohut, Mitchell, or Winnicott. An often reiterated Lacanian criticism of object relations targets what Lacanians see as a narrow focus on the mother–infant dyad. Such a focus, Lacanians argue, entails a denial of culture, for in Lacanian theory there is no subject before culture enters the scene in the form of the paternal function or third term that wrests the child from a fantasied unity with mother (the imaginary). To avert psychosis, the paternal function enforces the incest taboo and brings the child into the symbolic, the site of difference and lack (Mitchell and Rose 1985). This "castration," which also requires the child to assume one of two gender positions, is the founding moment of Lacanian subjectivity, for it is the entry into language that leads to the inevitable rupture between desire and its fulfillment, between meaning and being. A subject is internally divided, non-coincident with itself; only in fantasy is plenitude possible.

Foucault's (1973, 1979, 1980, 1982) version of postmodernism is a genealogy of the institutions and discourses that produce, construct, and maintain the modern subject, and one of his major contributions has been to clarify how the coming into being of the subject is a process that involves subjection to the power relations that criss-cross these institutions and discourses. Foucault's writings suggest that the modern individual exists as multiple and contradictory positions in discourse. Rather than experiencing cultural coercion as external, this sub-jected subject internalizes a cultural system of surveillance and thus disciplines and punishes his own body, sexuality, and consciousness in what seems like consensus with the dictates of culture.

Judith Butler (1990a, 1993), whose work represents one of the most interesting poststructuralist positions on gender and agency, has added that the process of becoming a subject with mind and body is one that dictates what kinds of minds and bodies are speakable, what kinds unspeakable; what parts of the body are sanctioned as erogenous zones, what parts are not; what counts as a gender identity and what does not; and which sexual practices have legitimacy and which do not. Butler (1995a) contends that the heterosexual subject is constructed upon a culturally enforced taboo against, and an ungrieved disavowal of, same-sex love. Her contentions go much further than feminist object relations critiques, which, until recently, have had as their subject middle class white male and female heterosexuals. (Chodorow's recent work [1994] interrogates the "normalcy" of heterosexuality. See O'Connor and Ryan [1993] for a discussion of the long history of psychoanalytic theory's heterosexist assumptions.) Yet, as other critics have pointed out (Abel 1990), Anglo-American relational psychoanalytic theories, which focus not only on intrapsychic processes but on the developing child's caretaking environment, take into account the specificity of the experiencing subject in the context of his/her relationships and thus have the potential to allow one to elaborate individual or group histories in a way postmodern theories, with their universalized schemas of power (Foucault) or the imaginary/symbolic/real (Lacan), or "différence" (Derrida) might not (see Dews 1987).

This tension between individual specificity and cultural processes has been much discussed among clinicians who are also gender theorists. Some Anglo-American relational feminists have argued that postmodernists and clinicians have a hard time communicating because they each address a different level of subjectivity. For example,

Jessica Benjamin (1994b) has recently pointed out that much of postmodern theory mistakenly equates the subject that is a position in discourse—a construct of multiple and contradictory discourses (for example, "the black middle-class female")—with the psychic self, the conflicted, experiencing self. Frosh (1994), a psychologist and an academic, makes the point four times in the first twelve pages of his book on sexual difference that gender is both a position in discourse, a category of culture to be contested, *and* an intersubjective and intrapsychic element of each individual's sense of self. The question Frosh poses is one that certainly vexes any clinician familiar with postmodern critiques of the gender binary that results from the compulsory assumption of one of two gendered positions: "What can we say or do that might challenge the received wisdom of what is appropriate to being masculine or feminine, whilst also recognising the way people's experiences of themselves are bound up with deeply felt but often implicit notions of what their gender should and does mean?" (p. 1). Chodorow (1995), too, argues that gender is both a cultural and a personal construct, and she implicitly critiques postmodern and other perspectives that undervalue the psychological experience in which one makes idiosyncratic meaning of gender. Her well-taken point is that too few clinicians are aware of the ways that culture constructs gender and too few feminist academics are sensitive to the way gender is constructed and experienced psychologically.

Benjamin, Frosh, and Chodorow underscore an important difference between two levels on which meaning is constructed. If we are to attempt an integration of postmodern and relational theories, however, we have to be clear that these different levels of discourse are not dichotomous: the cultural is psychologically constructed, and the psychological is cultural. The cultural meanings of "black middle-class female" will not exhaust but will be part of the way a girl makes meaning of her gender identity. No part of that identity will be free of culture. But the way a black middle-class girl construes a gender identity at any particular historical moment, the way she puts together the possibilities that circulate in her family and culture, in turn contributes to constructing the set of cultural practices that will define "black middle-class female." Clinicians have a lot to gain from understanding postmodern critiques of the cultural discourses that construct the subject, and postmodernists have a lot to gain from Anglo-American psychoanalytic theory's capacity to capture the specificity, construction, and experience of an individual's inner world and relational negotiations.

Subjectivity, Culture, and the Practice of Psychoanalysis

Like postmodern theories, Anglo-American psychoanalytic theories are also concerned with a general theory of subject formation (which they call developmental theory), and psychoanalytic practice interrogates certain of the discourses and includes at least one of the institutions, the family, that constitute the individual who has come for treatment. But, aside from feminist and Marxist psychoanalytic theory, Anglo-American psychoanalytic theory does not in general have a stake in altering the social status quo and thus does not question the fact that many of its assumptions are uncritically borrowed from the white middle-class dominant culture. For example, the cornerstone of most developmental theory is the heterosexual nuclear family, treated as though it exists in a cultural vacuum. For postmodernists, not only power inequalities between father and mother have to be addressed, but also the assumption that the family ought to *consist* of a father and a mother—or that the family is the best place for a child to grow.

Relational psychoanalytic feminists have deconstructed the Freudian oedipal scenario and pointed to less misogynist directions Freud might have taken in his theorizing (see Sprengnether 1990, 1995), and they have challenged the supposed normality of the monadic individual that is the oedipal scenario's product. Yet, few clinicians or theorists in the Anglo-American tradition of relational theory have talked about the fact that psychoanalysis is one of the many discourses/practices that construct the individual in particular ways (exceptions are usually feminist theorists, e.g., Harris 1995, and Benjamin's [1988] critique of the way psychoanalytic theory has always eliminated the mother's subjectivity). In postmodern discussions, psychoanalysis is not a discourse that helps a subject to discover an identity already presumed to be there. Rather, it is one of the many Western discourses that *produce* identity. Readers familiar with the various two-person psychologies that have been elaborated in recent years will see the connections between postmodern and relational psychoanalytic positions, which also assume that analyst and client co-construct the subjectivities that emerge from the clinical encounter. But relational theories do not generally concern themselves with what postmodern theory insists on as the coercive element of the psychoanalytic enterprise, the fact that psychoanalysis legitimizes some gender identities, sexualities, and ways of being, and delegitimizes others. Nor do non-feminist relational theories show much interest in the cultural strictures that allow some subjectivities to emerge and prohibit others. If we assume that psychoanalytic theories and practices play a constitutive role in producing subjects and theories about subject formation, clinicians need to be more aware than they have been of the kinds of subjects they participate in producing.

Self, Individual, Ego, Subject

A major source of tension between postmodern and relational theories lies in their conflicting definitions of *self*, *individual*, *ego*, and *subject*. Relational theories use *self*, *individual*, and *subject* interchangeably (see Flax 1996, for a critique). Postmodern theories distinguish *subject* from *individual*, *self*, and *ego*, and they tend to assume that *self*, *individual*, and *ego* are equivalent and are essentially narcissistic constructs. Let us look at Lacanian theory as an example. A prime target of the Lacanian theory of subjectivity is American ego psychology, which Lacan accused of having betrayed Freud's most radical discovery—the unconscious. In Lacanian theory, the ego originates in a mis-recognition in the "mirror stage": the baby denies its awareness of its own fragmentation by identifying with its idealized, unified mirror image and by taking this image as exhaustive of its subjectivity. This misrecognition marks the ego as an imaginary structure, a structure built on a fictional coherence. All of the later identifications that make up the ego involve such misrecognitions, and so the ego is constituted by narcissistic fantasies of wholeness and homogeneity that suppress awareness of the subject's heterogeneity and its existential condition of lack. The individual, sustained by the fantasy of indivisibility and conscious control, is the representative of the Lacanian ego. Most postmodern and poststructuralist accounts, psychoanalytic and non-psychoanalytic, share Lacan's understanding of the ego and the individual. As I said earlier, the condition of subjectivity—the incest taboo and the entry into language/the symbolic/culture—is conceived as a loss that splits the subject from himself. The truth of the subject—as distinguished from ego or individual—is that it is split, lacking. A Lacanian clinician, then, as well as a Lacanian critic, figures the cure to the ego's narcissism to be acceptance of the condition of lack.

In relational theories, the self has been defined in a multitude of ways, few of which reduce to the Lacanian view of the ego (indeed, Freud's view of the ego does not reduce to the Lacanian view; see Whitebook 1995). There is an error, I believe, in the postmodern assumption that the self is equivalent to what feminists and postmodernists have critiqued as the controlling consciousness of bourgeois individualism, the autonomous male subject. The postmodern disdain for the term *individual* seems to result from the postmodern conflation of the bourgeois individual (a self-identical entity that is not relationally formed and claims to be fully conscious) with the individual. While the process of subjectivation (becoming a subject) in Western culture certainly includes the internalization of this dominant version of agency and relatedness, I will argue throughout this text that this version does not exhaust even the conscious self. I want to distinguish between *self*, defined as multiple and contradictory and thus akin to Lacan's *subject*, and a *master self* (Fairfield 1996), that is, a self that always suppresses otherness and is pathologically narcissistic.

Versions of subjectivity elaborated by relational analytic theorists do not assume that pathological narcissism is the primary constituent of late-twentieth-century Western identity (see, for example, Benjamin 1988, Bromberg 1996, Mitchell 1988). Relational psychoanalytic theories posit a heterogeneous subject/individual/self who has narcissistic vulnerabilities, but they do not claim, as Lacanians do, that there is a universal structure of subjectivity, a necessary outcome of all people's development (the ego), that is pathologically narcissistic. When pathological narcissism is present, it does not arise from a denial of existential lack but rather from specific familially induced wounds. Clinical work in a relational paradigm suggests that the degree of narcissism that produces oppression and the suppression of otherness is quantitatively greater than and qualitatively different from the degree of narcissism that exists in every psyche. Pathological narcissism and narcissistic vulnerability may exist on a continuum, but the tendency for postmodern theories to equate the two may make it difficult for clinicians to incorporate postmodern theories into their work.

In distinction from postmodern theories, I use the terms *subject*, *self*, and *individual* interchangeably, reserving the term *pathological narcissism* to describe the inability to experience an other as a separate subject and to describe the suppression of heterogeneity both within the subject and between subjects. In distinction from relational theories, which tend to focus on pathological narcissism as an individual rather than a cultural problem, I follow those feminist relational theorists who have argued that dominant versions of femininity and masculinity are marked by pathological narcissism.

The Account of Agency

Because subjection to cultural forces is so central to subject formation in postmodern theories and so absent in relational theories, another source of tension between the two sets of theories concerns the way they conceptualize agency. Diverse theorists who draw on Lacan to critique the cultural status quo struggle to bridge the gap between what, in Lacanian theory, seem to be two different levels of subject formation and two different kinds of agency. In Lacan (1977), the components of originary subject formation—the mirror stage that inaugurates the narcissistic ego, the splitting of subjectivity that results from language acquisition, the compulsory assumption of one of two gendered positions—are set forth as universal, ahistorical processes. Because of this, it is no easy task to bring them into relation with contingent and historical processes of development, such as those that produce racial or class identities or those that produce narcissistic wounds, such as parental or cultural slights. In Lacanian culture criticism (see, for example, Mulvey 1975, Silverman 1996), one finds that wounds produced by parental pathology or cultural pathologies such as racism and sexism are often explained in the final instance as a defense against acknowledging the original wound: fragmentation in language, the inevitable rift between desire and its fulfillment. From a relational analytic perspective, this explanation itself appears as a rationalization that calls on existential necessity to circumvent the pain of acknowledging our dependence on loved ones and the hurt caused by them.

The early processes of Lacanian subject formation figure the subject as sub-jected to cultural systems. Culture and language alienate the subject in the expectations and desires of the other, which exist even before a baby is born. It is not at all clear how later processes would escape that same problematic, since Lacan asserts that all imaginary ego identifications are made on the model of the mirror stage; that is, they are all narcissistic in that they reduce heterogeneity and lack to coherence and unity. The agency of the ego, then, is located in subjects' capacity to deny their essential lack or fragmentation by identifying as whole and unitary. But what does the agency of the subject look like? Lacanian theorists who want to challenge the status quo have found this agency difficult to derive.

Smith (1988a), who has attempted this task, distinguishes between the individual, the subject, and the agent in his reading of Lacanian theory. Although in a footnote Smith recognizes two origins of *subject* (p. 164), one from political theory that focuses on subjection to the state, church, and other hegemonic discursive formations, and one from German philosophy that focuses on the capacity for autonomous critique of authority, he chooses to define *subject* only by the former and to reserve the term *agent* for the latter. He defines the subject as a colligation of seamless subject positions (such as race, gender, and class) provided by family and culture and (mis)recognized by the individual as positions to which s/he belongs.[2] Smith discovers agency in the contradictions and disturbances created in the "subject/individual" by the multiplicity of different subject positions imposed by the culture. Agency is defined as resistance to ideology. However, Smith does not challenge the Lacanian assumption that these subject positions, like originary ego formation, occur on the model of pathological narcissism (for challenges to Lacan's assumption, see Flax 1990; for a critique of Lacan that takes a different direction from mine but which also seeks a way out of narcissism, see Whitebook 1995). Because I challenge this assumption, I prefer to preserve the two origins of *subject* and not reduce the subject to internally coherent subject positions (see de Lauretis 1986). The contemporary subject internalizes more than one version of agency and relatedness, each of which is embedded in particular relational matrices. Conflict arises not from the collision of subject positions, nor from the fact that some of these subject positions are more pleasurable than others (a remnant, in Smith's work, of the influence of Freud's pleasure principle), but rather from the fact that internalizations are products of numerous conflicting relationships, relationships with different degrees of power to approve or disapprove, to give or withhold love.[3] The multiple versions of agency

---

[2]See Althusser's (1971) notion of interpellation, where the person is hailed by the culture as, for example, a gendered individual, and recognizes him/herself as the person who is hailed. How much choice this person has in recognizing or not recognizing the self in the cultural position offered is a subject of debate among those drawn to Althusser (see Morley 1980).

[3]My work, in its focus on the relational core of gender identity, owes a great debt to Goldner's (1991) article, "Toward a Critical Relational Theory of Gender," which brilliantly draws on systems theory, feminist theory, and deconstruction to elaborate the construction, experience, and consequences of the masculine/feminine binary. Goldner argues that "since gender develops in and through relationships with gendered others, especially parents and siblings, its meaning and dynamics must be located, minimally, in a three- or four-person psychology that can make room for the interplay between different minds, each with an independent center of gravity" (p. 262). Goldner's critical relational theory of gender focuses on how "personhood, gender identity, and relationship structures develop together, coevolving and codetermining each other" (pp. 261–262). Along with Flax (1990), Goldner

and relatedness that we internalize are not equally powerful contenders for self-acceptance or expression because they are also subject to cultural proscriptions or cultural approval.

Anglo-American relational theory/practice focuses almost exclusively on the contingent processes of development. The capacity for agency, presumed to exist from birth (Stern 1985), is first observed in the infant's multiple ways of relating (for a critique of Stern, see Cushman 1991). In this view, agency takes shape in relationships, in the various kinds of mutual encounters with early caretaking others.[4] In some of these encounters, agency is identified when infants match the other's affect and behavior or get the other to match theirs. In other encounters, agency is identified when infants resist the other's call to match affect and behavior. It is also identified in infants' attempts to repair a disruption in mutuality. There is little focus on subjectivity as sub-jection in these theories, except in cases where, for example, a narcissistic parent might demand the infant's subjection. The relational school's account of the development of agency does not necessarily conflict with postmodern theories and might provide these theories with more specificity (indeed, there are potential intersections between Stern's theory and Butler's use of performativity). But non-feminist relational theorists tend to omit the cultural context in which agency develops, and this omission obscures the questions postmodernists and feminist relational theorists ask about agency: what cultural functions does agency serve? why assume only one kind of agency? What versions of agency are allowed to develop and what versions are not? (An important feminist debate on agency takes place in Benhabib 1995.)

---

is one of the very few publishing U.S. clinicians who has made the integration of postmodernism and object relations theory her project.

[4] A difference between Smith's position and mine might be seen in the examples of agency each of us would highlight. Smith's model of someone who comes close to incarnating a subject who mediates between being sub-jected and agentic is Roland Barthes. He champions Barthes for constantly undermining his unitariness in relation to his objects (e.g., photos). I would turn instead to Pratt (1984), who constantly undermines her unitariness by interrogating her history in relation to that of others—men, blacks, Indians, lesbians (see Martin and Mohanty 1986).

Clinicians and developmental theorists of the relational school tend not to differentiate between the kinds of interactions that produce individuals and the kinds that reproduce them. Relational theorists thus presume that individuals might become less conflicted, might find more satisfying ways of relating, might feel less self-hatred, and might come to appreciate their own complexity and fluidity, but they tend not to wonder whether agency, affect, and relatedness themselves take shape in a particular cultural field that makes some versions acceptable and others not. In the worst case, this tendency not to wonder produces the individual who reproduces the cultural status quo—which should *not*, to my mind, be the project of psychoanalysis.

The different views of agency again highlight the tension between the postmodern focus on the cultural determination of subjectivity and the relational focus on the microprocesses of mutuality. An integration of the two might ponder the cultural constraints on the ways, for example, female parents and male babies, male clinicians and female clients talk, play, regulate affect, display affect, and so forth, thereby generating particular kinds of agencies.

The Account of the Other
and the Relation between Self and Other

Yet another source of tension between postmodern theories of subject formation and relational analytic theories, one that follows from the above, is the conceptualization of the other and of self–other relations. In most postmodern theories of subjectivation, the other—in the guise of culture, language, and family—is figured as coercive. In Lacan, paternal law wrests the child from a narcissistic fusion with the mother and brings him into the realm of the symbolic. Lacanian theory is called intersubjective by its proponents because the subject is constituted by intersubjectively shared, culturally determined linguistic structures that speak the subject. Those in the Anglo-American psychoanalytic tradition of intersubjective theory, however, will likely not recognize this usage of *intersubjective*, for in Anglo-American theory the term means that the subject's development and his/her desire are mutually negotiated with caretakers from birth, with the child's needs and desires exerting their own independent influence. Winnicott's (1974) "potential" or "transitional" space, a space created between mother and child, is where internal and external, difference and sameness, are continuously negotiated (see Benjamin 1995, Pizer 1992). In relational theories, the attainment of language is not seen to be motivated solely by compensation for loss, nor is language primarily used to cover over lack, as it is in Lacanian culture criticism (with roots in Freud's [1920] discussion of the *fort/da* game). Rather, in the relational school, language acquisition and use are equally motivated by the pleasures of attunement, creative play, a non-defensive liberation from dependence and helplessness (here again we must note the influence of Loewald 1980 and Winnicott 1974). Indeed, relational theories, unlike Lacanian theory, do not envision subject formation as motored solely by loss and the mastery of loss. Rather, the pain of loss and the pleasures of attachment are equally determinant. For instance, Benjamin (1988) roots the capacity both for intimacy and for erotic love in early parent–child moments of mutual attunement. And Winnicott (1965a) writes that the capacity to be alone grows not from mastery of the loss of the other but from persisting attachments to the other. (Winnicott has been egregiously caricatured by postmodern gender theorists.)

These differences in conceptualizing the relation between self and other bear directly on the relation between client and therapist in clinical work. Both postmodern and relational theorists would want the therapy relationship to make new versions of subjectivity and intersubjectivity possible. But they might have different ways of figuring the stance the therapist ought to take to accomplish this. The assumption of relational theory is that agency is structured by the quality of attachments (see Lyons-Ruth 1991). New kinds of attachments open the client to new ways of being a subject, so the presence and subjectivity of the therapist, the kind of relationship therapist and client forge, are stressed in relational theory. It is in relational negotiation, for example, that narcissism is confronted. Attachment is not the starting point of postmodern theories. Lacanian theory assumes that clients will place the analyst in the position of the one who knows, a position the analyst must refuse in order to enable the client to come to know his own desire and to know that he is lacking. The analyst's stance, then, does offer a different kind of attachment (one that refuses imaginary projections), but by the end of analysis the attachment to the analyst should not be constitutive of the client's desire.

Barratt (1993), an analyst who acknowledges a debt to Derrida, claims that the postmodern core of psychoanalysis is free association. Interpretations of any kind, on the other hand, are modernist attempts to re-establish the client within an identitarian logic and so encourage adaptation to the social status quo. Free association, curative in itself, is "a process that works against the fixities, priorities, certainties of every act of interpretive establishment" (pp. 14–15). In Barratt's version of postmodern analysis, the analyst's role is far less constitutive of the process than it is in contemporary relational theories. Ironically, Lacan's and Barratt's postmodern psychoanalytic therapies rely on what seem to be modernist one-person clinical models, while most relational therapies rely on what seem to be postmodernist two-person models (Aron 1990).

The Functioning of Categories

Related to many of the above tensions is the tension between postmodern discussions of cultural categories like *masculine* and *feminine*, and the place of such categories in clinical practice. Derrida's (1976, 1978) work focuses attention on the structural relation to each other of binary pairs of categories such as speech/writing or conscious/unconscious. His writings take aim at the binary logic at the core of Western metaphysics. Derrida contends that the wish to avoid uncertainty, to lay claim to a universal truth that would be the foundation of all we know (be that truth appealed to in the name of God, class struggle, evolution, or core gender identity) is a wish that produces rigid binaries in hierarchic relation. While clinicians have long been aware that black-and-white thinking characterizes such self-disorders as borderline and narcissistic, Derrida alerts us to the constricted black-and-white nature of Western thought in general, and thought is where ideology and power differentials operate.

What about masculinity and femininity? Until fairly recently I would guess that most people, including myself, thought they knew exactly what they were talking about when they evoked these categories; the pages of most psychoanalytic journals still suggest that a lot of people are clear about what masculinity and femininity mean.[5] In everyday language and in mainstream ideologies of all disciplines, including psychoanalysis, masculinity and femininity are presented as mutually exclusive opposites. But they are neither opposite nor are they equally valued: one member of any binary pair, in this case masculinity, is always in a superior cultural position to the other. Derrideans show the way in which masculinity and femininity actually co-construct each other and have meaning only in their relation. Maintaining the categories as mutually exclusive binaries keeps the hierarchical relationship intact. The dominant strand of "difference feminism," which informs much mainstream psychoanalytic writing on gender, argues that women's self structure, ways of knowing, ways of making moral decisions, and ways of using language are different from and as valuable as men's (see the work of Belenky et al. 1987, Gilligan 1982, Miller et al. 1991, Tannen 1990). A deconstructive politics, on the contrary, leads rather to an uncovering of the constitutive connection between men's and women's "ways," and opens the door to other gender/sex possibilities beyond male and female.

In most poststructuralist theories, categories like the master self and the coercive other are also oppressive because they impose unity on heterogeneity. This is one very important way that categories operate—but not the only way. Certainly femininity and masculin-

---

[5]Chodorow (1989) differentiates "psychoanalytic feminists," among whom she includes herself, from contemporary psychoanalysts who write about women and femininity, particularly about the way that femininity is constructed from female anatomy. Included in her discussion of the latter are Kestenberg 1968, Mayer 1985, and Tyson 1982. These defenders of primary femininity elaborate on early work by Horney (1924, 1926).

ity are often evoked defensively to suppress heterogeneity (see May 1986; cf. Thompson's [1995] discussion of clients' defensive use of race). Sexual difference can be used ideologically to obscure the relevance of other categories; for example, see Williamson's (1986) discussion of the way advertisements encourage men of all classes to bond in their domination over women, using gender difference to cover over potentially more explosive class differences. But another function of categories is to facilitate provisional unities that have the potential to transform both the individual and culture. I am thinking of the civil rights, the feminist, and the gay and lesbian movements (see Hacking's [1986] interesting position that categories and the kinds of persons they cover emerge historically at the same time). It is this facilitative function that poses a challenge to proponents of postmodern theories.

Throughout the text, I argue for the facilitating possibility of gender categories. In clinical work, therapists and clients grope for new categories to provide points of identification as they deconstruct the old ones that constrict possibility. Let us look more closely at the difficulties that postmodern views of categories pose for clinical work.

Fluidity and Coherence

When I spoke of the history of social movements, I noted that a central tension arose as theorists and activists sought to respect the histories of particular identities—gay, lesbian, female—yet simultaneously pointed to ways that those identities were not discrete, were co-constructed by what they excluded. This is a version of the problem of the category discussed above. Some postmodern feminists, Butler included, have found it difficult to defend their deconstruction of gender identity while maintaining an allegiance to women's political struggles. Here lies one of the main tensions between postmodernists and their critics. On one side are those who defend identity politics. On the postmodern side are those who find identity a necessarily oppressive and narcissistic construct, one, as we have said, that imposes coherence on multiplicity, that necessarily makes normative inclusions and exclusions. The debate often becomes quite complicated, especially when a group attacks an identity position as exclusionary and thereby in effect constitutes a new identity category. This occurred, for example, when feminists of color began to challenge the white subject of white feminism (see hooks 1981, Moraga and Anzaldúa 1983, and Smith 1984). Their position seems to be that the identity of feminists of color is a decentered, multiple identity that does not impose coherence, that embraces non-identity, and is thus a model for feminist subjectivity (note that some early feminist theory made this claim for women in general, e.g., Rabine 1988).

Butler (1992) has proposed a way to sustain allegiance to feminism while contesting the category *women* with her notion of "rifting," a way of both elaborating a "we" and letting it be open to what it necessarily excludes, which will continuously change the nature of the "we." This "double gesture," however, cannot work as a way to hold identity politics and postmodern politics in tension if each subject making up the "we," as well as the "we" itself, is seen to be exhausted by narcissism. Butler makes a similar point in *Gender Trouble* (1990a) when she speaks of coalition politics. If the people in a coalition do not recognize that their own identities are made up of repudiations of the identities of others in the coalition, the group cannot work. I read this as saying that it can only work if the subjects involved are capable of taking the position of the other, of respecting both difference and likeness. But where Butler seems to see narcissism as endemic to identity, I think that identities need not be mere defenses against difference (see Weir 1996 for a different argument toward the same conclusion).

A very important tension between postmodern and relational theories of identity concerns the dispute over whether or not there is anything about identity that is "core." Many Anglo-American psychoanalytic feminists accept Stoller's (1976a,b, 1985) idea that a core gender identity, that is, the conviction established by 18 months that one is either male or female, is essential to subject formation. In recent work (1995, 1996), Jessica Benjamin has begun referring to this as nominal gender identity. With this switch in terminology, she wishes to maintain the idea that children know by 18 months that they are either male or female; at the same time, she wants to integrate cognitive findings (e.g., Fast 1984) that make it clear that these categories are at first empty of meaning.[6]

The division into male and female is something I would guess few clinicians ever question. Yet such a binary "conviction" is precisely the kind of thing that a poststructuralist such as Judith Butler will challenge. She will want to establish the genealogy of this division and will ultimately want to replace it with other possibilities that she considers less homophobic. For she believes that the division into male and female is not a necessary but a culturally contingent decision, one that guarantees compulsory heterosexuality.

Butler's is a most important project. Yet clinicians meet with people who have at least in part been culturally produced to replicate the status quo. When these people do not replicate it, they usually find themselves in great pain, because they are not met with love and approval. And they want clinicians to make them "normal," they want to fit in. Indeed, clinicians find that those who do not have a conviction of being either male or female do not usually enjoy the fluid identity that postmodernists hold out as ideal but instead often hate themselves and are riddled with shame. A fluid identity is a desirable outcome, but clinical work suggests that fluidity is an accomplishment, not a given—and that achieving it may presuppose the experience of a core gender identity.

The tension between the way gender conflicts are conveyed to a clinician and the way gender is discussed in postmodern theory is the concern of this book. Much of the difficulty postmodernism poses for clinicians arises because postmodernists radically question the very categories that structure what most of us call our "identity," catego-

---

[6]Note the recent study by de Marneffe (1997) that shows that one's sense of gender is not necessarily based on one's bodily experience: children know what genital they have by 24 months but only later know that having it means they are male or female. When looking at anatomically correct dolls with no other gender-identifying features, they know which doll has genitals like their own and know which gender they are, but they don't know which doll is a boy and which a girl. De Marneffe argues that the fluidity between body representation and gender representation continues through life.

ries that anchor us psychologically and relationally: male and female, black and white, straight and gay. Indeed, there is a radical schism between postmodern celebrations of identity fluidity and what most people find it like to live an embodied, raced, and gendered life in contemporary America (see Hennessy 1995). Deconstructive theory and politics argue persuasively that the consequences of maintaining such dichotomous categories can be oppressive both intrapsychically and intersubjectively, but the contemporary uses of deconstructive theory and politics that I discuss in Chapter 5, for example, consistently ignore or underestimate the difficult work of extricating oneself from reified binaries.

Postmodernists charge that notions of a "core" are essentialist, that they fix identity in a way that denies cultural construction and emancipatory practices. But feminist relational theorists' conception of a "core" does not in fact assume the kind of unity postmodernists abhor, the kind that silences otherness (see Abel 1990, Flax 1990, Rivera 1989). In the relational paradigm, *core* does not mean *innate*, nor does it imply a true self. And it is not incompatible with cultural construction. Perhaps the relational and postmodern camps have been falsely polarized (see Brennan 1989, Fraser 1995). But "core" does imply something internal that recognizably persists even while it may continuously and subtly alter, and there are real differences between theorists for whom a constructed interior relational world motivates behavior and those, like Butler in *Gender Trouble* (1990a), for whom interiority is an appearance, an effect of discourse.

Because of what they see in practice, clinicians versed in psychoanalytic theories of self disorder and fragmentation find themselves uncomfortable with the celebrations of fragmentation and fluidity put forth in some popular versions of postmodern theory (for example, Haraway's [1985] cyborg subjectivity). Because of what they see in practice, psychoanalytic relational theorists assert that gender and other identity elements are culturally constructed pieces of an internal relational world that both evolves and is relatively coherent and stable (Glass 1993). It is this stance for coherence, I believe, that most garners the contempt of postmodernists for relational theorists.

CONCLUSION

Given these important differences, can we conceptualize a notion of the subject that is informed both by the postmodern emphasis on the general constituents of subject formation and by the Anglo-American emphasis on its specific, individual relational constituents? Can we find a way to theorize both the coercive and the non-coercive moments of subject formation? I maintain that "the subject" is both a position in discourse (sub-jected to the multiple and contradictory discourses of culture, including family) and a multiple and contradictory being whose negotiation of early relationships will shape the meaning that these discourses take on and so shape the discourses themselves. Of course, it is the nature of this being that is in question: A precultural true self, à la Winnicott? Fully constituted by discourse, à la Butler?[7]

I will define the self/subject/individual as neither a true self nor fully determined by existent discursive positions but rather as a continuously evolving negotiator between relationally constructed multiple and contradictory internal and external worlds. We are both subject to these worlds and create them as we engage in current relations with intimates, groups, and the social environment. We are born into families with their own histories and ways of mediating culture, and so we immediately engage in particular patterns of re-

---

[7]In feminist circles, debates are ongoing about whether the subject is fully constituted by discourse, and about how something new might be generated from what is culturally determined (see Adelson 1993). Judith Butler's position in her introduction to Bodies that Matter (1993) is at one end of the continuum: material reality is always already discursive. Newness is generated from the fact that meaning always exceeds the linguistic categories that try to fix meaning. Another view is propounded by Frankenberg (1993), who seems to equate discourse not with language but with dominant ideology and argues that a person can get a distance from discourse and evaluate it from another place. Frankenberg sees the discursive and the material dimensions of the category she investigates, whiteness, as connected but distinct. The connection generates experience: "Discursive repertoires may reinforce, contradict, conceal, explain, or 'explain away' the materiality or the history of a given situation" (p. 2).

lating. The way those patterns are internalized is conditioned by the
accidents of gender, race, and class and by the power differentials
that structure them at a given historical moment (see Collins 1994).
It is also conditioned by the bodies and temperaments of individuals and those with whom they come in contact. The meanings these
bodies, temperaments, and other individual identity elements take
on are not outside of culture; they are culture. Neither are they reducible to already existing discursive positions, because neither the
individual nor the discursive level is static. Rather they are mutually negotiated and renegotiated. Subjects idiosyncratically make
meaning of, identify with, disidentify with, take up parts of, or modify
these positions in accord with ongoing relational experience.

The fluidity inherent in subjectivity does not originate in the
fluidity of the language that speaks the subject, as poststructuralists
would have it. Rather, the fluidity of the subject and of the meaning subjects make results from the internalized multiple and contradictory relational patterns that both constitute the subject and are
negotiated by the subject. And the stability of these patterns as they
repeat over time accounts for the subject's coherence. This stability
in itself has coercive and non-coercive moments: coercive in that the
relational patterns will inevitably be informed by gender inequality
and other cultural and familial constraints, non-coercive in that the
stability of internalized attachments can be the very thing that opens
one to creative and emancipatory possibilities. Postmodern theories
suggest that oppression and hierarchies of all kinds are created and
sustained by defenses against uncertainty or against existential lack.
My assumption here is that they are created and sustained by defenses against relationally inflicted pain, that binaries in hierarchic
relation are the sequelae of trauma, and that the capacity to go
beyond binaries is a developmental achievement. To investigate relational patterns in their cultural context, we need the insights of
both postmodern and relational theories.

Each of the chapters that follow looks at a different aspect of
the possible integration of postmodern and Anglo-American relational psychoanalytic theories. Each mediates between the particularity of gendered individuals and the social formations that they

act upon and that act upon them. And each investigates the tension between the aspect of the subject that is modern, constituted by binaries, and the aspect that is postmodern and unravels binary distinctions. Chapter 2 proposes a model of gender, agency, and relationship that accounts for the cultural and psychic tensions between dominant and non-dominant versions of femininity and masculinity. Chapters 3 and 4 take a look at gender relations in contemporary popular culture and argue that variants that defend gender fluidity (gender benders) and variants that defend dichotomous gender identities (gender binders) are each best understood by combining a deconstructive and a relational analytic approach. Chapter 3 focuses on gender binding in romance and detective fiction. Chapter 4 takes a closer look at a gender bender, Madonna, and finds that one key to her popularity has been her particular way of holding in tension a modernist conception of identity ("I am in control") and a postmodernist conception (the continuous reinventions of self, each of which deconstructs the binaries that support the fantasy of the unitary individual in control). In Chapter 5, I look at the effects of trauma on gender identity and examine tensions between postmodern discourses that celebrate fragmentation and Anglo-American discourses that connect fragmentation with self-disorder. In Chapter 6, I turn to male development and analyze David Lynch's (1986) film *Blue Velvet*. Here, I show how the universal and ahistorical categories of Lacanian film theory do not capture the subtleties of self-disturbance. An integration of relational theory with postmodern concerns yields a historicized understanding of what postmodern theorists (e.g., Penley and Willis 1988) have called "male trouble." Continuing the "male trouble" theme, Chapter 7 brings postmodern critiques of the gender binary to bear on the stories of two of my male clients who had disidentified with masculinity and identified with femininity.

In many of the chapters, I use Kohut's (1971, 1977) understanding of pathological narcissism as a way to bridge postmodern and relational gender critiques. Kohut's notions of the healthy self, on the other hand, are more problematic. Chapter 8 deconstructs some of Kohut's assumptions to show the gender bias at the core of his theory of the self. Finally, Chapter 9 provides a closer look at the gender theory of Judith Butler, another theorist whose work is central to the book. Here, I examine the evolution of Butler's concept of gender performativity to show how it has become more and more psychoanalytic. Arguing for an integration between Butler's work and relational analysis, I use the connection Butler makes between performance and melancholia to shed light on the social and psychic dynamics of chronic depression. Whether looking at popular culture, clinical material, or theory, the book's analyses all suggest that an integration of relational and postmodern theories provides the best explanatory model for what it is like to experience gender in our particular cultural and historical moment.

2

Beyond Narcissism:
Toward a Negotiation Model
of Gender Identity

In this chapter, I discuss several models of gender that have been proposed by psychoanalytic feminists in the object relations or intersubjective tradition (whom I shall call relational feminists) and by psychoanalytic and non-analytic postmodern feminists. To state my thesis in advance, I want to argue that all of them are interested in gender identity formation only as it informs a larger project: to ground the possibility of a fluid, agentic, heterogeneous self that recognizes its own multiplicity (gendered and otherwise), that does not defensively foreclose on its own (or another's) multiplicity, and that can recognize and be recognized by an other both like and different from the self. While few of the theorists use the term *narcissism*, my sense is that what their projects have in common is their search for a way out of the narcissistic binds that sexism and other forms of oppression impose. All are seeking an intersubjective mode of being, acting, and relating to another, which requires what Kohut (1971, 1977) has called the capacity to experience both self and other as separate centers of initiative and awareness.

While Kohut's theory itself ultimately fails the test of intersubjectivity (see Chapter 8), I mention him because he elaborates a the-

ory of narcissism in which pathological narcissism—the incapacity
to experience self and other as separate centers of awareness—is not
part of the human condition but rather a product of traumas in
development (Kohut also has a concept of healthy narcissism, which
I do not find useful). Because, like Kohut, I take pathological narcissism to be an outcome of developmental traumas and not an originary state to which one regresses or which one never fully leaves, I
want neither to abandon developmental theory nor to abandon a
claim that the outcome of healthy development can be a non-narcissistic mode of relating to self and others. At the same time, I want
to expand the range of developmental traumas beyond the familial
ones Kohut and most psychoanalysts explore to include sexism, racism, homophobia, and class inequality.

As I described in the introduction (Chapter 1), when I use the
word narcissism I have in mind a disturbance in the capacity to
experience both self and other as separate centers of awareness, as
subjects. Pathological narcissism results from various kinds of interferences in the processes of negotiating connection and differentiation, dependence and independence. An overly intrusive parent or
a very neglectful parent, for example, will likely cause narcissistic
injury. Kohut sees pathological narcissism as a problem affecting the
regulation of self-esteem, and he tends to limit the definition of self-
esteem to a particular version of agency: the capacity to work well,
to achieve one's goals and ambitions, to feel energized rather than
empty or depleted (see Chapter 8). In my view, however, self-esteem
problems generally reflect difficulties in negotiating a sense of agency
while maintaining connection. The two processes may be separable
operationally, and, as I shall argue in Chapter 8, they appear as separate in narcissistic disorders. But from a developmental perspective,
capacities for assertion and connection proceed in tandem. Disruptions in attachment cause disruptions in agentic capacities and vice
versa.

Relational feminists like Chodorow (1978) and Benjamin (1988)
have suggested that a culture marked by gender inequality produces
certain kinds of interferences with the negotiation of connection and
differentiation that reproduce hegemonic or normative femininity

and other kinds that reproduce hegemonic masculinity.[1] Gender identities, then, become inextricable from particular modes of self-assertion and relating (Goldner 1991). Gender inequality, located in such social practices as the sexual division of labor and the organization of the work world, the sexual division of bodies, media representations of men and women (see Connell 1987), and the different patterns found in male as opposed to female parenting of boys and girls, is experienced internally as narcissistic injury. Narcissistic wounds are caused when cultural and familial gender expectations restrict the many ways that one can be agentic and relational to two ways: those that define hegemonic masculinity and femininity. These wounds are powerfully conveyed and sustained when parents and other important figures make the giving and withholding of love contingent on a child's gender or on a child's meeting gender expectations. But they are also conveyed in more subtle ways, for example, in the different ways parents hold, play with, or talk to boys and girls. These differences, too, create subjects whose relational and agentic possibilities become constricted and organized in particular ways. Normative

---

[1]What I am after here is a way of translating to the psychic level what theorists talking about culture call dominant or hegemonic (see Hall 1980, and, more recently, Connell 1995). Despite warnings that the use of normative is tricky because so few people incarnate it (Connell 1995), I use it interchangeably with dominant and hegemonic. These terms all refer to what version of, in this case, gender identity has the most cultural clout. Hegemony is sustained by the intertwining of the many social practices that organize a society; a dominant male gender identity involves a particular class and race position as well as a gender position. Connell (1987) speaks of the inequalities in the organization of labor, power (authority), and sexuality (including emotional attachments) that generate gendered experience and thus characterize a particular gender order. The hegemonic version is the one that wants to impose coherence, wants to claim that it exhausts the definition of gender identity. But, both intrapsychically and culturally, other versions compete for dominance and always pose a threat to the continued hegemony of the dominant version (see Gramsci [1971], who first discussed bourgeois hegemony as something that must constantly be re-won in conditions of social struggle). Psychologically, this appears as internal struggle, conflict between multiple gendered, relational, and agentic positions.

gender socialization itself, then, produces narcissistic disturbance and in fact produces differently gendered versions of narcissism (see Layton 1988, Chapter 3 this volume, and the discussion of Benjamin below).

What do these gendered versions of narcissism look like? Hegemonic masculinity is defined by a model of agency that defensively splits off dependency to appear defiantly separate and independent. Benjamin (1988), who discusses the pseudo-separation that characterizes masculine development, makes it clear that hegemonic masculinity qualifies as a disorder of differentiation. Pollack (1995a,b) roots this disorder in the damaging relational sequelae of a too early and too severe abrogation of the boy–mother holding environment, and Kaftal (1991) roots it in the lack of a nurturant preoedipal father. As I said previously, and as the latter theories underscore, gender, agency, and connection develop in tandem, so the hegemonic masculine model of agency goes along with particular modes of connecting. When connection is interfered with and dependency needs are split off, dependency and longings for intimacy do not disappear, but only particular kinds of intimacy—those marked by both dread and longing, devaluation and idealization—become possible.

A hegemonic female model of relationship offers approval for connecting in submissive ways and withholds approval for wishes to differentiate. Autonomy strivings that are not approved of get split off and disavowed, or at least hidden. Again, agency does not disappear, as some early feminist accounts suggested, but it takes particular forms, for example, finding a powerful mate on whom you can depend psychologically and economically. When a girl splits off autonomy strivings or a boy splits off dependency needs, an other is needed to fulfill a function that the self cannot fulfill, and this other is experienced as part of the self and not as a separate subject. Subjects marked by the narcissistic injuries that bring forth these modes of connection and agency, then, do not have a differentiated experience of self and other and thus have great difficulty experiencing their own multiplicity and recognizing that of others. Narcissistic injury and the splitting that follows from it internally perpetuate the reduction of multiple gender/agency/relational options to two polarized but co-implicated complements. Subjects whose gender experience is marked by severe narcissistic injury can oscillate between the two poles but cannot break free of them. The degree of narcissistic injury determines how capable one will be of achieving a mode of relating and differentiating that does not depend on disavowal or splitting.

The above discussion of the processes of defensive splitting makes it clear that there is a difference between hegemonic masculinity and femininity as social structures (sometimes referred to by postmodernists as discursive positions) and as psychic structures. On the discursive level, hegemonic masculinity and femininity present themselves as coherent and non-contradictory—although, as I shall argue, they are always forced to compete with other cultural positions that contest their hegemonic status. But on the psychic level, where splitting is a defense against loss of love or approval, what is split off remains in the psyche and engenders conflict.

My views are clearly indebted to work that has been done before (Benjamin 1988, Chodorow 1978, Dimen 1991, Goldner 1991). I repeat and elaborate on this work here for several reasons. First, after Benjamin and Chodorow were critiqued for essentialism and for the presumption that all psyches are structured like middle-class white psyches (see, e.g., Spelman 1988), the narcissistic structures of masculinity and femininity that they had elaborated seemed to disappear from discussions of gender. Even their own recent work (Benjamin 1996, Chodorow 1994) is more focused on possibilities for what Benjamin calls gender ambiguity than on hegemonic masculinity and femininity. In my view, the shift toward exploring multiple gender and sexual options, while important, ought not lead theorists away from the content of the gender polarities created by gender inequality. For one thing, gender inequality is still very much extant, and for another, these internalized polarities are damaging to the psyche and highly resistant to change.

Second, as recent work by Connell (1987, 1995) suggests, everyone in a culture, not just the white middle class, deals psychically and socially in some way with hegemonic femininity and masculinity (Connell [1995] speaks of several possible negotiations with hegemonic structures, among them the complicit, the marginal, and the subordinate). Despite the critiques of essentialism and universalism leveled at Chodorow and Benjamin, I find that the women and men I see in clinical practice (who range in age from 15 to 55; are all middle-class; mostly, but not all white; homosexual and heterosexual) and many of those I read about in fiction or view in cinema (produced by white, non-white, hetero- and homosexual authors or directors) have psychic constellations similar to those Chodorow and Benjamin described—and this has not been satisfactorily explained away for me by postmodern or other critiques of their work.

Many who write about non-white groups focus on the conscious way these groups resist dominant white culture. But, while those outside the dominant culture may have a different psychic structure from those within, and a potentially critical perspective on the dominant culture, few will psychically escape the narcissistic injuries imposed by white dominance. A relational theory of gender identity has to account for the way dominant and nondominant groups build identity in relation both to their own reference group and to those groups with the power to define what will pass as "normal." Although white middle-class heterosexual femininity may be built on repudiations of stereotypic masculinity, black femininity, and lesbian femininity, the dominant versions that Benjamin, Chodorow, and others describe appear to be internalized in some form by most members of U.S. culture. For this reason, the contributions of Benjamin and Chodorow are no less relevant to the study of gender today than they were ten or twenty years ago.

Finally, I have chosen to continue to work this ground because I have not found many of the poststructuralist psychoanalytic, Foucaultian, or Derridean discussions of gender psychologically convincing. My argument is that the narcissistic wounds that result from gender inequality are an obstacle to the fluid, heterogeneous subjectivity that does not foreclose upon either its own or another's difference, a kind of subjectivity necessary to what I would consider ethical modes of connection and agency. These wounds interfere with development, damaging capacities to tolerate ambiguity, ambivalence, and otherness.

In Part 1 of this chapter I review the early work of Chodorow and Benjamin for what it told us about the narcissistic structure of gender polarities and the narcissistic structure of dominant modes of agency and connection. Then I look for what it is within us that contests these structures. Several theorists have proposed ways to go beyond narcissism. Benjamin (1996) proposes a model that roots the possibility of gender ambiguity in preoedipal development; Sweetnam (1996) suggests a Kleinian oscillation between paranoid-schizoid and depressive gender positions. Poststructuralist theorists have turned to Freud and Lacan to argue for the fluidity within and between gender positions (e.g., Adams 1988, Rose 1986) or to Derrida to argue that the fluidity of language guarantees that gender performances will not obediently cite gender norms (Butler 1993). My argument does not rest on fluidity, gender ambiguity, or oscillation, although pieces of each of these theories have influenced my thought. Rather, in Part 2 I propose that we are products of multiple internalized relational patterns, some of which are marked by narcissistic injuries that reduce multiple options to two and some of which are not. Because the culture designates us and those with whom we interact "male" or "female," every internalized relational identification and every internalized attribute is potentially gendered. This gives rise to diverse possibilities of gender/agency/relationship, many of which contest narcissistic constellations. For example, the cultural division of subjects into male and female has led to social practices such as feminism, practices built from identifications that contest gender inequality. From these practices come new gender/agency/relational options that make it possible to experience one's own multiplicity without defensively foreclosing on the multiplicity of another. Gender identity, then, is a product of relations informed by gender inequality and relations that counter gender inequality; it emerges from the constantly negotiated conflict between these sets of relations.

PART 1: GENDER IDENTITY DEVELOPMENT
AND THE TRAUMATIC IMPOSITION
OF A GENDER BINARY

In their early work, Chodorow (1978) and Benjamin (1988) used psychoanalytic developmental theories to trace the origins and content of gender differences. Like their postmodern counterparts, they worked not only on the individual but on the cultural (although not linguistic) level, arguing that conditions such as the fact that women are primarily responsible for childcare produce particular versions of masculinity and femininity. Chodorow adopted Stoller's hypothesis that when a mother is the primary caretaker—an assumption of both psychoanalysis and the culture at large—her child's first internalized self-representation will be "protofeminine." This insight made it clear to Stoller (1964, 1965, 1968, 1976a,b) that Freud was wrong: the development of gender identity would be far more difficult for a boy than for a girl. Chodorow also agreed with Greenson (1968) that a boy establishes a male gender identity in part by "dis-identifying" from the mother. Where Greenson found this normal, however, Chodorow saw it as a damaging cultural prescription, one that produces a particular version of autonomy. Hypothesizing that both boys and girls develop the capacity for primary relatedness and mutuality in the early relationship with the mother, Chodorow argued that mothers and fathers allow only girls to continue to develop and experience that capacity. To become men, boys must suppress primary relatedness and everything else the culture codes as feminine. Because of father absence, boys tend to take on a gender identity by identifying not with a person but with (sexist) cultural constructs of masculinity. Thus masculinity is constructed in relation to femininity—but as a repudiation of it. The masculine self that develops from these cultural conditions, Chodorow argued, has rigid boundaries, defends against intimacy because intimacy raises the specter of loss of identity, denies its embeddedness in relationship, and maintains a detached and dominant position toward women and its other objects. The masculine sense of self draws self-esteem primarily from successful autonomous activity.

Note that autonomy, in this account, is a product of the afore-mentioned defenses of the masculine self, and not to be confused with how it was understood in Enlightenment tradition, that is, as the capacity for critical reflection and the refusal to submit blindly to authority. For postmodernists, the Enlightenment subject and its autonomy are oppressive. Benjamin, Chodorow, and others (see Benhabib 1995, Weir 1995), including myself, want to preserve the Enlightenment notion of autonomy as the capacity for critique, but want also to differentiate a form of agency cognizant of its embed-dedness in relationships from the hegemonic male model of autono-my that is produced and reproduced from gender, race, and class inequalities.

Chodorow argued that mothers find it more difficult to see their daughters as separate from themselves than to see their sons as sepa-rate, and in fact push their sons toward greater independence, pre-maturely oedipalizing the relationship as well. Using as her data base clinical cases of very narcissistic mothers and their daughters (a clear methodological problem that nonetheless does not necessarily falsify her conclusions), Chodorow argued that mothers tend to keep their daughters enmeshed. Fathers tend not to allow daughters to iden-tify with their autonomy. Since daughters do not have to break the tie of primary relatedness to become women, girls develop a sense of self that has permeable boundaries and that draws esteem from creating and preserving intimate relationships. What women crave, men cannot give; only with children (and other women) can they recreate the longed-for intimacy.

A major problem with Chodorow's theory is that although she identifies mother–daughter enmeshment, the girl's difficulty in be-coming separate, as a problem, she does not integrate this finding with her thesis: that the girl's capacity for relationship is superior to the boy's defensive autonomy. In fact, Chodorow's theory shows that relational and agentic capacities are damaged in both girls and boys when mothers are primary caretakers in conditions of gender in-equality. Chodorow's followers magnified her oversight when they elaborated themes of women's relational superiority and paid no attention to the girl's conflicts with agency or saw these conflicts as separate from the girl's relational capacity. Chodorow (1989) went on to describe a process of differentiation that does not deny its embeddedness in relationship, and she distinguished this from the masculinist process of separation/autonomy, which does. Her project here was to conceptualize a relational form of agency.[2] But still she claimed this form as female, which does not make the problem of the daughter's conflicts around agency go away. In a cultural system in which autonomy and relatedness become binary—and gendered—opposites, what we will find psychically is that both agency and connection will be highly conflictual in men and women, but the conflicts will take different forms. A case in point is Pollak's and Gilligan's (reported in Gilligan 1982) work on the differences in the stories men and women make up when presented with TAT cards, pictures designed to evoke unconscious wishes and fears. More men than women saw danger in cards that show a man and a woman in "close personal affiliation," and more women than men saw danger in cards that show "impersonal situations of achievement" (p. 41).

To me, the implications of Chodorow's theory are that a daughter's conflicts about agency will express themselves not only in her work life but in her relational life, and this is what I see in clinical practice. Some years ago, at the height of the popularity of feminist relational theory, I saw a white, 30-year-old chronically depressed female client who, in her first three sessions, described what she perceived to be a career failure, a hypersensitivity to the judgments and achievements of others, and an incapacity to advocate for herself in either personal or professional situations. She felt that she was so focused on the needs and views of others that she just could not achieve what she wanted to achieve. In between the third

---

[2]Weir (1996) argues that Chodorow repudiates autonomy and separateness, that the self in Chodorow's theory always suppresses otherness. Weir misses the fact that Chodorow is critiquing a particular model of separation, not separation *tout court*. When Chodorow uses the word *autonomy*, she does not mean, as Weir does, the Enlightenment ideal of critical reflection but rather a psychological model of individuation that denies or claims to "outgrow" relatedness (see, for example, Mahler et al. 1975). This is quite clear in Chodorow's (1989) essay, "Gender, Relation, and Difference in Psychoanalytic Perspective."

and fourth sessions, she read two things: a magazine article about the relational theory then being developed at Wellesley's Stone Center (see Miller et al. 1991) and a course catalogue with a description of a course I was going to teach on the family in contemporary women's literature. In my description, I had included among the readings Stone Center theorists, Nancy Chodorow, and Jessica Benjamin. My client came to her next session very upset. "About the last thing I need," she said, "is to be more relational. I can already barely make a move without worrying how it will affect someone else. If this is what you're about, I'm leaving."

She was right about herself—and wrong. Her version of being a good female did indeed mean that putting forward her own agenda had to come second to worrying about how things she did would affect her intimates. But her version of relationship bore little similarity to the models proffered by the Stone Center or by Carol Gilligan (1982), where women are described as healthfully basing their desires and moral decisions on maintaining relationship, or, as Gilligan puts it, on an ethic of care. My client's incapacity to act on her own behalf in fact made her simultaneously a very giving and a very angry and demanding woman. She had as much difficulty recognizing an other, getting recognition, and sustaining mutuality as she had advancing her career goals.

Just as boys are narcissistically injured by the cultural demand, mediated by subtle and not-so-subtle parent–child relational patterns, to abjure dependency, emotionality, nurturance, and the primary affectional tie with their mothers (see Kaftal 1991, Lisak 1991, Pollack 1995a,b), so are girls narcissistically injured by the cultural demand to abjure separateness, to put the needs of others before their own, to restrict to the "feminine" the kinds of things they can do with their bodies and minds. Both hegemonic white masculinity and hegemonic white femininity demand a splitting off of key capacities and attributes associated with the other, and for this reason assuming a normative gender identity is a narcissistic blow. If gender identity is in part forged via assumptions about what girls and boys can or cannot do or be, and in what context, then it is clear that gender is an important element in the personal experience of a sense of agency. A male model of agency that denies the need for others and denies mutuality develops alongside a female model of relationship that denies the need for separateness. Translated into clinical terms, normative masculinity looks like phallic narcissism, where only the self and not the other is experienced as a subject, and normative femininity looks like self-effacing narcissism, where only the other and not the self is perceived as a subject.

Identifying these gendered versions of narcissism calls to mind the work of Jessica Benjamin (1988). Benjamin mixes several sources in her model of development and gender development, including Abelin (1980), Chodorow (1978), Fast (1984), Mahler and colleagues (1975), Stern (1985), and Winnicott (1965, 1971).[3] Like Chodorow, Benjamin has a model of what development ought to be and a model of what it looks like when it breaks down; like Chodorow, she claims that the ideal model is "woman's desire" (because its intersubjective attributes run counter to the dominant phallic model). Benjamin calls for the kind of intersubjectivity sketched in Daniel Stern's (1985) theory of development, where the baby is not originally merged with the parent, not originally narcissistic. This assumption sets Stern apart from just about all other psychoanalytic theorists of development.

Stern reviews a plethora of infant observation studies that suggest that babies assert some form of self from the beginning; the so-called autonomy "phase" of, for example, Eriksonian theory (Erikson 1968), is in fact not a discrete stage but rather a negotiation with others that is ongoing throughout life. At 3 to 6 months, caretaker and child mutually regulate gazing, at 7 months gestures and vocalizations, at 14 months running away, and at 2 years, language. Ba-

---

[3]Benjamin's model mixing leads to a few contradictions in her work that are not paradoxes but inconsistencies. For example, in some places she calls omnipotence a breakdown product of relational problems rooted in gender inequality (1994a); this fits with a relational model of development such as Stern's. In other places, however, omnipotence is a child's originary state and is overcome only when the other can withstand the child's destruction of him/her in fantasy (1994b). This fits better with some of Winnicott's views or with other psychoanalytic models that assume an originally merged mother–baby dyad.

bies turn away from a gazing game with the mother when they no longer want to engage, or they will play a game of increasing emotional intensity with the mother up to a point and then decrease the intensity. These incipient assertions of the baby are met with actions and reactions on the part of the other; mutual recognition of self and other as separate but related centers of awareness emerges as the relational outcome of healthy development. For Benjamin, this intersubjective possibility depends on the mutual capacity to hold in tension assertions of the self and recognition of the other as a separate subject—what she calls the dialectic of assertion and recognition.

Stern's model gives Benjamin a developmental rationale for the possibility of non-narcissistic relating. But in her early work Benjamin argued that, because of gender inequality, the dialectic of assertion and recognition breaks down in the rapprochement phase of development (Mahler et al. 1975). In *The Bonds of Love* (1988), she writes that mothers are not endowed by the culture or by psychoanalytic theory with subjectivity; traditional middle-class gender polarities place the mother in a position the child associates with its dependence, the father in a position associated with its independence. In rapprochement, where the child struggles with dependence/independence, a gendered pseudo-solution takes place in which the boy opts for an independence that denies its roots in dependence: normative masculinity emerges as pure assertion, omnipotence, individualism. And the girl opts for submission to an all-powerful other: normative femininity emerges as self-effacing and as drawing subjectivity only from attracting and being loved by an idealized other. The girl's solution comes about not only because of her identification with the devalued mother but because her father does not allow her to identify with his autonomy. Seeking recognition of her agency by identifying with his, and not finding that recognition, a girl can express her agency only by gaining the love of an idealized male. Thus, the gendered breakdown of the dialectic of assertion and recognition results in two subtypes of narcissism that need each other to exist, two subtypes constructed in such a way, as postmodern theorists might claim, that they shore up compulsory heterosexuality. Normative gendering is narcissistic, for, as Goldner (1991) asserts and Butler (1995a) elaborates, it involves two different strategies for not dealing with losses and disappointments. The strategy of femininity is to seek recompense in idealized love for the loss of agentic capacities; the strategy of masculinity is to seek recompense in autonomous activity for the loss of relational capacities.[4]

The Psychic Interdependence of Gender Polarities

The early work of Chodorow (1978) and Benjamin (1988) focused on white middle class families of the '50s, where mothers were largely at home and in charge of child care and fathers were away at work. In these families, Chodorow and Benjamin asserted, fathers were the exciting, out-in-the-world figure, but their autonomy left them isolated and threatened by dependency and emotionality. Mothers submerged their agency beneath the needs of children and husbands. Their agency was located by the culture almost solely in their maternal and reproductive capacities. Associating masculinity with autonomy and femininity with relationship, the culture splits two capacities that originate in the same relational matrix. But both sides of the split continue to operate psychically. Benjamin argues, for example, that dominant masculinity is not independent but pseudo-independent. Demonstrating in heterosexual couples' work how this pseudo-independence plays out, Levenson (1984) found that a married man's relationship to his wife often replays the rapprochement child's relationship to his mother. Her male clients denied their dependence on their wives, but it was clear that what made them able to function autonomously was the unacknowledged background presence of their wives.

---

[4]I am not at all talking about the narcissistic blow allegedly caused by discovering that one is limited by anatomy and does not have all possibilities at one's disposal: breasts, penis, reproductive capacity (see Fast 1984). I frankly do not think these blows are nearly so detrimental as those imposed by a sexist limitation on agentic and relational possibilities, by the different ways that parents interact with boys and girls, and by prohibitions on same-sex love.

If men are always haunted by the primary relatedness they had with mother and were forced to repudiate (Chodorow 1978), so, too, are women haunted by the white male model of autonomy. I think that the model is internal to most women, along with the cultural and/or parental demand to repudiate it. Because I believe that each of us contains both sides of the gender binary, I find compelling Benjamin's revision of Freud's notion of penis envy: that for a white, middle-class woman, heterosexual love may reflect a choice to love in men agentic options she wanted for herself and was disallowed. Hard-core women rockers like Courtney Love say that they started out dating guys in bands and only slowly realized they didn't want to date the guy in the band, they wanted to *be* in a band (Apramian 1995). I recall telling a friend that my psychoanalysis was making me aware that many of the characteristics I had attributed to men (negatively, to be sure) were also part of myself—for example, strong wishes to be alone, the capacity to separate emotional attachment from sexual desire, putting the needs of self before those of others, the open expression of anger or disapproval. She replied by sending me a postcard that suggests that a lot of other women were having the same experience: a sexy cartoon woman scowls and thinks, "Oh my God, I think I'm becoming the man I wanted to marry!" My inability to risk disapproval and loss of love for acting on these desires kept them largely unconscious; consciously, I repudiated, unconsciously, I envied. I sought men who could do these things and then hated them for being rejecting and self-centered.

With Benjamin, I want to argue that the internalization of hegemonic femininity and masculinity involves a violent imposition of an agency binary that is psychically entwined with the gender binary, a dictum of what girls and boys are allowed and not allowed to do. A Lacanian might say that my personal example above reveals a fantasy of plenitude or completeness, a denial of lack, a refusal to accept castration. Such an interpretation gives ideological support to a sexist status quo. I understand my dilemma rather as a longing to have multiple agentic and relational positions available and equally valued, a rebellion against being forced into one relational or one agentic position. As Benjamin (1994a) has written, the culturally imposed and internalized splitting of agentic and relational options *results* in fantasies that another will complete you, *results* in a lack of differentiation from an other.

This understanding of the agency binary produced by gender inequality makes me skeptical of psychoanalytic theories, postmodern or relational, that do not take gender into account. In the introduction, I mentioned Barratt's (1993) assessment that what is postmodern about psychoanalysis is free association, which he sees as a counterdiscourse to the identitarian logic of most other language uses, including all therapeutic interpretations. His exemplary vignette involves a woman who appears to have built an identity around her selfless caretaking capacities. In one session, her analyst suggests to her that she fears being damaged by a penis. In the next session, she free-associates and produces a sequence that suggests that her self-denying caretaking masks wishes to damage the penis (here she is taking *good* care of her therapist!). Barratt notes that every analysis necessarily deconstructs the phallocentric assumptions of culture, but he focuses on the language of the sequence because he wishes to underscore the way that free association reveals a desire that always contradicts the coherent narratives of everyday speech. His thesis is that the liberating potential of psychoanalysis lies in the way free association makes us aware of our multiplicity.

From my feminist perspective, Barratt's sense that it is less liberatory to interpret the content of what the woman says than to allow her multiplicity to unfold is problematic. For the content exposes the two poles of the gender/agency/relationship binary that I have been exploring. The woman's conscious gender identity is that of hegemonic femininity. To achieve it, she splits off agentic strivings that emerge in rage against men, a wish to destroy rather than nurture. The guilt about the wish to destroy makes her redouble her efforts to be a good caretaker. What Barratt calls the woman's unconscious desire, the wish to destroy the penis, is dialectically related to her conscious narrative and is every bit as constructed, coherent, and historically determined as the conscious narrative. So what is liberating? To understand that we are a jumble of contradictory wishes? Or to understand that these particular two options—the self-denying caretaker and the castrating bitch—*are* the options available to women in a culture of gender inequality? If, like Barratt, we are looking for a "left-minded" psychoanalysis, we cannot assume that the process of free association itself will liberate; we also need to interpret the content that free association produces and interpret it in the context of a culture built on structural inequalities of all kinds.

Postmodern Feminist Views of Gender Polarities

Benjamin's view of the way normative gender development becomes entwined with thwarted forms of agency and relationship bears some similarity to certain postmodern accounts. For example, Jacqueline Rose, a Lacanian in her 1986 work, feels that the cultural command to line up on one or another side of the phallus as "having it" (male) or "not having it" (female) is a command violently imposed on boys and girls, who continuously struggle against this homogenization.[5] For Rose, the unconscious is the way out of the narcissistic binds of gender polarities, for it is the place from which constant disruptions of seemingly unproblematic identifications emanate. In her view, the task of psychoanalysis is not to redo development more successfully or enforce traditional narratives of development but to uncover psychic resistance to cultural norms of femininity and masculinity.[6]

Benjamin's views might also be compared with the early work of the French feminist Luce Irigaray. In "The Blind Spot of an Old

---

[5]While Benjamin and Rose suggest that gender polarizations are oedipal products imposed later on a more fluid developing child, I would argue that it might just as well work in the opposite way: a person might have a family highly invested in gender polarizations and only later, in school, or by watching TV or reading books, come into contact with other ways of being a girl or boy or girl-boy. Of course, the more highly invested the family is in polarizations, the greater the narcissistic injury and the harder it may be to allow in significant others who might approve and permit other ways of being. Regardless, I do not think stage theories that place gender polarizations later are tenable.

[6]While it is true that the early work of Chodorow and Benjamin captured neither the sense of ongoing struggle important to Rose's account nor the sense of multiple versions of femininity and masculinity, Benjamin's recent work shares with Rose's the view of culturally imposed polarities and tries to ground resistance to them in preoedipal identifications with both genders. Both Chodorow (1994) and Benjamin (1996) champion fluidity and multiplicity in their recent writings.

Dream of Symmetry" (1985), for example, Irigaray interrogates Freud's (1933) essay "Femininity," which, she argues, accurately describes the normative path for women whose development takes place within a phallic cultural order. Irigaray charges that within the phallic order women have not been able to symbolize their relation to their genitals. She shows how both Freudian and Lacanian theory endow the phallus (transcendental signifier of the symbolic) with the status of origin, defensively wresting that status away from the mother, origin of us all. In so doing, the phallic order does not allow girls to symbolize their own relation to their origin-mothers (recall Freud's [1925, 1933] idea that the girl turns from her mother in hate when she realizes she does not have a penis/phallus; although Freud [1931] also acknowledges a girl's ongoing ambivalence toward her mother, the "hate" side remains rooted in what she lacks). Irigaray too, then, describes processes of gendering in terms of loss and damage to the self. Like Chodorow and Benjamin, she also proposes an ideal model, a counter-symbolic based in women's construction of their relation to their bodies and to their mothers. In a masculine symbolic, woman is figured not as different from man, but simply as not male, as a lacking male, as a deficient version of the same: the phallic little girl is a little man, the woman is a deficient man. Real difference emerges only when women elaborate a new symbolic that changes the equation from male = A, female = −A to male = A, female = B (Grosz 1990).

Benjamin, Chodorow, and Irigaray all propose that something particular to women gives them the capacity to contest a masculine economy that imposes narcissistic gender binds. Each believes that there is something more to the psyche than hegemonic femininity and masculinity—at least to the female psyche. If we believe that all there is in the psyche and the culture are gender polarities, however, there is no way out of narcissism. This dilemma exists in certain uses of Lacanian theory, for example, in Laura Mulvey's (1975) pathbreaking analysis of how classic Hollywood film positions spectators to line up on one or the other side of the phallus. The male protagonist and spectator are culturally allowed to be bearers of the gaze, to be subjects; women are allowed only to be looked at, as objects. Cultural apparatuses, such as film, work to suppress other possible identifications. In Mulvey's appropriation of Lacan, the ego is all there is, and in Lacan's work the identifications that make up the ego are always imaginary/narcissistic. Thus, in Mulvey's model, all the culture offers are the narcissistic polarities of domination and submission.[7]

As many critics have pointed out, Mulvey's model never exhausts the possible interpretations of a film, but her theory usually provides one plausible interpretation. And I think this is because gender polarities based on gender inequality are both the dominant version of gender that people internalize in this culture and the dominant version that structures the major apparatuses of culture, including film. Interpretations that undercut Mulvey's model also work, however, not only because the meanings of language and images can never be fixed, not only because gender intertwines with race, class, and other identity elements, but also because gender identity is not exhausted by the splits and disavowals that issue in gender polarities. Indeed, theories that suggest that women are not (yet) subjects, and that their agency consists only in dutifully playing their role in a masculine symbolic, critically undervalue women by ignoring both the active forms (the comings and goings of a mother, for instance) and the passive forms (e.g., nagging to get the other to enact her desire) that her self-assertions might take.

---

[7]Another model has been proposed by Sweetnam (1996), one in which, as in Benjamin's, gender polarities are normative but do not exhaust gender possibilities. Drawing on a Kleinian framework, Sweetnam argues that in the paranoid-schizoid position, gender identity is experienced as binary; in the depressive position, gender identity is experienced as fluid. Throughout life, we oscillate between fixed and fluid gender identity positions. Sweetnam's argument does not take culture into account; what she describes as paranoid-schizoid is close to what I have described as culturally imposed binaries. Nor does she make distinctions between the relative degree of the two positions in a given psyche. Although all people are narcissistically vulnerable throughout life, I would argue that there is a point where quantitative differences tip over into qualitative ones. The capacity to spend most of one's waking hours in the depressive position is a developmental achievement that emerges from non-narcissistic relating; Sweetnam's theory obscures the differences between what gender may be like for someone who functions largely at the paranoid-schizoid level and for someone who does not.

Judith Butler, who proposes one of the most sophisticated accounts of gender acquisition in a poststructuralist paradigm, has also discussed the narcissistic binds of gender identity. For Butler (1990a), an internal sense of masculinity or femininity is an effect of constant citings and re-citings of the normative gender practices of one's culture, practices that include how one speaks, how one plays, how one dresses. Gender is brought into being in the performance of a gender identity. Performativity is not a voluntaristic activity; gender norms dictate what performances are possible and how they are to be performed. Citings of the norm include what gender one is allowed to identify with and what gender one is allowed to love. In our particular culture, assuming a sex and a gender identity involves not only identifications that are allowed within the cultural norm, but also repudiations of those that lie outside the cultural norm. Thus identity is based as much on disidentifications as on identifications. What is repudiated and disavowed, however, always returns to threaten the boundaries of the subject.

As rich as it is, Butler's work offers few ways out of the problem of narcissism, for her theory assumes that splitting and disavowal are intrinsic to subject formation, a conceptual necessity rather than, as I would see it, a historical or developmental contingency grounded in gender inequality (see Fraser's [1995] critique). Gender categories are figured as imaginary ego structures that are always about the business of imposing coherence on multiplicity. For Butler, resistance occurs because of the impossibility of faithfully citing gender norms. In her early work, she does not ground resistance in psychological motivation.

Benjamin's Ways Out of the Narcissistic Injuries of Gender Polarities

Before returning to my own thoughts on how to ground possibilities that take gender identities and gender relations beyond narcissism, I want to review the three possibilities that Benjamin has offered: (1) She uses Stern's and Winnicott's developmental theories to show what must happen to achieve non-narcissistic relating; in

The Bonds of Love (1988), she calls the resulting version of intersubjectivity "woman's desire." (2) She (1991) demands that mothers be valued as subjects and be able to experience themselves as subjects, not objects, and that a father allow his daughter to experience her agency as like his. (3) She looks to preoedipal identificatory processes to ground gender fluidity.

The history of dominant male–female relations involves the narcissistic assumption that women's interests are coincident with those of men. For this reason, a feminist psychoanalysis insists that a criterion of health is the capacity to see the other as a separate subject. Because her concern is how one achieves the differentiation necessary to be able to be a subject in relation to another subject, Benjamin over and over again invokes Winnicott's essay "The Use of an Object and Relating Through Identifications" (1971).[8] In brief, the essay claims that an other becomes differentiated from the self when the self has been able to destroy the other in fantasy and then perceives that the internal and external other survives that destruction without retaliating or withering. Retaliating would occur from a position of omnipotence, and might include abandonment or harsh punishment; withering would occur from a position of constant submission to a child's demands. The external other can survive destruction only when he or she feels differentiated enough, enough of a subject to withstand the anger and the neediness of the child, and unequal gender, race, and class arrangements make that non-narcissistic position no small achievement. Nonetheless, Stern's and Winnicott's developmental theories clearly envision the possibility both of the mother as subject and of versions of agency and relating that maintain the tension between attachment and differentiation.

In Benjamin's later work (1996), the content of normative masculinity and femininity takes a back seat to, as she puts it, a "de-

---

[8]Few commentators have picked up on this aspect of her work, and many feminist critics of Winnicott, I would argue, depict him as conservative because they have misunderstood or missed the radicality of this essay and of his notion of potential and transitional space. For a misreading, see Doane and Hodges 1992. For a positive and postmodern revaluing of Winnicott, see Marike Finlay's (1989) comparison of what she calls Winnicott's mirror stage with Lacan's mirror stage.

fense of gender ambiguity" (p. 27). In this more postmodern strain of her work, Benjamin wants to ground possibilities for cross-gender identifications in normal development, and she does so by drawing on Fast (1984), who argues that children have an overinclusive sense of gender possibilities until they are capable of understanding difference. Difference becomes a narcissistic blow: girls realize they will never have a penis; boys realize they will never have babies. In her recent work, Benjamin suggests that the possibilities of this bisexual preoedipal period, where bisexuality is defined to include cross-gender identifications of all kinds, are never given up, even after oedipal "realities" assert themselves. While oedipal gender dictates are polarized and dichotomous, one can later draw on the more fluid early possibilities to counter them. Postmodern in her concern for gender fluidity, Benjamin yet adheres to a stage theory of development and still works within the cultural confines of male and female, with identifications with father defined as male and those with mother as female.

Schwartz's (1992) critique of Benjamin and Benjamin's (1992) reply offer an interesting insight into the tensions between Schwartz's non-Lacanian postmodernism and Benjamin's object relations. Schwartz is uncomfortable with Benjamin's preservation of categories like *penis envy, preoedipal,* and *oedipal,* and he is critical of her stage theory with its crucial moments of separation–individuation in rapprochement; he criticizes her for gendering the attributes boys happen to have as male and for associating these attributes in any way with a penis, and he seems to feel that Benjamin works in the confines of a gender binary. Benjamin replies:

> "Both/and" means that girls should no more have to sacrifice femininity for masculinity anymore than the other way around—whatever femininity or masculinity may be.
>
> However we address this unanswerable question—what are femininity and masculinity?—we know that we want to get beyond either/or thinking. I know that I work with a kind of tautological answer, to wit, that they are constituted by identifications with maternal and paternal, female and male significant others. . . . The binary system of gender complementarity that

prevails in our culture and informs much of our social life seems to reflect and resonate with the psychic structure of the oedipal phase, in which either/or predominates. [p. 421]

Benjamin's unwillingness to throw out developmental theory, as well as her sense that we cannot, in this culture at least, psychologically transcend the categories male and female that mark the way we make meaning of our identifications with men and women, may make her work unpalatable to postmodernists. But her work is important to clinicians whose clients are disentangling themselves from gendered and non-gendered identifications with parents and from their parents' gendered projections onto them.

There is a problem, however, with Benjamin's adherence to stage theory. Grounding gender ambiguity in early cross-gender identifications suggests that the child does not feel the effects of culture until a later age, rapprochement or beyond, which does not seem plausible. In *The Bonds of Love*, Benjamin compellingly deconstructs the kind of agency that develops in a culture whose norms include the dictum that a male must disidentify with his mother to be masculine. Yet, in her theory of identificatory love (1991), which provides a way to ground early cross-gender identifications, she puts forward what within her own system would be a precultural version of agency, defined merely as a father's investment in the outside world. She claims that the preoedipal father's agency is non-phallic, not caught in the dominance–submission paradigm, and this seems idealized to me. In Kaftal's (1991) alternate account of masculine development, for example, preoedipal fathers are not different from oedipal fathers. The unavailability of a preoedipal nurturant father encourages the boy's envy and repudiation of women and offers only a competitive, hostile identification with an isolated monad who continuously struggles to redo failed attempts at separation.

Rather than appeal to a stage theory that differentiates the good (and precultural) preoedipal from the bad oedipal, a very problematic move, I propose that men and women maintain multiple gender identities, and each gender identity is associated with its own modes of agency and relationship. Hegemonic masculinity and femininity are likely to be the most powerful internalizations, but they are not the only ones. To ground ways of connecting and of being agentic that are not marked by narcissistic injury, I suggest we look in two places: to stage-free relational developmental models such as Stern's (1985) and May's (1986), which we must resist calling "female," and to alternative ways of relating and asserting agency that have arisen from the division into male and female.

PART 2: TOWARD A NEGOTIATION MODEL OF GENDER IDENTITY

In a paper on gender that synthesizes an object-relational view of how gender is internalized with Lacanian concerns about how identity imposes a constricting coherence on multiplicity, May (1986) writes that each of the self-and-object patterns of relationship that we internalize in the course of development is gendered. A girl may internalize numerous self–other patterns, among which we might find the following: athletic in relation to an active mother or father, passive and small in relation to a caretaking mother or father, flirty in relation to a seductive or distracted mother or father. We have within us, then, a plethora of gender identities. May argues that when people try to constrict their vision of their gender identity to normative femininity or masculinity, a defensive reduction takes place; one shrinks one's multiplicity to a narcissistic polarity. May's theory is relational, assumes the lack of differentiation that characterizes narcissism to be defensive and not a necessary outcome of development, and suggests that gender experience is not fixed at a particular stage but rather evolves with our evolving sets of relationships.

May does not account for the effects of gender inequality, namely that many gender internalizations are internalized with gender proscriptions (e.g., it is not quite so okay to be a tomboy in relation to dad as to be a flirty little girl). Internalizations that derive from repeated relational patterns as described by Stern (1985) and May take place within a particular culture that sets up their conditioning framework (e.g., women mother, babies are reared in families, babies in heterosexual nuclear families are named after their fathers, girl babies are given pink clothes at baby showers even before they are born, and so forth). Babies are born into raced and classed families, which also determines how gender and agency will become intertwined for them—a working-class white girl, for example, will get very different messages about what she can do in the world from those given to an upper-class white girl. And this has everything to do with power differentials that are internalized as part of one's definition of gender, agency, and relatedness.

Nonetheless, May alerts us that there are multiple and competing gender internalizations. Benjamin is right that gender identifications get tied up with dependence and independence. But breakdowns in the assertion/recognition dialectic are a product of ongoing relational disturbances, not of a critical moment. And other gendered relational processes, where the dialectic just may not break down, occur simultaneously. Narcissistic gender disturbance, then, is a matter of degree; no one escapes it, but not everyone is incapacitated by it. Gender identity, agency, and relationship involve ongoing processes of negotiation between outcomes of narcissistic relating and outcomes of non-narcissistic relating, between products of gender inequality and possibilities that counter gender inequality.

I propose that what happens psychically is analogous to what British Cultural Studies theorists of the Birmingham School (see Hall 1980, Morley 1980) have proffered as a model for the study of how people make meaning of culture. In this model, those who produce cultural messages have limited control over how these messages will be interpreted for two reasons: (1) language is polysemous, that is, the nature of language is such that it generates multiple meaning possibilities; and (2) people are made of multiple and conflicting identity positions, which means that different subcultures or individuals interpret messages in ways different from how those who produce the messages may have wished them to be interpreted. In this view, culture is always a site of struggle over meaning, where dominant and non-dominant interpretations compete for hegemony. Dominant interpretations may appear to have hegemony, but their hegemony is contingent and always needs to be re-won against competing interpretations. The only certainty is the struggle.

The same process occurs intrapsychically. In a complex culture such as ours, in which a multiplicity of positions are visible in cultural products, on the nightly news, on the streets, and within our own families, we engage in and take in multiple versions of gendered subjectivity, agency, and relatedness, differentially valued and differentially conflictual for boys and girls. The less conflictual, the greater the degree of flexibility for future identifications. At the beginning of this chapter, I suggested that the division into male and female both constricts and facilitates gender options. We have looked closely at the constriction, and what we have seen might make us wonder how these same binary structures could produce anything but narcissistic injury. Yet the division into male and female results historically in a multitude of different and conflicting social practices, some of which have allowed subjects and collectives to bring forth non-narcissistic agentic and relational options. One of the psychic consequences of the division into male and female is the experience of core gender identity, discredited as illusory in postmodern theory. Experiencing oneself as female and locating oneself in relation to other females, however, can be an important way of contesting the hegemony of the narcissistic structures of femininity and masculinity. I begin with a personal example to show that one source of resistance to gender inequality, a source underplayed in many postmodern accounts, is identification with and attachment to other women.

The Facilitating Possibilities of Gender Categories

My mother graduated from Bryn Mawr in the mid-'40s, married a year before graduation, and became a mother and housewife in 1950. Since she lived through the war experience where women were called upon to take on men's work roles, I would guess that she grew up with conflicting and multiple messages about female agency (cf. May 1988). She mediated gender inequality to me less by deferring to my father than by clearly preferring my brother to me—a narcissistic wound that became inextricable from my experience of gender. When she went to work as a preschool teacher in the late 1950s, she would occasionally report that the boys were ever so much more interesting than the girls. Later, around 1971, she criticized me for not putting my husband's career plans before mine ("Feminism, schmeminism, somebody has to compromise and I still think it should be the woman"). She was quite upset that women were competing with men for places in professional schools. "Why do they have to be a veterinarian when they can marry one?" she once asked, angry that my brother hadn't gotten into a school that had accepted 50 percent women for that year's class. And while I think she is quite pleased with my intellectual achievements, she still does not much like it when I remove myself from a social situation to read.

Judging from my unwavering commitment to feminism since first I heard of it in 1969, I would guess that my defense against my mother's confusing mix of intellect, strength, breadwinning, idealization of males, and negativity towards females was a "feminine protest," an insistence that women were just as good as men. Turning away from women and towards ideal love or identification with men, then, is not the only possible defense against gender pain. My particular defense drew me to the kind of feminism that said women could do the same things men could (equality feminism) rather than to the kind that lauded women's relational superiority (difference feminism). Through school, I identified with smart female teachers and thrived on their approval. I always had a lot of female friends. When I look back on my history, I can clearly see how my mother's conflict and the culture's sexism made me hesitant and timid about what I could do, but I also see how I looked not to men but to women—including my mother—to show me just what women could do. For me, the feminist movement was a lifesaver, a cultural source of approval for what had always been lurking in me but was able to make only intermittent appearances. The male/female binary places women not just in a world of inferiority to men but also in a diverse world of women, a world with different social practices that at times produce narcissistic wounds (especially from self-hating women) but at other times produce defiance of sexist norms and create new, more liberatory possibilities. The feminist movement itself shows that there must be more to the psyche than narcissistic gender binaries.

In 1984, de Lauretis drew attention to the important difference between the cultural construct *Woman*—which emanates from the fears and fantasies of men—and *women*, female subjects constituted by their practices and by the representations they create of themselves. Gender categories are elaborated in social practices and from particular positions in a race-, class-, and gender-stratified culture, and these categories both create agentic and relational options and constrict them. To the best of my conscious knowledge, as painful as it was not to be as highly regarded as my brother, as painful as it was later that the male faculty in graduate school did not regard me as highly as they did my male counterparts, I have never wanted to be a male. I have wanted their privilege, their mobility, their economic advantages, the love they got for simply being male, but I did not want to be a man. And I do not think that my attachment to women was only defensive. My sense is that it is not just the coerciveness of inequality that creates resistance, but also attachment to and recognition from caring and agentic women.

Such attachment and recognition come from relationships both to people in our lives and to cultural representations by and about women. One effect of the social movements of the 1950s, '60s, and '70s is that many more women have had the opportunity to represent themselves in novels, poetry, music, and, now finally, film. In recent books and movies, contemporary young women rockers talk about how important Patti Smith or Joan Jett was to them, just as their fans talk about the "permission" to rock hard that comes from watching Kat Bjelland, Courtney Love, and Donita Sparks (Raphael 1996). Women rappers like Salt 'n' Pepa rework sexist stereotypes and spit them back in response to misogynistic representations in men's music. Gloria Naylor (Naylor and Morrison 1985) reports that she took a college course in creative writing where the instructor had them read great fiction. It was only when they got to Toni Morrison's *The Bluest Eye* that she realized she had a story worth telling, because she could see herself in another black woman who dared to tell a story and told it beautifully. Reading women's literature, listening to women's music, and watching women's films gives the sense that there are multiple ways of being a woman *and* that women's experience is worth articulating.

I would like to give a few more examples of women expanding the category *woman* and transforming themselves in their relations to other women, because this possibility for escaping narcissistic wounds increases in significance as the number of women representing their experiences increases. Finding approval for multiple versions of female agency heals wounds caused by disapproval, and possibilities for finding that approval are greater at this historical moment than ever before. Sara Evans (1979) writes about how black women active in civil rights in the south were important as models not only to young black women but to the white college females who went south in Freedom Summer. De Lauretis (1994) writes that Helene Deutsch permitted her homosexual clients to enjoy same-sex sexual activity, and she calls for cultural apparatuses such as literature and film to do the same. One of the things that hard-core women's bands permit is a pleasure in physicality; another is anger. In most male representations of women, the angry woman is the crazy woman (*Fatal Attraction* [Lyne 1987], for example). In Veruca Salt's hit song "Seether" (1994), the female songwriter and singers represent woman's anger as painful but as a central part of themselves. The song makes it clear that anger is still difficult to reconcile with hegemonic femininity, but anger is not split off and dissociated; angry women are neither rejected nor rendered psychopathic.

Cross-cultural facilitations of female transformation such as those Evans (1979) reported have become a topic of great interest in women's writing. In Sandra Cisneros's (1992) story "Woman Hollering Creek," a Mexican who marries an abusive Mexican-American male sees more options for femininity after a brief encounter with a Chicana who is like no other woman she has ever met (see Wyatt 1995). In like fashion, an Asian client of mine identifies with what she perceives to be my more autonomous version of Anglo womanhood as a way to free herself from cultural stereotypes that keep her enmeshed in a patriarchal family (see also Moraga's [1986] description of her own similar border crossing).

While I criticized assumptions of women's relational superiority in the first section of this essay, there is no doubt in my mind that women's friendships are qualitatively different from men's and are worthy of male envy. Some have argued that women become relational because of the narcissistic wounds of gender inequality: women have to be able to read body gestures and facial expressions, know what everyone is feeling, read between the lines in order to survive. Whatever the origin, these bonds are a sustaining force and yet another source for mitigating narcissistic wounds. I occasionally see female clients who have had very untrustworthy mothers and who have made all the male-inspired cliches about women their own: women can't be trusted, they're gossipy and catty, they're stupid and uninteresting, and the like. But most of my clients have at least some strong female friendships that are not fraught with the same kinds of problems as their relationships with love partners, male or female. These friendships are often sources the clinician draws on to decenter a client's constricted view of her possibilities.

Finally, although there is no female way of doing art, I do find that there are things in the texts of Toni Morrison and Gloria Naylor, black women writers; Dorothy Allison, a white working-class lesbian; and Mary Gordon and Anne Tyler, white middle-class heterosexuals, that mark them as likely to have been written by women, and these texts, too, then, become sources of identification and resistance to cultural norms: perhaps a focus on being a daughter, on being a sexual object to men, on being responsible for childcare or tending to the needs of others, on developing breasts, on being a sexual subject, on worrying about getting fat, on the strong bonds between women. These topics are dealt with in a multitude of ways, but they are definitely, and for specific socio-historic reasons, women's concerns. When I was in graduate school in the early '70s, works that dealt with such issues were just beginning to exist in greater number and were not yet deemed worthy of inclusion on syllabi. Olsen (1978) has talked about how such cultural silencing of women's experience perpetuates what I have been calling narcissistic injury.

It is clear that women seek and find other women to help them out of the painful confines of the gender binary. In this process, they identify with women because they are similar in sex but crucially different in capacities (see Stacey 1989). Engagement with other women offers female recognition and validation of the category *woman*. It also gives permission to question the legitimacy of gender inequality, which leads to change. As long as power differentials continue to exist between masculinity and femininity, any theory that claims to transcend binaries or looks only at continuities between them risks keeping the power hierarchy intact. It is the power difference between women and men (of all races), the different social positionings they occupy, and the different meanings they construct of those positions that make the male/female binary continue to be politically and personally meaningful.

Indeed, several feminists in the mid-'80s worried that just as women had begun to speak, to multiply their agentic options, male postmodern theorists declared the death or radical decentering of the subject (see Miller 1986, Modleski 1986a). The postmodern impulse to deconstruct binary oppositions risks erasing the specificity and creativity of those who have elaborated a group identity over many years. The tension between appreciating the richness and specificity of categories as lived and resisting the way categories constrict is a challenge both to academic discussions of gender and to clinicians working with gendered clients. For the people who come to therapy live within the constraints and pleasures imposed by the binary categories male/female, masculine/feminine, straight/gay, black/white, and, at the same time, they defy, undo, and remake these categories.[9]

---

[9]In a defense of gay identity against the deconstructive impulse of queer theory, Leo Bersani (1995) writes:

> In spite of the oppressive intent in the social manipulations of the category, "homosexuality" was also received as an opportunity for self-fashioning. Even if the targeted men and women forged their own identity and culture in "the same categories by which [homosexuality] was medically disqualified," the homosexual personality could also be experienced as a psychic enrichment. [pp. 34–35]

I would insist that the same can be said for male and female, and my insistence is compatible with the postmodern claim that sex assignments need not be limited to these two.

Grounding Other Non-Narcissistic Possibilities

The strategic identification of females with other females is one relational pattern and social practice that can contest hegemonic femininity and masculinity both within the psyche and within the culture. Let us look at other situations that show how gender identity becomes a product of the negotiation of narcissistic and non-narcissistic agentic and relational options.

When I was a 4-year-old, I used to stay overnight with a friend whose mother was my mother's best friend. We'd jump up and down like crazy until we heard our mothers threateningly coming up the stairs, at which point we'd yell, "Here come the mommies" and dive under the covers, pretending to be angelic sleepers. In jumping, I was experiencing some of what my body could do, raising the intensity of physical activity to frenzy, and doing it in the company of another girl in the same state. Perhaps the enjoyable physical feeling was enhanced because we were not supposed to be jumping; whatever the origin, jumping like this and feeling its effects became part of what I thought a girl could do and feel (see Grosz 1994; for a further discussion of body agency, see Connell 1995).

Flash forward forty years. I'm power walking down a dirt road in rural Florida at midday. I've got my walkman on, and I'm throwing my whole body into the exercise, listening to P. J. Harvey (1992) sing about Sheela-Na-Gig, the song's exhibitionist. Then I see a car drive down with a man inside. Immediately, my arms return to my side; I make sure my breasts aren't jiggling; I constrict. Even when two young boys ride down on bicycles, I constrict. I'm angry, but I know how to keep myself safe. I have always enjoyed moving my body freely. Yet I learned at some point that it was unladylike to be physically wild, to enjoy all the things my body could do. And at another point I learned that it was okay to flaunt my body in some situations and unsafe to do so in others. I internalized the cultural prohibition against autoerotic enjoyment of my body, a narcissistic wound that interferes with that enjoyment but does not necessarily annihilate it. Autoerotic enjoyment of the body does not line up with the demands of hegemonic femininity, but it is nonetheless an important element of gendered experience, one of many that can be called on to contest hegemonic femininity.

British Cultural Studies theorists propose a model of subjectivity in which a subject develops by taking up or being interpellated into a variety of discursive positions; for example, one is simultaneously a national subject, a racial subject, a classed subject, a religious subject (Morley 1980; see also Higginbotham 1992). Any mix of these positions might come into contradiction with positions of hegemonic femininity or masculinity and create something more fluid. A white upper-class student of mine told me that her parents' highest value is education, and they impressed this equally on her and her brother. She felt entitled to the finest educational possibilities, but at some point in school she realized that girls were treated differently from boys in the educational process. This was confusing to her, and she struggled with the mixed message. Yet, fundamentally, she and her parents saw no reason that being a girl should have anything to do with educational possibility, and they contested attempts to impose restrictions. This and my jumping example suggest that when you put together what appear to be two facts of your experience, "I am a girl" and "I do particular things or have particular capacities," you may come up with something quite different from what hegemonic femininity aims to impose as natural, and so you create or construct alternate versions of "femininity." The values of a particular family, or some of its values, may contest those of the dominant culture, which will make one's gendered experience contain possibilities that go beyond gender polarities. The struggle between dominant and non-dominant versions of femininity is a gendered form of intrapsychic conflict.

I am proposing a theory of gender identity that focuses on competing gender internalizations and competing cultural norms. But I spent a lot of time discussing hegemonic gender positions because these positions and their psychic effects are the major obstacles to postmodern and relational feminist goals of intersubjectivity. Dominant gender positions aim to secure hegemony by gendering all experiences and attributes only in those ways that maintain gender inequality. Alternate possibilities circulate both in the culture and in the psyche, but hegemonic positions have a great deal of power, in part because they offer the love and approval that go with social sanction. What often keeps us from being unconflictually free to choose among multiple gender options is the fear of losing love.

For this reason, a most important legacy of the civil rights movement, feminism, and gay and lesbian movements is the visibility and social sanction they gave to numerous non-dominant gender, race, and sexual options. These permissions are relational events. They are also deconstructive events—writings by and about women and men of color, gays and lesbians, and women of all classes have irrevocably challenged the hegemony of the singular, universalist point of view and have been a major force in decentering hegemonic and narcissistic versions of gender identity. But because the power relations of racism and sexism and classism continue to dominate, these versions are still with us and are still a major source of pain for men and women alike. Social movements reveal a tension in the way identities operate: people may take up the identity ascribed to them, rework it in the context of many other identity elements, or refuse it. Gender identity works in much the same way—it is a negotiation, within relational matrices, between the constricting and facilitating consequences of gender categories.

3

Gender Benders/Gender Binders: A Psychoanalytic Look at Contemporary Popular Culture

Jacqueline Rose (1986), defending psychoanalysis from British feminist attacks against it, argued that feminists have used psychoanalysis in two ways, one that she considers conservative and one radical. In the work of Nancy Chodorow and other object relations feminists, Freud's developmental theory is adopted and/or adapted to explain how people take on masculine and feminine identities in patriarchal culture. In Rose's view, this is a rather conservative use of psychoanalysis, for she feels that the radicality of psychoanalysis is Freud's discovery of the unconscious, which functions to disrupt any fantasy that identities might be assumed in an unproblematic way, that femininity and masculinity are univocal. Rose argues that this second version of psychoanalysis is every bit as radical as Marxist theory, for the unconscious disturbs a complacent bourgeois culture by consistently undermining cultural demands to reproduce a sexist status quo.

Postmodern and Anglo-American relational feminist culture critics have both looked to popular culture as one of several sites where struggles over the meaning of gender identity (and other aspects of identity) take place. In contemporary American mass popu-

lar culture, gender identity and gender relations are generally depicted in two ways, each of which resonates with one of the two
different uses of psychoanalysis sketched out by Rose. A gender-
bending strand of popular culture, represented by artists such as
Madonna or Prince, and the films *The Crying Game* (Jordan 1992)
and M. *Butterfly* (Cronenberg 1993), seems to want to turn up the
heat on anxieties about gender, to deconstruct gender identity, to
refuse binary constrictions. Here, as in postmodern theories, disruptions of normative connections between anatomy, gender identity,
and sexual preference are in the foreground.

For example, Dil, in *The Crying Game*, is an anatomical male
with a female gender identity and a sexual preference for men. Her/
his two lovers are a black and a white man linked to each other
homoerotically. Cronenberg's M. *Butterfly*, based on the play by
Hwang, is the story of a white, Western male's love obsession with
someone he thinks is a Chinese female opera star but is really a male.
This film weaves criticism of cultural imperialism together with gender criticism as the opera singer asserts that what the Western diplomat loves is not her, but Asian submissiveness, the fantasy of a
Butterfly who would kill herself over love for her Western master.
She tells him that he would never find compelling a story where a
white woman's obsessive love for a Japanese man would cause her
to commit suicide. The opera singer later explains to an agent of the
cultural revolution that the reason men played female roles in traditional Chinese opera is that only a man knows how he wants a
woman to be and to act. A man falls in love not with a subject, the
opera singer implies, but with an object of his own making. Positioned as the master in race and gender, the diplomat can only fall
madly in love with cultural representations that corroborate his race
and gender superiority. This recalls Irigaray's (1985) assertion that a
masculine representational economy requires that women have penis envy, for, when men become aware of their own insufficiency,
penis envy reassures them that there is a reason why they have
power. The film exposes love, and the gender/race constructions that
secure love, as thoroughly political, not natural. Works of this kind
challenge fixed gender roles, question rigidly conceived notions of

sexual preference, and emphasize the social construction of genders and gender relations.

A different take on gender identities and gender relations occurs in genres that I call gender binders. These genres try to turn down the heat on gender anxieties by mixing one part heat to two parts Valium. They insist on gender difference and largely present men and women who incarnate the normative versions of masculinity and femininity that I referred to in Chapter 2 as narcissistic. I would include in this category most male buddy films, such as *Lethal Weapon* (Donner 1987) and *48 Hrs.* (Hill 1982), classic heavy metal, classic hard-boiled detective fiction, and classic romance fiction.[1]

In this chapter, I focus on gender binders, in which characters struggle to manage longings for agency and connection within the constraints of the narcissistic binds of traditional gender identities. Classic romance and hard-boiled detective fiction show that attempts to live out one side of the gender binary are threatened and undermined by the internalized other side of the binary, by what has been split off. The impossibility of banishing what is split off is manifest in the repetition that is the essence of formula fiction, a repetition compulsion meant to heal the wounds of dichotomized gender socialization and gender inequality (Modleski 1982). In recent versions of romance and detective fiction, there are attempts to overcome the splits and integrate longings for agency and connection. In some, heroes and heroines are represented as both agentic and connected; in others, women are placed in traditionally male positions. Yet we will find that the persistence of seemingly natural links between

---

[1]A third strand looks like a mix of the first two, in that it generally occurs within genres yet does a lot of gender bending. In this strand, however, which includes serial-killer novels and the recent rash of films about women who kill (e.g., *Basic Instinct* [Verhoeven 1992] and *The Last Seduction* [Dahl 1994], the gender bending has a misogynist, regressive cast. Susan Faludi (1991) has referred to such works, which use feminist theory to enforce a misogynist message, as "backlash" popular culture. Yet other versions of gender and gender relations, ones that resonate more with the model of gender multiplicity explored in Chapter 2, appear in popular culture that tends not to have a mass audience, for example, women's independent cinema.

gender binaries and particular forms of agency and connection limits these attempts both to love and to work well, to achieve gender
relations based on mutual, intersubjective recognition.

The gender binders are of interest because they show many of
the psychological difficulties that get in the way of achieving the kind
of multiplicity and fluidity called for in postmodern theories and incarnated in the gender-bending strand of popular culture. Unlike the
gender benders, these genres acknowledge that men and women in
our culture are socialized differently, so differently that Maxine Hong
Kingston (1990) once quipped that every time a man and a woman
get together it's a cross-cultural experience. To understand the persistence of traditional gender identities, I rely on relational analytic
feminism. As we shall see, however, the binaries within which the
gender binders hope to remain fixed continually undermine each
other and therefore call as well for deconstruction. In the next chapter, I look at Madonna as an example of a gender bender, and there
we will see that the ease of her stance for gender and identity fluidity is consistently undermined by the psychological consequences of
the binaries that a modernist identity paradigm imposes upon her.
While the concerns of postmodern theories resonate with the gender benders, and the concerns of relational theories resonate with
the kinds of struggles over agency and intimacy depicted in gender
binders, an integration of postmodern feminist and relational feminist versions of psychoanalysis is necessary to understand fully what
each of these strands of popular culture tells us about contemporary
issues of gender identity, agency, and relationship.

As I said above, the gender-binding strand of popular culture
seeks less to heighten anxieties about gender than to manage them.
We see this in genres that maintain traditional gender dichotomies
and often appeal primarily to one gender or the other. These genres
try not to blur boundaries between male and female, straight and
gay. As an example of the way that they insist on gender difference,
let us look at a description of a masculine space from Kathleen
E. Woodiwiss's enormously popular, steamy romance, *The Flame and
the Flower* (1972). Heather, the heroine, is looking for her Mr. Right,
Brandon:

Seeking Brandon's presence, she went to his study and found it
in the heavy chair that sat before his massive walnut desk. Test-
ing the chair, she found it hard and uncomfortable, as if it re-
sented her imposing upon its masculine stature. She rose and
gazed about the room and despite its lack of order, sensed that
here was where the Birmingham men sought their ease. The room
was neat and clean, yet the huge chairs seemed to stand where
they had been last used and where they would again serve a
manly mood. Books arrayed great shelves in no apparent order,
simply replaced as they had been read. A tall rack held a score
of guns whose well worn sheen spoke of common usage, and a
great roebuck stared silently from above the fire-place. The only
hint of a woman's touch in the room was a large portrait of
Catherine Birmingham hanging where the sunlight fell upon it,
seeming to set the gentle figure aglow. [pp. 247–248][2]

Such descriptions are quite common in romance fiction: having once
forgotten my Woodiwiss on the eve of a lecture, I went into a mass-
market fiction store and asked the clerk to find me a description of
a room or landscape that is clearly feminine or masculine; she knew
exactly what I was talking about, went to the bookshelves, and immediately accommodated me with numerous examples.

Popular genres are perhaps better than high art at revealing not
only differences in the ways that men and women are socialized but
also the tensions that result from culturally imposed gender differences. And popular genres allow the reader to manage the anxieties
that arise from changes in gender relations and from the never fully
successful attempts of culture to impose one standard of femininity
and masculinity. Lending support to the feminist object relations
theory of Chodorow (1978), genres such as the classic hard-boiled
detective novel embody a fantasy of masculinity in which identity
and self-esteem are rooted in separateness and an isolated form of
agency, which I have been calling the hegemonic male model of au-

---

[2]Catherine is the hero's mother, an interesting deconstructive touch to the intent
of the paragraph. The paragraph stresses the radical difference between men and
women but suggests that the men's vaunted autonomy, their independence from
women, depends on the background presence of the mother.

tonomy; romance fiction, on the other hand, embodies a fantasy of femininity in which identity and self-esteem are rooted in a self-effacing creation and maintenance of intimate relationships—the hegemonic female model of intimacy. As I said in Chapter 2, these are only two possible modes of connection and agency, but they are both dominant positions in discourse as well as internalized structures with which most men and women must contend.

I certainly do not mean to say that intimacy is female and agency male, that men do not yearn for intimacy and women for agency. Indeed, one problem in contemporary pop culture theory is that theorists unwittingly tend to label any work that centers on agency as masculine, and on nurturance as feminine; in so doing, they reinforce the pathological splitting at the core of gender identity formation. For example, in a book on heavy metal, Walser (1993) makes the argument that the core of metal is guitar virtuosity, and he traces the history of musical virtuosity back to Baroque masters such as Bach. Walser sees the kind of individualism embodied in this musical structure as masculine, and he can draw on one line of feminist theory to support this argument. But to label virtuosity or any other attribute male or female is to accept gender dichotomies, and this move usually results in a limiting of options for women. This was clear in male press reactions to *Thelma and Louise* (Scott 1991), and in some feminist reaction as well. When women break from the domestic sphere and are placed in positions or genres that have typically been encoded male—the buddy film, the road film—critics become anxious that lines are being blurred, that women want to be men, and so forth. This obscures the fact that what women want is a chance to be agentic, sexual, and aggressive, too—without being raped for it. If women were not raised to be submissive, they, too, might make guitar virtuosity their own, might revel in power chords, as we can see in some recent hardcore female bands (e.g., the women in Courtney Love's band, Hole) and in the activism of Riot Grrrls. For this reason, I prefer the integrative model I have proposed, in which we recognize that women also internalize the autonomous male model of agency and then struggle in their own way with the conflicts it engenders.

In Western culture, both genders develop capacities and longings for agency and intimacy, but social taboos—and, as I will argue, the limited way agency and intimacy are defined and gendered—make it hard for women to feel unselfish about fulfilling agentic needs and hard for men to feel manly about their needs for intimacy. What results is a tumultuous struggle between men and women who try to meet each other's radically different needs in heterosexual relationships. No less tumultuous are those struggles that take place within the individual, straight or gay, when internal desires for agency or intimacy come into conflict with tabooed versions of masculinity and femininity.

Popular genres try both to maintain the gender status quo and to alter it in ways that would make our gender conflicts less painful. While many contemporary works in these genres show great concern to maintain the gender status quo and, if anything, exaggerate gender difference to do so, they also reflect wishes to integrate various versions of agency and connection. Hard-boiled detective fiction works within a fairly constricted model of male autonomy, but its texts try to manage the pain of rigidly adhering to such a model, particularly the pain of isolation. A romance is a romance only if falling in love is the core of the action, but recent romance fiction has tried to make love include the hero's recognition of the heroine's agency. Indeed, a central conflict in contemporary forms of these genres is how to hold onto a traditional gender identity while integrating agency and connection. The fantasy invariably hits an impasse, for, in our culture, agency and connection are not only coded as masculine and feminine respectively but are constructed in such a way as to be impossible to integrate. If relationship requires self-effacement and agency requires a splendid heroic isolation, how can the heroine of romance fiction be agentic and how can the hero of detective fiction carry on a love life with not an object but a subject?

Gendered genres do reveal that men and women have different fantasies, different fears, and different levels of tolerance for emotions like sadness and anger. But many of these differences are products of the defensive splitting that constitutes normative masculinity and femininity. For example, there are many men's genres that feature a lone, tough male hero. Cultural and historical factors influence how that toughness and isolation will be enacted and whether it will be most popular in the generic form of the western or hard-boiled detective fiction. Jane Tompkins (1992) has convincingly argued that to understand the generic conventions of the western you have to go outside of the text and look at what forms preceded it in popularity. In her view, the early twentieth-century western can be understood only when read against the very popular domestic and Christian fiction of the late nineteenth century. Motivated in part by anxiety about the contemporaneous movement for women's rights, writers of the western constructed a version of masculine space, character, and plot in direct opposition to what they considered the more feminine world of their predecessors.

Tania Modleski's groundbreaking *Loving with a Vengeance: Mass-Produced Fantasies for Women* (1982) shows both the facilitating and the constricting nature of the gender binary. An example of the facilitating side: in her study of the soap opera, she notes that the viewer is positioned in the role of mother, positioned to empathize with each of the multiple perspectives presented by the characters/children. The mother's intersubjective stance contests a subject–object domination paradigm. On the constricting side, Modleski elaborates some of the core fantasies and anxieties of women's genres, many of which stem from women's lower status in relation to men. Writing about romance fiction, she argues that the novels incorporate revenge fantasies that reverse the gender order in women's favor but maintain a paradigm of domination. An example: whereas in life it seems that women spend a lot more time thinking about relationships than men do, romance fiction writers make the hero obsess over the heroine and think about her all day long. Modleski thinks that the rape scenes reflect not wishes to be raped, but rather anxieties about rape. These anxieties are managed by having the menacing hero turn out to have loved the heroine all along. Finally, Modleski and others have noted that the men of romance fiction appear at the outset to be stereotypes of cultural masculinity: cold, distant, hard, muscular, gorgeous, ladies' men. Nonetheless, their coldness and distance turn out to be due to misunderstandings; for example, a jealous other woman told him that the heroine was a scheming little adventuress, and it takes him the whole book to discover that the heroine is really a patient, nurturant, selfless, domestic wonder. The reader knows all along that both heroine and hero have hearts of gold. Thus, Modleski argues, romance writers and readers create the kind of men they long for, men who are very macho but who, in the end, are as sensitive as your best girl friend.

Of course, a romance heroine doesn't have a best girlfriend because other women, unless old and asexual, are not to be trusted. Indeed, Modleski and the Lacanian critic Alison Light (1984) point out that these scheming peers incarnate the versions of femininity that a good bourgeois feminine gender identity represses. Female villains are often more interesting to the heroine than is the hero; in du Maurier's *Rebecca*, for example, it is the hero's ex-wife Rebecca, not the hero, who obsesses the nameless, drab heroine, the second Mrs. de Winter (see Light 1984). The female villains are allowed to act out an aggressive female sexuality and a suppressed female rage that good girls are not supposed to know about. But the representation of this dilemma in romance is far different from its representation in the gender benders: Madonna, for example, makes it look easy to claim the good girl and the bad girl. In romance, the conflict is so great that it is dealt with by splitting good and bad into two characters, one of which is consciously repudiated (and for good reason; a typical male audience reaction to Madonna's autoerotic sexual enjoyment is to label her a slut).

Traditional romance heroines have all the virtues of bourgeois femininity: they have sexual feelings, but they are not allowed openly to acknowledge and act on them; they put the needs of others before their own; their whole world focuses around the hero. Is there any evidence of longings for agency? Jessica Benjamin would argue that the evidence is in the heroine's identification with the hero's autonomy. But Janice Radway's (1984) study of actual romance fiction readers found that the resistant moment of romance is the act of reading itself. Women, who tend to put the needs of others before their own, take a fairly substantial amount of time out of the week to read romance fiction, an activity in which they receive the nurturing (see Juhasz 1988) and sexual pleasure (see Snitow 1979) usually denied them.[3]

In recent years, again spurred on by feminist activity, women's increased entry, compelled or otherwise, into the work force, and fan demands, romance heroines have become much more agentic-looking than their predecessors. Harlequin heroines are mechanics, accountants, retail managers, and the like, and part of the struggle in the text involves their wish to be recognized by the hero as an equal. The texts, however, rarely if ever can sustain the demand to be both loved and regarded as an equal. A formalist critic might say that this is because the essence of a romance is the love relationship, that if the heroine's agency shares the focus, the novel will no longer fit into the genre. This explanation does not quite satisfy because it reverses cause and effect. The form of the genre is determined by hegemonic gender conventions and not vice versa. No less than in M. Butterfly, the romance novel's version of love depends on particular gender conventions, and its version of love does not tolerate female equality. The novels cannot sustain the heroine's wish to be an equal because the male model of autonomy and the female model of intimacy that still underwrite romance fiction are incompatible with intersubjectivity.

What do I mean by this? First is the problem with the female model of intimacy. All over romance fiction we find that underneath the manifest fantasy, which is that relationships provide security, is latent anxiety that relationships not just with men but with women as well are quite unreliable. As noted earlier, the universe of romance fiction includes few other sources of nurturance besides the hero. In classical romance fiction, mothers are often dead, and fathers, when alive, are not usually able to love the heroine the way she needs to be loved. Girlfriends are rarely to be trusted. So the hero has to make up for all the love that the heroine never got. Unlike the universe of much of male popular culture, a hostile universe wherein no one

---

[3]In Radway's sample, 33 percent of the women read 5–9 romances a week, 22 percent read 1–4 a week, and 4 women read 15–25 per week. Carol Thurston writes, in 1987, that 1 in 4–6 American women read 4 or more per month.

can be trusted, the romance is in part about coming to trust one other person, the man of your dreams. This man is to be parent, friend, lover, everything, and the heroine is to be the center of his universe.[4] Yet the underlying fear of this fiction is the flip side, abandonment, the return to the state of isolation, of not being understood, the state that preceded meeting the hero. How indeed did this heroine become so relational if she never got any love? The fear of abandonment and the willingness to enter self-effacing relationships are two sides of the same coin. The rhythm of the texts alternates between seduction and abandonment, and the texts often make an explicit connection between the heroine's inability to assert herself and her history of parental abandonment. The novels suggest that it is not love, not an ongoing sense of reliable connection, that makes a woman ready for a self-effacing relationship, but rather the anxiety, born of experience, that connection is unreliable, conditional— and that her own assertiveness might be the reason the relationships fail. Somewhere along the developmental line, as Gilligan (1982) has argued, females get the message that female agency poses a threat to connection.

Autonomy, too, would have to be redefined if it were to be compatible with an intersubjective mode of relating. Autonomy, as practiced in our culture, just about requires isolation. As we saw above, one fantasy of romance texts is to have thoughts of the woman so obsess the hero that he is drawn away from his work. These texts in fact require both the hero and the heroine to forgo autonomy or at least to make it quite secondary to love. One recent way romance

---

[4]Ernest Abelin's (1971) studies of gender differences in rapprochement suggest that girls exit rapprochement denying gender difference but aware of generational difference. Generationally, their fantasies are around taking care of and being taken care of; in terms of gender, their core fantasy is uniqueness. Boys exit rapprochement denying generational difference, but with a heightened awareness of gender difference. Boys' core fantasy is that they are omnipotent like father. It is interesting to think of this blend of Lacanian and Mahlerian theory in light of the fantasies at the core of male and female popular genres such as romance for women, where the woman demands to be the only object of the hero's universe of desire, and action films for men, where pleasure is found in the hero's indestructability.

writers have tried to hold autonomy and intimacy in tension is to have the heroine and hero work together. In Charlotte Lamb's *The Threat of Love* (1992), the heroine's father wants to take over the hero's family department store, and the heroine, an accountant, is sent to go over the hero's books. After the usual rhythm of misunderstanding, rage, protest, and surrender cedes to love, hero and heroine fly off to the States to start a department store together. Work is permissible, so long as it does not herald the hero's turn to other pursuits, which is read as abandonment of the heroine—and which returns us to the discovery that women see relationships as anything but reliable. Proof of reliability requires that the hero forgo autonomous pursuits.

Ann Rosalind Jones (1986) argues that the dictates of hegemonic femininity come into conflict with romance fiction's desire to incorporate into its texts feminism's calls for female independence. I would say that this is so, but I would add that the dictates of femininity include not only a cultural pressure to maintain relationship, not only a proud refusal to be autonomous on male isolationist terms, but also a psychic state of uncertainty about the durability of relationship, particularly about whether a woman can be loved if she is in touch with a nonconventional desire and agenda. One of my patients used to worry that if she asserted herself at work she would be thought of as a bitch. She had every reason to worry.

Before leaving romance fiction, I would like to challenge another received idea, this time about the workings of identification between reader and text. In Radway's study, women romance readers expressed a very strong identification with the heroine, so strong that they indicated they might read the last few pages of a novel before purchase to make sure there was a happy ending. When I teach romance fiction, I ask my students to read an erotic scene to themselves and write down what makes it erotic. Nine out of ten women students will say that they identify with the heroine being seen and made love to by the hero. Nonetheless, I would argue that romance fiction, on the surface purely heterosexual, in fact has a strong homosexual subtext.

Critics such as Ann Barr Snitow (1979) and Alison Assiter (1988) write that romance fiction is pornography for women. Snitow notes that the books are one long scenario of (heterosexual) fore-play and that heroines are in a constant state of sexual readiness. In fact, every opportunity is taken to titillate the reader with visions of the heroine's body. In Kathleen Woodiwiss's classic *The Flame and the Flower*, heroine Heather's breasts are constantly slipping out of her clothes or half revealed as she lifts her arm, half seen through a transparent gown. In the text itself, her body is looked at not only by the hero but by dressmakers, and her aunt, in short, by women and men. Although my women students insist that in these scenes they identify with Heather and imagine themselves being looked at longingly by a male, I would say that since romance readers are just about exclusively female, these omnipresent breasts must also be meant to give pleasure to a female spectator. Like my students, nearly all feminist critics of the romance focus exclusively on the reader's identification with the heroine rather than her desire for the hero-ine. To do so is to collude with a heterosexist binary, for I think that the pleasure of these texts is both hetero- and homosexual. Thus here, too, as in the gender benders, we have a deconstruction of the heterosexual/homosexual dichotomy, but in the binders this deconstruction is, we might say, closeted, whereas in the benders it is openly celebrated. Again, as with the villain/heroine dynamic, what the culture repudiates, what it demands women disidentify with, gets split off and goes underground but re-emerges to haunt the good white, middle-class, heterosexual subject.

Classic hard-boiled detective fiction works the other end of the autonomy–connection gender dichotomy. The first hard-boiled de-tectives appeared in the early '20s; Dashiell Hammett's Continental Op made his debut in the dime magazine *Black Mask* in 1923. Hard-boiled detectives, urban loners, have much in common with other isolated heroes of male popular culture; critics trace Sam Spade's and Phillip Marlowe's characteristics back to those of James Fenimore Cooper's Leatherstocking. As Tompkins alerts us, we must see these characteristics not as what men are like, but as fantasies that men elaborate against what they perceive as a constricting reality. This reality includes responsibilities to spouse and family (Dashiell Hammett felt he had to move out from his wife and children to begin to write), fears of intimacy, and also the requirements of an increasingly bureaucratic and unadventurous work existence, in which chances for autonomy are in fact few.

The world of the classic hard-boiled detective is thoroughly corrupt and hostile; time and time again the novels prove that no one can be trusted, least of all the beautiful women we have come to know as *femmes fatales*. The detective is a tough but ordinary guy, who chooses to be marginal because the mainstream, which includes the police and the moneyed classes they protect, is rotten to the core. While I think that the primary pleasures of these texts come from identification with the hero's autonomy, even classic hard-boiled detective fiction struggles with the pain of the hero's isolation. Raymond Chandler's work deals with this in an interesting way, one not atypical of male popular genres. In just about every one of his works, the plot is motivated by Marlowe's strange attraction to another character, an unknown male. For example, in *The Long Goodbye* (1953) Marlowe has a mysterious pull toward Terry Lennox, who in fact treats Marlowe quite poorly. Terry disappears early in the novel, and only when he returns at the end does Marlowe let himself recognize how Terry has played him for a fool. Nonetheless, all of Marlowe's autonomous action, the detective plot itself, is undertaken out of loyalty to the absent Terry. *It is connection that makes autonomous action meaningful.*

Yet, because it must not threaten the isolationist model of male autonomy, it is a peculiar kind of connection we see here, what I call connection on the sly. This kind of connection is rather typical of male genres; another example is the slam dancing, head banging, and stage diving of a heavy metal audience. Male bonding has always been central to metal, both within the band and among the fans. On the surface, metal suggests that pleasure comes just from autonomous action, from playing guitar or air guitar. But under the surface lies the suggestion that what a man really needs in order to take real pleasure in autonomy is connection and recognition—not from a woman, but from a man (see Leverenz 1991). Women are in fact quite peripheral to male genres, whereas, as we have seen in our look at romance fiction, men are absolutely central to women's genres.

Recognition, however, even from a man, is impossible to get directly, because no one can be trusted in the world of male genres, which makes a certain subgenre of the buddy film extremely interesting. Buddy films became popular in the late '60s, when masculinity was threatened on at least two fronts, the Vietnam War front, and the women's liberation war front. A subgenre that includes such classics as *Midnight Cowboy* (Schlesinger 1969), *Midnight Run* (Brest 1988), *Lethal Weapon* (Donner 1987), and *48 Hrs.* (Hill 1982) involves a relationship where two men are thrown together against their will. The films struggle with the problem of forging a bond between men taught to trust no one but themselves. Again, recognition is sought in the relationship between the men, and women are often denigrated in the service of helping to forge the male bond. As different as male and female fears and fantasies may be, one thing common to both gender's genres is a world in which one must struggle to establish basic trust, the requirement of Erikson's (1968) first stage of healthy development. Further, both men's and women's genres suggest that each gender seeks trust and recognition only from those with the power to confer it: men. In classic hard-boiled detective fiction, anxieties about closeness to other men, and competitive anxieties about the greater power of other men, are dealt with by denying the need for recognition. Indeed, celebrations of autonomy are constructed from this denial of the need for recognition. Chandler's detective is hostile towards powerful men, but he reserves his greatest hostility for women and other others with less power than the more threatening white male elites.[5]

---

[5]In his fascinating book *White Guys* (1995), Fred Pfeil suggests a model for understanding masculinity in both classic hard-boiled detective fiction and contemporary detective fiction. He sees a dynamic in which the hero resists and yields to indulgences considered feminine, and he feels Chandler's Marlowe yields much more than Hammett's Op. The detective's task is to "rescue masculinity and restore male-dominant order" to a "feminine and pre-oedipal morass" (p. 112); the pleasure is in both holding back from and yielding to the morass (p. 113).

The problem I see here is that these "feminine" indulgences have nothing to do with women but are rather male projections of what is "feminine." While Pfeil is aware that this is the case, his theory does not really grapple with the problem

Toward the end of *The Long Goodbye*, there is a scene between Marlowe and his love interest, Linda Loring. Linda asks him to marry her and he refuses. Although it first looks as though he refuses because he covets his independence, it turns out that his primary reason for saying no is his fear that she will someday abandon him. Marlowe says the marriage wouldn't last six months:

> "For two people in a hundred it's wonderful. The rest just work at it. After twenty years all the guy has left is a work bench in the garage. American girls are terrific. American wives take in too damn much territory. Besides—"

> "I want some champagne."

> "Besides," I said, "it would be just an incident to you. The first divorce is the only tough one. After that it's merely a problem in economics. No problem to you. Ten years from now you might pass me on the street and wonder where the hell you had seen me before. If you noticed me at all."

> "You self-sufficient, self-satisfied, self-confident, untouchable bastard. I want some champagne." [pp. 362–363]

Just as Marlowe expresses his abandonment anxiety, Chandler has Linda, in a *non sequitur*, accuse him of self-sufficiency and self-confidence! Although the works are outwardly so different in content and character structure, the same fear of abandonment is in fact at the base both of *The Long Goodbye* and of romance fiction; what differs is the way the protagonist defends against that fear. In popular

---

that these projections conceal as much as they reveal. My guess is that neither then nor now was middle-class masculinity threatened by women; the threat came instead from wealthy white guys who own both the means of production and the goods offered for consumption. Pfeil's historicization of the dynamic, however, is quite interesting. He argues that the classic detectives embody the two sides of what he calls "Fordism," a routinized, instrumentalized system of capitalist production and a glamorized world of consumer goods (pp. 119–121), both, I would argue, run by upper-class white guys.

genres, the female defense against her fear of abandonment is to give up agency. The male defense is to avoid intimacy.

At the novel's end, Terry appears in a disguise that makes him hateful in Marlowe's eyes: he is Mexican, he is elegant, he is perfumed, and his eyebrows are "damned dainty" (p. 370):

> "You bought a lot of me, Terry. For a smile and a nod and a wave of the hand and a few quiet drinks in a quiet bar here and there. It was nice while it lasted. So long, amigo. I won't say goodbye. I said it to you when it meant something. I said it when it was sad and lonely and final. . . . You're a very sweet guy in a lot of ways. I'm not judging you. I never did. It's just that you're not here any more. You're long gone. You've got nice clothes and perfume and you're as elegant as a fifty-dollar whore." [p. 378]

This is almost romance fiction in reverse. Marlowe fell in love at first sight over nothing and describes phase one of their relationship as though he were Terry's whore. Now that Terry is back and a relationship is possible, it's over. The cross-gendered simile that ends the paragraph is not uncommon in Chandler's writing; nor is the misogyny. Terry is no longer worthy to be a male buddy; for one thing, he's present, and for another, he's a woman—and a non-white woman at that. Racism and sexism explode at the end to cover over the repudiated femininity and homosexuality, the repudiated dependency, and the repudiated wish for white-male recognition that pervade the entire novel. The ending of the novel tells it as it is: if you have a deep distrust of connection and feel the only way to maintain moral purity and self-sufficiency is in isolation, then all you are going to have in the end is isolation. It is hardly a happy ending, hardly a paean to the male model of autonomy.

As we saw in the romance novel, the evolution of the hard-boiled detective novel also shows men and women groping toward new ways of defining and trying to integrate the male model of autonomy and the female model of intimacy. In the early '70s, Robert Parker's Spenser appeared on the hard-boiled scene, a tough guy with an unshakeable commitment to his psychologist girlfriend, Susan

Silverman. The fantasy that Parker elaborates in his Spenser series is one in which an enduring and meaningful love relationship does not drain the hero of one ounce of toughness, and a love respectful (if not fully comprehending) of the male code facilitates rather than interferes with getting the job done.

Spenser draws attention to the fact that he is the namesake of the author of *The Faerie Queen*, but he also often reminds us that he is every bit as tough as Phillip Marlowe and Sam Spade. He lets us know that he reads feminist classics, is a great cook, and can be quite a sensitive guy. Whereas toughness, isolated autonomy, and the male code of honor are defended, elaborated, and largely assumed to be reasonable by Spade and Marlowe, Spenser often finds himself in situations that throw the sense, viability, and desirability of this male code into question. Two issues are raised and explored in the novels:

1. Is there something wrong with Spenser's code, and thus with the very definition of male autonomy?
2. Can one who lives by this code have intimate relationships?

Spenser, like Marlowe before him, wonders about what it means to be tough. But Parker extends this wondering. He frequently has the detective plot itself raise questions about the efficacy of hard-boiled manhood; moreover, Susan, alien to Spenser's code, continuously confronts him on the code's presuppositions and blind spots while trying to understand the code from Spenser's point of view.[6]

---

[6]Pfeil's (1995) analysis of Spenser is quite different from mine and much more negative. He describes Spenser's version of masculinity as "mastery-in-relation," an apt phrase that captures what I have described as the fantasy of being as tough as Spade but still connected to people and to the social world. Susan and Hawk, his black sidekick, function as ciphers in Spenser's "ongoing negotiation between . . . his feminine and his hypermale sides" (p. 125); the real violence and primitive indulgences are displaced onto the Black man, Hawk.

In Pfeil's structure, Spenser represents "Sonyism," the phase of capitalist development that follows "Fordism." Here, consumption is okay for men, and Pfeil sees Spenser's consumption as well as his distaste for collectives as the core of what Pfeil calls his narcissism. While I agree with Pfeil that Spenser is not a collective

In *Looking for Rachel Wallace* (1980), the sixth book in the Spenser series, Spenser confronts his issues with both gay and straight women. He is hired as a bodyguard to protect the prominent lesbian feminist author Rachel Wallace, during her speaking tour in Boston. In the first pages, Rachel's Brahmin, intellectual publisher, Ticknor, probes to see whether Spenser is tough enough for the job:

> "I am told that you are quite tough."
>
> "You betcha," I said. "I was debating here today whether to have lobster Savannah or just eat one of the chairs." [p. 3]

Toughness is the first theme sounded, but Parker has Spenser quickly upset presumptions that a man whose work is physical is a macho dolt; not only does Spenser describe the food and wine in loving detail, but he is also well read. And well read not just in the male canon, but also in feminist classics:

> "Do you know very much about Rachel Wallace?"
>
> "*Sisterhood*," I said.
>
> "Really?"
>
> "Yeah. I have an intellectual friend. Sometimes she reads to me."
>
> "What did you think of it?"
>
> "I thought Simone de Beauvoir already said most of it."
>
> "Have you read *The Second Sex*?"
>
> "Don't tell the guys down the gym," I said. "They'll think I'm a fairy." [p. 4]

---

player, I would argue that neither does he qualify for the clinical label of narcissism. In clinical terms, narcissism is a self-esteem disorder, not a definition of high regard for the self. Consumption is narcissistic when it is used to regulate self-esteem. My argument, which Pfeil might consider part and parcel of what he calls the therapization of the hero and the social world (p. 150), is that Spenser sheds his narcissism in the course of the series and learns to appreciate others as separate subjects.

Ticknor goes on to warn Spenser that Rachel, aggressively gay, is difficult and humorless (feminists and gays are not always accorded the same opportunity to challenge stereotypes as Spenser). As Ticknor tells Spenser that he physically looks like everything Rachel Wallace hates, Spenser retorts: "'What you want . . . is someone feisty enough to get in the line of someone else's fire, and tough enough to get away with it. And you want him to look like Winnie-the-Pooh and act like Rebecca of Sunnybrook Farm. I'm not sure Rebecca's even got a gun permit'" (p. 7).

This is one of the book's central conflicts: sometimes women need something of a man that is more in line with a traditional machoism and incompatible with niceness and sensitivity, and sometimes even incompatible with the laws of a democratic society. Spenser is more conflicted about all this than he lets on. While he deconstructs the binary of toughness and sensitivity in the first passages cited, he nonetheless puts his sensitivity aside when he does his work, with consequences that form the series' other major conflict: the incompatibility of the male model of autonomy with the kinds of relationships Spenser wants to have with women.

In novels such as *Looking for Rachel Wallace* (1980) and *A Savage Place* (1982), independent women confront Spenser with the limits of his code. The problem is that Spenser's way of going about doing his job, exercising his autonomy, virtually erases the autonomy of the women who hire him. In a central scene of *Rachel Wallace*, Rachel, a lesbian feminist author, is speaking to a group of corporate women at corporate headquarters. As the male bosses come to throw her out, she decides she is going to resist passively. In part because young, sexy girls are watching him, and in part because his idea of protection holds no place for another's agency, Spenser slugs Rachel's assailants. Once outside, Rachel lets him have it. Spenser retorts:

> "What kind of a bodyguard stands around and lets two B-school twerps like those drag out the body he's supposed to be guarding?"

> "An intelligent one. One who understands his job. You're employed to keep me alive, not to exercise your Arthurian fantasies." . . .

"Back there you embodied everything I hate," Rachel said. "Everything I have tried to prevent. Everything I have denounced—machismo, violence, that preening male arrogance that compels a man to defend any woman he's with, regardless of her wishes and regardless of her need." [pp. 81–82]

Rachel fires him, and, after she enters her hotel, Spenser confides to the doorman, "The hell of it is . . . I think she was probably right" (p. 83). Nonetheless, the book goes on to suggest that Spenser's way of doing things is the only way that gets the job done. The fantasy is that you can live by the code, have an intimate relationship, and even be liked by lesbian feminists.

The problem of erasing a woman's agency eventually occurs in Susan's and Spenser's relationship as well, and several later novels are devoted to Spenser's attempt to rework the code so that it allows Susan the freedom necessary to remain in a relationship with him. Susan recognizes that Spenser chose his field because he needs people who need protection. Beneath the attraction to hard-boiled detecting we once again see a longing for a certain kind of connection. While this protective way of connecting fits well within the western model of male autonomy, it does not work at all when deployed on a woman who herself wants to be recognized as autonomous. And this is the major problem with this model of autonomy. Inherent in it, as well as in the female model of self-effacing intimacy, is the fact that only one person in any pair can be a subject; the other is a non-subject, property of the subject, a "dependent," in short, an object. Even when the property owner is a benevolent master, a knight, as is Spenser, he still does not accord his partner the status of a separate subject. Susan and his female clients challenge Spenser's code precisely on its central tenet: these women demand to be subjects, to be recognized as having their own agency.

Spenser is no less an individualist than Marlowe and Spade, but Spenser's world is much less hostile than theirs; it's a soft-boiled world, a kinder, gentler America. Intimacy is not on the sly as it is in Chandler. The novels reveal differences in what each gender deems intimate (talking for Susan, acting for Spenser), and fewer and fewer attempts are made to resolve or apologize for these differences as the series evolves. At the same time, the relationship between Susan and Spenser does cause an important shift in Spenser's code. Because of his respect for Susan's difference, Spenser becomes less and less judgmental, less and less likely to impose his morality and view of normalcy on others. Spenser's authoritarian humanism, his tendency to speak for all individuals, falls slowly away, replaced by his sense that different people want different things, that maybe you don't fully have to understand to be able to empathize and to help another out.

Another challenge has recently been posed to the conventions of the hard-boiled detective novel. Women, active in the detective genre from its beginnings, have turned from writing amateur and classic detective fiction to writing the hard-boiled variety. And their protagonists—Sue Grafton's Kinsey Millhone, Linda Barnes's Carlotta Carlyle, Sara Paretsky's V. I. Warshawski, to name the best known—are tough-talking, hard-drinking, hard-living women. What happens to the hard-boiled world when a female occupies the position staked out by male fantasies of autonomy? Why is this position desirable? What are its pitfalls? How does it alter the genre? How does the genre constrain it?

Paretsky's hard-boiled V. I. and Grafton's Millhone first appeared in 1982. Both Millhone and V. I. are without parents (a convention in hard-boiled detective fiction), without husband or significant other (each is divorced, Kinsey twice), and without children. Each to some degree follows in her father's footsteps. Despite their heroines' lack of biological parents, both Grafton and Paretsky provide families of sorts for them, particularly older men and women who function as parent surrogates. Here, as in lesbian detective fiction and romance fiction, families are absent but longings for a good family are evident.

In Parker, Spenser's heterosexual relationship is what humanizes him, keeps him in contact with warmth, trust, and care. Heterosexual relationships are far more problematic for hard-boiled female detectives. Divorces happen because their husbands could not tolerate these women's strong needs to be independent. And love relationships in the novels are often with men who turn out to be *hommes fatals*. The primary fantasy and pleasure for the female reader probably centers on the heroine's demand to be recognized and valued for her autonomous activity. V. I.'s autonomous life is described as immensely pleasurable: "I took the portable phone from the bedroom into the bath with me. Once I was in the tub with whiskey at close reach I checked in with the answering service. Jonathan Michaels had tried to reach me. . . . I stuck the phone up on the sink and leaned back in the tub with my eyes closed" (Paretsky 1988, p. 122). Nothing could be further from the version of femininity expressed in romance fiction.

Like Spade, Marlowe, and Spenser, V. I. keeps her knowledge to herself, often frustrating allies who want more information. V. I.'s appropriation of male prerogative is exciting; she is not afraid to go out into the mean streets alone at night (probably because she packs a gun and knows how to use it). Readers may worry more for V. I. than for Spenser; V. I. herself doesn't often worry.

But the romance heroine is right to fear that if she is too autonomous others will reject her; V. I.'s version of femininity often causes others, even her intimates, to bristle. She has many conflicts with people who put her on the defensive about her version of autonomy. A family friend and policeman, Bobby Mallory, pleads with her to settle down and have children like a "normal" "girl":

> Mallory looked around in disgust. "You know, if Tony had turned you over his knee more often instead of spoiling you rotten, you'd be a happy housewife now, instead of playing at detective and making it harder for us to get our job done."

> "But I'm a happy detective, Bobby, and I made a lousy housewife." That was true. My brief foray into marriage eight years ago had ended in an acrimonious divorce after fourteen months: some men can only admire independent women at a distance. [Paretsky 1982, p. 24]

While the female hard-boiled detective shares loner status with her male counterparts, there is a lot more pressure on her to connect. The male model of autonomy makes of isolation a virtue, a sign of successful masculinity and moral purity; that same model sees female needs for career and alone time as pathological, unfeminine. Sue Grafton's heroine Kinsey Millhone plays down the heroic isolate nature of detecting: "There's no place in a P. I.'s life for impatience, faintheartedness, or sloppiness. I understand the same qualifications apply for housewives" (Grafton 1986, p. 33). Nonetheless, both V. I. (who is quite sloppy and obviously does not see her job as in any way like that of a housewife) and Millhone treasure their independence and alone time and actively choose not to be in relationships that require too much of them. And people are always trying to make them feel that they are pathological for exercising this preference. (While I am about to deconstruct the driven way that V. I. exercises what I would call her "counter-dependence," I in no way mean to suggest that needs for solitude are pathological.)

There are those who argue that Paretsky's work upsets the conventions of male hard-boiled detective fiction in a number of ways, for example, the refusal to adopt a voice of authority and drown out other voices, the refusal to isolate the heroine, and the refusal of a linear plot (see Godard 1989, Reddy 1988). While I do not fully agree, I'd say that one thing that cannot be contested is that the job that motivates the plot of these novels almost always involves people V. I. is close to as friend or family. Thus, critics argue, where Spenser's clients are not part of his personal circle and he is paid for his work, V. I. does her labor out of loyalty to relationship and often does not get paid. What these paeans to the unselfish relational woman miss is that V. I. is usually quite reluctant and resentful about taking these jobs. When V. I.'s reluctance is factored in, a slightly different story about autonomy and connection emerges.

Indeed, criticism of V. I.'s rabidly defended autonomy does not come only from outsiders. Several novels have as subtext her own conscious and unconscious conflicts about defying the conventions of "normal" femininity; through dreams, arguments, and self reflection, Paretsky explores the toll a male model of autonomy takes on a female model of connection. In *Bitter Medicine* (1987), for example, Consuelo, a pregnant Hispanic teenager, dies after giving birth to a stillborn baby she names after V. I. Ironically, Consuelo got pregnant at age 16 in defiance of her mother's pressure that she be autonomous, that she make something of herself and lead their poor, Hispanic family to the American dream. Her baby goes on to haunt the text, both as the baby that the rebel V. I. is unwilling to have and as the needy baby that V. I. once was and still, on some level, is. The novel is full of all V. I.'s usual hard-living exploits, but the subplot suggests that, for a white woman, her kind of autonomy is something that must be won and re-won not only in struggle with devaluing men but in constant struggle with oneself.

The baby first appears in Chapter 4:

I hadn't seen Consuelo since she'd passed through the double steel doors six hours ago. In my mind she appeared as I'd last seen my mother, small, fragile, overshadowed by the machinery of an indifferent technology. I couldn't help picturing the baby, a small V. I., unable to breathe, lying with a shock of black hair, lost in the medical maze. . . .

In my sleep I tried to find the source of an anguished wailing. I went up the stairs in my parents' old house and found my ex-husband snoring loudly. I shook him. "For God's sake, Richard, wake up—you'd rouse the dead with your noise." But when he got up the sound continued, and I realized it came from a baby lying on the floor next to the bed. I tried to comfort it, but it wouldn't stop wailing. It was baby Victoria who would not stop crying because she couldn't breathe. [p. 24]

The baby, her parents, and her marriage are dead. Is it due to some fault of her own? Shortly after this, her surrogate mother, Dr. Lotty Heschel, tells her that she doesn't have the temperament for clinical work. V. I. is not flattered; she reads this as a suggestion that she is "too detached and analytical to be good with people" (pp. 27–28).

V. I. is worried that there is something wrong with her relational capacities, and this worry follows her throughout the book, giving rise to the dreams. It also makes her take on the case, for she agrees to do it only after several people who want her to investigate accuse her of an unnatural detachment. In her dreams, in fact, the baby is dead because V. I. won't claim her. In one baby dream, she relates, "I realized it was my child, but that . . . she would come to life only if I gave her my name" (p. 31).

V. I.'s guilt about not having a baby strongly colors another of the book's subplots, in which Lotty's clinic is nearly destroyed by a group of rabid anti-abortionists led by a creep who, when taken by the police, is freed by the efforts of his slick corporate lawyer—V. I.'s ex (now with a second wife and children). Unconscious guilt about murdered and unborn babies is all over this text.

The dreams focus also on V. I.'s relationship with her parents, and they express a fair amount of guilt about her agency. In one, V. I. connects one of her happiest moments as a girl jock with her mother's illness and death:

> I was on my way to the hospital. My mother was sick. She might be dying but Dad and I were being brave for her sake. After winning the state high-school basketball championship, the other girls on the team and I had sneaked off with several pints of whiskey. The ten of us drank it all and were vilely sick. Now I had to go see my mother. She needed me alert and cheerful, not aching and hung over. [p. 60]

If you do the kind of things V. I. likes to do, the kind of things that give her female readers great pleasure, will your parents and children get sick and die? Can you be a relational woman if you are too autonomous? If you have a baby, can you take pleasure in physical and other autonomous pursuits? Another dream suggests the answer is no:

> I was outside the high, cyclone fence surrounding my high school's athletic field, watching a baseball game. Bill Buckner was on third. He turned and saw me and beckoned to me to climb the fence to join him. I started to climb but my right leg was paralyzed. I looked down and saw the mute mournful face of the baby staring at me as she clutched my pantleg. I couldn't dislodge her without hurting her and she would not let go of my jeans. The scene switched, but wherever I went, whatever else was going on, the baby clung to me. [p. 70]

Such dreams, fantasies, and fears do not haunt the texts of male detectives.

Indeed, subtexts in Parker usually reveal that Spenser is worried about how tough he really is. Anxiety about toughness is just under the surface of every novel; should the reader's identification with Spenser waver for a moment, the reader would find himself lost among the untough. For toughness is the axis on which Spenser judges all males. The novels are peopled with—or rather manned by—short men who think they're tough, high school preppies who think they're tough, loud-mouthed gangsters who think they're tough. He laughs at his own accoutrements of toughness, but he eventually is compelled to show all of the other guys that they're just not quite tough enough.

As in Parker, once Paretsky's detective plot goes into high gear, the dreams and doubts disappear and the reader is again allowed to take pleasure in V. I.'s often hilarious ways of getting what she wants. But the book ends by reminding us that V. I.'s relational capacities are limited, that her autonomy is bought at the price of an ability to be nurturant and caretaking. The *homme fatal* kills himself, leaving his dog Peppy an orphan. V. I. "adopts" her, and so she gets her baby at the book's end. But Mr. Contreras, her surrogate father/landlord, knows who is going to take care of Peppy, and his is the last word. He begins his final oration by talking about the kind of man V. I. needs. V. I. stiffens, offended but wondering herself whether her unmarried status is bothering her. Contreras continues: "'And look at the good side. We got a dog. At least, you got a dog, but who's going to walk her and feed her when you're out to all hours, huh?'" (p. 259).

Readers of Paretsky's later novels know that Mr. Contreras is quite right. He is V. I.'s mother and wife, and mother and wife are what you need to have your male model of autonomy and your connection, too. Though the book ends with V. I. and Peppy enjoying their physicality together, the book's subtext does not let the reader forget the price a woman pays for such enjoyment.

Thus I think that those feminist critics (e.g., Reddy 1988) who claim that Paretsky's work exemplifies a female, relational style are wrong. The genre conventions of hard-boiled detective fiction, like those of romance, rest on gender conventions that define autonomy and relationship in certain ways. Placing a woman in the position usually occupied by a man does challenge generic conventions and brings different issues to the fore. For example, Paretsky's work shows how the world is a dangerous place for particular subgroups—for women, minorities, and the working class—and she tends to show the effects of corruption on the everyday lives and the bodies of its victims; her work also reveals how heterosexual relationships constrain rather than enhance female agency. These differences reflect Paretsky's feminist expansion of the category *femininity*, what I referred to in Chapter 2 as the liberatory effects of the gender divide.

Nonetheless, V. I. explicitly says in *Blood Shot* that it was her mother's death that made her terrified of dependence, of needing help. Lotty has just reprimanded her for coming to her for help, then disappearing: "You involved me in your problems, and then you disappeared without a word. That isn't independence—that is thoughtless cruelty" (p. 252). V. I. responds:

> "Lotty, I'm scared. I've never been this frightened, not since the day my dad told me Gabriella was dying and nothing could be done for her. I knew then that it was a terrible mistake to depend on someone else to solve my problems for me. Now I seem to be too terrorized to solve them for myself and I'm thrashing around. But when I ask for help it just drives me wild. I know it's hard on you. I'm sorry for that. But I can't get enough distance right now to do anything about it." [p. 253]

What makes V. I. compatible with a male model of autonomy is her dread of dependence, a dread based on actual loss (we will see the same dynamic in the next chapter on Madonna). But it also makes her a problematic friend and lover. The dread of dependence draws her to the male model of autonomy and this model does indeed protect her from getting too close to others. The male model of autonomy and the female model of relationship make holding autonomy and connection in tension barely feasible even in fantasy, regardless of whether the autonomous figure is male or female. In both models, only one person gets to be a subject, and the other is an object. Yet gendered genres such as romance and the hard-boiled detective novel reveal clearly and poignantly both longings for integration and the gender conventions that make integration impossible.

Let us return to Rose's distinction between conservative and radical uses of psychoanalysis. What I hope to have shown here is that both the descriptive and the deconstructive psychoanalytic approaches are necessary to understand what is going on in contemporary struggles over the meaning of gender identity. The more conservative-looking gender binders, like the more conservative-looking use of psychoanalytic theory, grapple with the consequences of the internalization of gender norms, particularly as they restrict each gender's possibilities for a variety of modes of agency and connection. Men's and women's genres present different kinds of struggles and conflicts that reflect the different ways agency and connection are constrained for each gender. Contemporary romance and detective fiction portray the struggle between internalized norms (so well described by Chodorow and other relational feminists) and resistance to the constraints of these norms (the terrain of the postmodern deconstructive approach). Unlike the benders, however, gender binders suggest that fluidity and resistance to gender norms cannot be won without great struggle.

In the next chapter I look at one of postmodern feminism's icons of gender and identity fluidity, Madonna, and suggest that in her work, too, when you look just beneath the surface you find a struggle between the effects that gender categories have on psychic structure and a postmodern resistance to those categories and effects.

4

Who's That Girl?: Madonna*

In a touching moment in her documentary *Truth or Dare* (Keshishian 1991), Madonna, who rarely shows hesitation, stammers as she admits to her female dancers/singers that sometimes she feels insecure about her abilities:

> I'm in my dressing room sometimes and I think to myself, Who do I think I am? Like trying to pull this off. You know. And I sometimes, I'm very much, but I can only allow myself to think it once in awhile because if I do I'm, I'm, I'm gone. And that is, I think of you guys and thinking, sitting in your dressing room going, you know, Who this bitch think she is? . . . But I know that I'm not the best singer and I know I'm not the best dancer but, but, but [the women are interrupting here] I'm not interested in that. I'm interested in pushing people's buttons and being provocative and being political.

*This chapter is adapted from Layton 1993 (copyright © 1993 by Adam Sexton, used by permission of Delacorte Press, a division of Bantam Doubleday Dell Publishing Group) and Layton 1994b (copyright © 1994 by Westview Press and used by permission).

And provocative and political she is. Madonna is one of the best known gender benders in the pop universe, and her continuous self-reinventions are designed to challenge the gender binaries produced by gender inequality. In her *Like a Virgin* video (1984b), for example, she upends the virgin/whore dichotomy that the Church and her grandmother taught her to regard as exhausting the options for an unmarried female sexual identity. The video blurs the lines between the two and suggests that there is no reason to regard virginity as good and sexual aggressivity as bad. Here she reveals how feminine gender identity constricts rather than enhances one's possibilities. Indeed, when I have shown the *Like a Virgin* video to college audiences, men not infrequently say, "She's a slut" to describe the segments in which she sexily dances, showing that they equate female sexuality with "badness." Madonna's work brings to the mainstream postmodern feminist suggestions that even though only one version of femininity may be culturally sanctioned as good, several versions circulate within the culture and within individuals. Madonna wants the right to lay claim to them all, and her fans do, too.

In her *Erotica* video (1992a) or *Justify My Love* (1990a) she deconstructs the straight/gay dichotomy, again asking her audience to notice how homosexuality turns heterosexuality on, showing how each is constructed out of the other. Her work suggests that homo- and heterosexuality are intermixed in people; she does not allow her heterosexual audience to divide the world into straight and gay, to hide safely in a heterosexual identity and declare homosexuality other, abnormal.

Madonna also subverts what Laura Mulvey (1975) saw as a rigid rule of Hollywood, that the camera always enables the male spectator to feel that he controls who is looked at and how she is looked at. The gendered nature of looking relations are central in many of her videos. One of the earliest ones, *Lucky Star* (1984a), is framed by Madonna taking off and putting on dark glasses. With this technique, she suggests that she is in charge of how she will be looked at by the camera, and the part of her body that is most frequently on display is her bellybutton, hardly a traditional object of male desire in the west. Indeed, at the time of that video, she claimed in interviews that her bellybutton was the part of her body she found most erotic. In both form and content, Madonna's work is on the gender bending end of contemporary popular culture. Her capacity continuously to reinvent herself and so to question the notion that identities of any kind are stable and enduring constructs is one of the things that marks her as a subject of controversy.

Another part of what makes Madonna so controversial—hated and loved, defamed as a talentless manipulator and hailed not only as an artistic genius but as a feminist—is her repeated insistence that she controls her life, her work, and her image. I contribute to this myth by letting Madonna control my title, for *Who's That Girl?* (Foley 1987) was the title both of the 1987 film in which she starred and, in the usual Madonna publicity tie-in, the 1987 concert tour that preceded and promoted the film. I chose this title not to add to the myth, which I intend rather to challenge, but to suggest that in Madonna's life and work we see crystallized some of the tensions in the ways we currently think about gender identity and other aspects of identity (cf. Dyer 1991).

What I want to explore in this chapter is how the gender bending of Madonna's performances is complicated by what she has let us know about herself. Madonna's life and work suggest that while the multiplicity of one's gender internalizations makes it possible to disrupt gender binaries, the internalization of gender binaries—and the splitting it entails—also disrupts fluidity. On the question of identity, then, Madonna's two projects, the assertion of individual control characteristic of a masculine model of autonomy and the postmodern challenge to that same secular humanist notion of a controlled, rational, ego-centered self, are contradictory. On the individual level, Madonna provides an excellent example of the conflicts that emerge when a woman internalizes and expresses two competing versions of agency, each marked on a cultural level as belonging to one of two mutually exclusive gender positions. An understanding of Madonna's contribution to contemporary struggles over gender identity and agency thus requires that we again turn to both postmodern deconstructive theories and relational theories. It is the very contradiction between Madonna's two projects, I think, that has accounted for her enormous popularity, a popularity that crosses lines of gender, race, class, and, perhaps most curious, education. For Madonna is not only the darling of young girls of all classes and races, of lesbians, of black, Asian, Hispanic, and white gay males, but also an icon for academic feminists immersed in postmodern theory.

I begin with some biographical material relevant to an understanding of Madonna's work and of her image (which all, including Madonna, agree is a major part of her work). Although she clearly has a lot of control over her image and may indeed wish to convince us that behind every one of her masks lies only another mask, I do not agree with those who say that all we know of Madonna is what she chooses to reveal. This is, I think, a trivial claim, for in some sense, all we ever see of people is what they show us. Yet people are not transparent to themselves; they always reveal more than they think they reveal, and Madonna is no exception. Thus we are dealing here with various and contradictory levels of Madonna: those parts of her work and her image that she consciously fashions and those that lie outside her conscious control.

Madonna was born Madonna Louise Veronica Ciccone on August 16, 1958 in Bay City, Michigan, the first daughter of Silvio and Madonna Louise Fortin Ciccone. She says that her name in part determined her sense that she was destined for something special: "I sometimes think I was born to live up to my name. . . . How could I be anything else but what I am having been named Madonna? I would either have ended up a nun or this" (quoted in Hirschberg 1991, p. 200; see Walkerdine 1986 for a discussion of how the names and nicknames others give us become constitutive of the identity we fashion).

Madonna has two older brothers, two younger sisters (about whom one heard very little until Madonna's pregnancy), and a younger brother, Christopher, who works as her artistic director. In interviews, Madonna repeatedly talks about the death of her mother from cancer (when Madonna was 5) as the pivotal event of her psychic life: "I knew I could be either sad and weak and not in control or I could just take control and say it's going to get better" (quoted in Skow 1985, p. 77). Like Paretsky's V. I. Warshawsky (see Chapter 3), Madonna claims that her mother's death made her fear abandonment and dependence and thus reinforced an internalization of the male model of autonomy: "The part of me that goes around saying 'Fuck you! Fuck you! I'm throwing this in your face!' is the part that's covering up the part that's saying 'I'm hurt. And I've been abandoned and I will never need anyone again'" (Sessums 1990, p. 214).

Madonna has also said many times that her insatiable craving for love and approval is a result of her mother's death and her own guilt at the thought that she may have played some role in it (she often repeats an anecdote about forcing her mother to play with her when mother was already quite sick): "[When she died, I] said, 'Okay, I don't have a mother to love me; I'm going to make the world love me'" (quoted in King 1991, p. 246). Part of Madonna's mania for "control," then, arises from loss, and her wish to have the largest possible audience love her is a wish to negate that loss. Her denial of the vulnerability brought on by dependency and loss manifests itself both in rigid self-control and in a hierarchical one-down or one-up way of connecting with others (visible in just about every song and every interview). As we shall see, the concept of control structures not only Madonna's autobiographical narrative but the narratives of her biographers as well.

Madonna has acknowledged an early envy of male privilege and an identification with masculinity, which she attributes both to seeing her brothers' real privilege and to not having a mother:

> I know if I'd had a mother I would be very different. It gave me a lot of what are traditionally looked upon as masculine traits in terms of my ambitiousness and my aggressiveness. Mothers, I think, teach you manners and gentleness and a certain kind of, what's the word? I don't want to say subservience, but a patience, which I've never had. Then, when my mother died, all of a sudden I was going to become . . . the best singer, the best dancer, the most famous person in the world, everybody was going to love me. I've been to analysis and I understand that about myself. [quoted in Deevoy 1991, p. 20]

The second blow to Madonna's sense of being loved was the remarriage of her father to one of the family's housekeepers (who had two children of her own) when Madonna was about 8: "It was then that I said, okay, I don't need anybody. . . . No one's going to break my heart again. I'm not going to need anybody. I can stand on my own and be my own person and not belong to anyone" (quoted in Andersen 1991, p. 27). When Madonna announces she needs no one, she distances herself not only from her own view of femininity but from the brand of feminist psychology that defines connection as the core of female selfhood (see, for example, Chodorow 1978, also Miller et al. 1991). Yet, *Truth or Dare* (Keshishian 1991), the interviews she gave to promote the film, and several of the songs in her album *Like A Prayer* (1989b) center on longings for family connections, and particularly on her image of herself as maternal.

In interviews, Madonna and her friends and family members frequently cite her lifelong need to be the center of attention and the early scapegoating by siblings angry at how she forced attention onto herself. Madonna claims her stepmother made her feel like Cinderella when she required her, as eldest daughter, to take care of her younger siblings; on at least one occasion, her stepmother smacked her in the face hard enough to cause a nosebleed. Throughout Madonna's work there is an uneasy tension between her maternalism/familism/communalism and her competitive individualism, a tension that seems to reflect the way she internalized both a male model of autonomy and what Gilligan (1982) has called a female ethic of connection and care. Often she expresses the conflict in scenarios where the spotlight is on her as the agent who, because of her ability to identify as both insider and outsider, brings warring groups together: black and white, working class and upper class, male and female, father and daughter (see Freccero's [1992] discussion of the *Like A Prayer* video).

Madonna's disciplinarian Catholic father impressed her with the sense that leisure opens the door to the devil; along with the need to make up for loss, Madonna cites her father's philosophy as a source of her workaholism. As for early training in gender identity and sexuality, she reports that her grandmother and the Catholic church made her believe that it was wicked to be with men, and that women have to choose between being either virgins or whores. She seems to see her mother as soft and angelic, but her mother was also sickly and unable to do much, and her body had deteriorated by the time Madonna was 5.

Madonna's own legend has it that she felt ugly and not special until she met her dance teacher, Christopher Flynn, at age 14. Not only did he tell her she was beautiful and make her feel special, but he introduced her to the gay discos of Detroit, to life on the margins, and to fun. Her subsequent devotion in her life and work to people on the margins—young girls, blacks, Hispanics, gays—attests not only to her connection to Flynn but to her own lifelong feelings of somehow being different and unloved.

Madonna attended the University of Michigan for awhile on a dance scholarship and there met Stephen Bray, her future songwriting partner. She left the University to pursue a dance career in New York. Next came a few years of living in poverty (punctuated by a brief period of luxury in Paris under the tutelage of two French producers who wanted to make her into their version of a star; it was not Madonna's version, so she left). There are those who, from her first public appearances in discos, could not stand Madonna (for example, Michael Musto of the *Village Voice*, who with foot in mouth recalls in a 1990 documentary his early premonition that Madonna wouldn't go anywhere because she was such an egocentric bitch). But most of the people who have been part of her success machine from the beginning remain in awe of her drive and her charisma.

Her first album came out in 1983 (*Madonna*), and when videos later appeared to promote it, sales soared and eventually reached nine million. Six of the songs on her first album became top-ten dance hits. Everyone agrees that Madonna and MTV, which began broadcasting in 1981, are a match made in heaven, that music video is Madonna's medium. In September 1984, her second album was released (*Like a Virgin*) and sold eleven million copies. Already enormously popular with gay and black disco audiences and with young girls, Madonna got the attention of the white adult audience when she co-starred with Rosanna Arquette as Susan in Susan Seidelman's 1985 film *Desperately Seeking Susan*. The Virgin Tour (later to be a video) promoted this film, and Madonna's song in the film, *Get into the Groove*, promoted both album and tour. This familiar pattern of intertextual promotion peaked in 1990, when Madonna's Blonde Ambition Tour promoted her 1989 *Like a Prayer* album (already promoted not only by MTV but by the canceled Pepsi commercial version of the title song, which, although shown only a few times, netted Madonna five million dollars and a lot of publicity). Simultaneously, the tour promoted Warren Beatty's film *Dick Tracy*, in which she played Breathless Mahoney. *Dick Tracy* in turn promoted *I'm Breathless*, Madonna's (1990b) album of songs inspired by the movie.

If that wasn't enough Madonna for one season, she also appeared on the cover of almost every major magazine in the spring and summer of 1990, with interviews promoting her entire oeuvre and high fashion photographs by the likes of Helmut Newton that were yet another showcase for her talent of self-reinvention. And then of course the Blonde Ambition Tour became the basis of her 1991 documentary, *Truth or Dare: On the Road, Behind the Scenes, and in Bed with Madonna* (Keshishian 1991). This kind of career control left the staff of *Forbes* magazine breathless as they vainly sought an interview for the October 1990 issue, which featured Madonna on the cover and a story titled "A Brain for Sin and a Bod for Business" (Schifrin 1990).

I have left out a few Broadway plays, the scandal attending the unauthorized publication of nude pictures taken in Madonna's early years in New York when she made money by posing for artists, the movie flops, and, of course, her highly publicized marriage to Sean Penn in 1985 and equally publicized divorce in 1989. What I do not want to leave out is what people wrote about her during these years, and I begin with two of the three unauthorized biographies that appeared in 1991 (Norman King's *Madonna. The Book*; Christopher Andersen's *Madonna Unauthorized*; the third, David James's *Madonna* is really little more than a photohistory with a bit of laudatory biographical filler).

Although these biographies tell us very little about Madonna beyond a chronology of events in her career, they tell us a lot about what pop biographers think people want to know and how these biographers conceptualize lives (Andersen and King seem much more concerned with getting a book out fast than with checking even factual information like how many brothers and sisters Madonna has). Andersen's book is, I think, typical. It is held together by the thin red thread of Madonna's relationship with Sean Penn. The book begins with the marriage and ends with the question of what she saw in him. In between are two entirely contradictory narratives: in one, Madonna goes from rags to riches almost overnight and with no work; in the other, Madonna goes from rags to riches because of her devotion to work and her extraordinary discipline.

David Lusted (1991) describes this contradiction as lying at the heart of the U.S. myth of individualism. I agree, with one amendment. The no-work side of the myth has a slightly different twist when male critics apply it to Madonna. In a male artist's story, biographers attribute meteoric rises to genius. Madonna's biographers, on the other hand, attribute her rise to the many important men she slept with and the many men and women she seduced and abandoned; in short, she is famous because she is a bitch and a slut. The no-work narrative is thus nasty gossip, the discipline narrative a boring chronology of career events. The only genius Madonna is granted is a genius for making money. Although the tone of the second narrative is awestruck, the tone of the first is damning and the overriding effect of the whole is negative. King, for example, ends with a chapter called High Priestess of Hype; Andersen's (1991) last paragraph cites the same material with which I opened this chapter, but he takes it out of context and, in so doing, he reveals his disdain:

> Today, however, she is very much alive and millions pray at the altar of Madonna, Our Lady of Perpetual Promotion. She is ubiquitous, part of the furniture of our lives. More than merely reflecting her times, Madonna is a virtual fun-house hall of mirrors, casting back distorted and fragmented images that both dazzle and disturb. In her film *Truth or Dare*, she says, "I

know I'm not the best singer. I know I'm not the best dancer.
But I'm not interested in that. I'm interested in pushing people's
buttons."

Believe it. [p. 334]

Elsewhere I have argued that the anger with which male critics often dismiss Madonna reveals more than mere worry about a lower-
ing of artistic or moral standards (Layton 1990b, 1993). The anger
always seems to refer back to how much money Madonna makes,
to how much power she has. What seems to be going on here is that
disturbances in white male identity caused by the economic disloca-
tions of contemporary capitalism issue in angry displacements onto
powerful women (as well as gays and minorities). As Jane Flax (1990)
and Judith Williamson (1986) have argued, it is in the interest of the
white male powers-that-be that disgruntled and disempowered
middle- and working-class males take their anger out not on them
but in gender and race wars (Levinson's 1994 film *Disclosure* exemplifies this). Thus Williamson warns us that we always need to be
alert to how gender difference is used to mask other differences, such
as those of class, which, if grasped, might be more explosive of the
status quo.

Power is central to Madonna's biographers, and their narratives,
like Madonna's autobiographical one, celebrate the individual in control of her destiny. On the surface, nothing could be further from
this reverence for control and power than what postmodern feminist critics have to say about Madonna and identity. And when you
contrast male anger towards Madonna with the celebratory tone of
postmodern feminist critics, you get some idea of the role gender plays
in critical responses to her.

As a postmodernist, Madonna is both celebrated and reviled,
a paradox that reflects two of the different meanings of *postmodern*
that currently circulate in the culture. One sense of postmodern, the
one I endorse in this book, refers to the project that critiques notions of universal truth, inevitable progress, male domination, and
innate heterosexuality, in short, a project that reveals the social
construction of reality and the varied interests that are served by

particular constructions. Another sense of postmodern, which I critique in this book, refers to imposture, posing, inauthenticity, pastiche (what Teresa Ebert [1992-1993] has referred to as ludic postmodernism/feminism). Although the two senses are related, in that a pose often reveals the constructedness of what one has taken to be the original (see, for example, Butler's [1990a] discussion of drag, or Cindy Sherman's art), the two camps that use postmodern in this sense are not really adherents of postmodernism as critique. One camp is represented by cultural conservatives who despise what they see as the mocking inauthenticity of the postmodern; these are people who still believe in a non-constructed original—for example, that heterosexuality is normal and homosexuality unnatural. On the other hand, the camp that identifies with this version of postmodernism does not seem to believe in anything; this camp fetishizes the pose and thereby loses the sense of postmodernism as critique. For them, nothing is serious, everything is play (for further elaboration of these differences in the context of psychology, see Kvale 1992, and in the context of feminist debates, see Ebert 1992-1993, Flax 1990, and Nicholson 1990, 1992; see also Jameson 1983; I explore this in more detail in Chapter 5). Madonna is adored by many who engage in postmodern critique, reviled by the cultural conservatives, and iconized by devotees of the pose (see, for example, Schwichtenberg 1993b).

Postmodernism as critique targets commonsense notions of identity. Lacan's work, for example, is an attack on ego psychological fantasies about the integrity of the ego. As we have seen, Lacan's ego is a fictive entity, an entity that fantasizes itself whole and solid, that tries to claim for itself a fixed identity, but that really knows itself to be fluid, fragmented, lacking. Lacan restored to prominence the Freud who discovered the innate bisexuality and polymorphous perversity of children, the Freud for whom the Oedipus complex violently forces social constructions of masculinity and femininity onto children. Although children are socialized to adopt their culture's version of gender identity (as well as other aspects of identity), Lacan (1985) emphasized that repressed versions remain in the unconscious and constantly destabilize the ego's wish to keep these lost possibilities at bay.

Enter Madonna, darling of Lacanian and other postmodern feminists. Madonna's continuous self-reinvention, her adoption of a variety of characters and voices, her gender-bending crotch-grabbing, cross-dressing, bisexual enjoyment of the most polymorphous of perversities upset those who feel that authenticity and family values are slipping away, while they delight those who feel that authenticity and family values have always been code words used by one group to oppress another. An example of Madonna as deconstructionist: in the *Like a Virgin* video, she sets one narrative, in which she is a bride in white, against a second, in which she sings the song while sexily writhing in her trademark Boy Toy Belt, with midriff revealed and multi-crucifixed top. As critics such as John Fiske (1989) and E. Ann Kaplan (1987) point out, Madonna here takes familiar signifiers like the crucifix and wrenches them from their familiar context (the purity of the church), placing them instead in juxtaposition to things that signify the cultural opposite (sexiness). In this way, Madonna takes the lesson of her grandmother, that women are either virgins or whores, and rewrites it so that women can be both sexy and virginal; the culturally-approved version of femininity is not allowed to exhaust the possibilities in Madonna's universe. Madonna deconstructs tired concepts and tired oppositions, oppositions that limit choice for women (and men) not only by allowing no combination of the two, or no third or fourth alternative, but by setting up one side of the opposition as good and the other as evil. She claims the right to be both bad and good and thus makes us question what is so good about good and what is so bad about bad. And that is why young girls love Madonna; as Judith Williamson (1985) wrote, "[S]he retains all the bravado and exhibitionism that most girls start off with, or feel inside, until the onset of 'womanhood' knocks it out of them" (p. 47), that is, until the culture codes these feelings "bad" and makes girls feel ashamed of having them.

Perhaps the most provocative claim for Madonna's postmodernism comes from Susan McClary (1990), a musicologist. McClary not only pointed out how Madonna's video narratives upset a western narrative musical tradition in which sexually provocative females must die at the end of the story (e.g., the operas *Salome* and *Carmen*) but also claimed that the musical structure of some of Madonna's songs performs a destabilization of identity and of the male/female hierarchy. In McClary's view, Madonna's *Like a Prayer* and *Live to Tell*, for example, begin like most musical narratives with a dominant chord (read "male") answered by a nondominant (read "Other," "female") that sets the narrative conflict in motion. Rather than resolve back to the dominant at the end as in most musical narratives, Madonna's songs end by alternating between the two, refusing to resolve in favor of the male, refusing to vanquish the voice of the female.

The controversies surrounding Madonna thus reflect the tensions of a culture in which some cling for dear life to a notion of stable identity and others do what they can to destabilize the notion because they are convinced that it has been used to define as deviant anything that is not white, middle class, and heterosexual male. The voices of disapproving critics betray this tension: There is Tom Ward (1985), who referred in the *Village Voice* to Madonna's multiple identities as a "multiple hedging of bets" against what will sell best (p. 55). Jon Pareles (1990), in an otherwise positive assessment in the *New York Times* of Madonna's "evolving persona," wrote: "The only constant is the diligent effort that goes into every new guise, which made her the perfect pinup in the careerist 1980s" (p. C-11); Michael David (1989) argued in *Manhattan, Inc.* that postmodern pastiche (the ironic putting together of incongruous existing elements) creates nothing new and has no passion, and he concluded: "She's the ultimate postmodern pop star: her creation is herself, not her music" (p. 98). And Jay Cocks (1990) in *Time*: "The deliberate artfulness of her various personas stresses artificiality above all. The common coolness of each role she plays keeps everything at a safe distance, stylizing all the sensuality out of passion until only the appearance remains" (p. 75).

Noteworthy is a tendency among male critics to deny that Madonna is sexy, to assert that her sexuality is about power and not about passion. Apparently, for these critics, power is not sexy when wielded by a woman. Writing in the *New Republic*, Luc Sante (1990) epitomized this tendency: "Between the teasing simulation of carnality and the real passion for efficiency lies Madonna's bona fide erotic territory. . . . All the sexual imagery in the show, behind its rococo and vaudeville trappings, was single-mindedly fixated on power and its representations" (p. 27). This response shows better than any the gender gap in the Madonna polls, for her female fans love her precisely because she is both sexy and powerful and because she makes them feel sexy and powerful. In the mid- '90s, however, few official voices affirm sexuality in girls. On the contrary, Madonna's (1992b) *Sex* book was released at a time when a puritanical government was lashing out against the National Endowment for the Arts and "obscene" artists everywhere. The press has been negative toward just about everything that Madonna has done since.

Lest one think all Madonna's critics are male, I cite Ellen Goodman (1990), who, in her response in *The Boston Globe* to Madonna's (1990a) *Justify My Love* video, represents a liberal and humanist conception of identity, one in which stability and consistency are paramount virtues:

> But what bothers me is a belief that she offers the wrong answers to the questions, or the crisis, of identity. Especially female identity.
>
> If the work of growing up is finding a center, integrating the parts, Madonna spotlights the fragments and calls them a whole. If the business of adulthood is finding yourself, she creates as many selves as there are rooms in her video hotel. If we must evolve as grown-ups, she switches instead, like a quick-change artist between acts. And if there is a search among Americans for authenticity, Madonna offers costumes and calls them the real thing. . . . The star of this show makes little attempt to reconcile the contradictions of her life and psyche. She insists instead that all the fragments of a self be accepted. [p. 13]

What critics and fans elucidate in these critical fragments is a controversy about the very nature of contemporary identity, and my own opinion as fan–critic is that both sides have appeal, intellectual as well as popular. For I believe that Madonna is popular because she reflects our own uncertainties about identity: Is it stable, fragmented by pain, open to continual reinvention? On the one hand, she is the female in control, exercising a variant of male autonomy mixed with her own version of the maternal. Then, too, she is the fragmented daughter of a dysfunctional family, who publicly exposes her pain, propounds her own version of family values, and is as much caught up as the rest of us middle-class women in the kind of self-doubt that drives us to lose weight, change costume, and go shopping. Finally, she is a liberated, highly successful postmodern artist, who in performance transcends her pain by playfully and politically arranging and rearranging the fragments. Fans eagerly take in her symbolic messages (for example, the line in *Express Yourself* [Madonna and Bray 1989] that tells girls not to go for second best), but they also seek out any autobiographical fragment they can find to see how Madonna makes sense of her life. By deliberately making her life a part of her work, Madonna presents us with both a public and a private persona; from a psychological perspective, these two personae often contradict one another. The contradiction reveals how gender identity evolves as a negotiated struggle between the way each of us internalizes gender, race, and class polarities; the effect of being culturally designated as either male or female; and relational internalizations that make it possible to transcend polarities.

Madonna as artist, playing her multiple roles in multiple relational contexts, well exemplifies May's (1986) object relational view that at our healthiest we carry within us "a fund of . . . contradictory images and fantastic aspirations" on which our "capacity for change and development depends" (p. 188). Following Lacan, May asserted that there is no such thing as unity when it comes to identity; she who clings to a fixed notion of feminine identity, for example, is both resistant and impoverished. In the course of development, we internalize relational patterns in which we play all kinds of roles vis-à-vis important others, for example, tomboy to aggressive father, little mommy to big mommy, *femme fatale* to heroic mother and father, and so on. As May writes, "These disparate identifications, these various and shifting images of self and other, this chaotic and contradictory jumble of wishes and worries, *this* is in fact our characterological treasury" (p. 188). Madonna's own words about her project, spoken as she looked up at a gigantic image of herself on the set of the *Who's That Girl?* tour, echo those of May: "Oh God, what have I done? What have I created? Is *that* me, or is *this* me, this small person standing down here on the stage? That's why I call the tour "Who's That Girl?": because I play a lot of characters, and every time I do a video or a song, people go, "Oh, that's what she's like." And I'm not like any of them. I'm all of them. I'm none of them. You know what I mean?" (Gilmore 1987, p. 88).

To a great extent, this is the Madonna of those postmodernists who celebrate fragmentation and the fictiveness of ego identifications. Madonna's postmodernism, however, is more in the tradition of critique. While, as I noted in Chapter 2, May's (1986) version of object relations (like most non-feminist versions) says nothing about the power differentials of the internalized relational patterns, Madonna's work is focused at all times on power differentials. And because of this a modernist Madonna always peeks through the postmodern curtain. For, while Madonna plays a multitude of gendered roles in her photographs, interviews, songs, and videos, never does one lose sight of the fact that she plays them as a woman, insisting on the discreteness of that category, enjoying her own version of femininity. In *Papa Don't Preach* (1986b) she plays the frightened but determined pregnant teenager to a potentially angry father, searching for the father's approval but not willing to change her behavior to get it. Dressed as a Parisian gamine, she asserts that she's keeping her baby. In *Material Girl* (1985), she plays her Marilyn Monroe sexy golddigger role to a horde of adoring, less powerful because interchangeable males. As in so many of her videos, she ironically comments on the main narrative by using a second narrative that throws the first into question. In the second narrative of *Material Girl*, the "real" Madonna asserts that money can't buy her love and she falls for the "poor" Keith Carradine, who courts her with daisies and a workman's truck (of course, as E. Ann Kaplan has pointed out [1987], Carradine is merely posing as poor). In *Burn-

ing Up (1983b), she plays the abject admirer of a man who doesn't know she's alive. "Down on [her] knees," she strikes many poses of panting humiliation, culminating in a road scene where she offers herself up to be run over by the lover's car. Again, a final scene makes a joke of what came before: Madonna is behind the wheel of the car, alone, laughing and carefree. In *Like a Prayer* (1989a), she gives herself stigmata, embodying herself as Christ and as the white savior of a black male victim of racism (see Freccero [1992], who stresses Madonna's frequent positioning as the daughter in an Italian patriarchal family). By playing a multitude of roles, Madonna restores to consciousness versions of femininity that women and girls are forced to repress in order to get social approval. By playing these roles from the embodied position of a woman, she attacks male supremacy in a way that makes her more popular with women and other marginalized cultural groups than with straight white men. Madonna enjoys being a girl and so not only challenges the gender binary but celebrates the fact that a woman is posing the challenge.

But, less wittingly, Madonna also reveals the narcissistic wounds of the gender binary. She wants to show us ever more of her off-stage self and needs to test our love for her by showing us, and hoping we will accept, what she considers her "bad" side. This is the driven, often bitchy, self-destructive Madonna of *Truth or Dare*, and this Madonna is perhaps better described by such diverse commentators on identity disturbance as Otto Kernberg (1976), Heinz Kohut (1971), John Bradshaw (1988) on the dysfunctional family, and Christopher Lasch (*The Culture of Narcissism*, 1979) than by postmodern celebrations of fragmentation. For this is the totally scheduled, not the playful Madonna, the Madonna who has dyed her hair so many times that her hairdresser warns her it will fall out (Sessums 1990), the Madonna who works out for two hours each day and who points to a picture of a woman squeezing her stomach and says, "That's like me . . . . Always looking for fat" (quoted in Hirschberg 1991, p. 200), the Madonna who can be abusive to those around her. This Madonna conceives all relationships in terms of power and hierarchy, and although she claims loudly in video and interview that she is always in control and thus on top of any conceivable hierarchy, our look into her private life shows that sometimes she is on top and other times she is in despair at the bottom. This is the Madonna whose concept of religion can be entirely self-serving, as when she prays before each concert that her show will be better than ever. This Madonna injects a dose of sadomasochism into most of her songs and videos (lately there has been a distinct upping of the dose; most critics seem to regard her as having o. d.'d), and, contrary to her self-perception, this Madonna is not exactly what most of us would call maternal. This is the Madonna whose dream of being loved has clearly not yet come true, despite her own myth-making. And although this Madonna is the one who claims loudly that she is in control, she is decidedly not in control. Indeed, this second Madonna exemplifies a kind of fragmentation that most psychologists would not want to celebrate, the kind shown by those who have difficulty constituting a self, whose internal world is harsh and split as a result of early traumas or losses. It is precisely this painful state of fragmentation that engenders a craving for control and power, power that may be fleetingly experienced, but at a great price to self and others (see Chapter 5). Madonna challenges male supremacy as a woman, but she also reinstates many of its power dynamics. In her work, the individualism of hegemonic masculinity competes with an ethic of care and an insistence on gender, race, and class equality.

Each of these Madonnas has popular appeal, exemplified here by the views of two fans. My hairdresser, who is incredibly thin, tells me that she preferred the pre-aerobics Madonna who acted as if she loved her body, which at the time did not fit cultural stereotypes of thinness. Madonna's lawyer's daughter apparently felt the same way. He told Madonna, "You've lost weight; my daughter's going to be so upset. You finally gave girls who are voluptuous a new lease on life. Don't get any skinnier, okay?" (quoted in Chase 1987, p. 193). I remember feeling similarly when I saw her in *Desperately Seeking Susan* (Seidelman 1985), my first encounter with her. I thought that it was amazing that this woman who was not gorgeous and did not have a great body could strut around as though she were God's gift to the world. Indeed, several critics have suggested that it is the very way Madonna treats her ordinariness as special that accounts for her popularity. This Madonna is so self-assured that she can try out various roles and challenge fixed identities that have constricted women (and men) for centuries. This Madonna is as comfortable in a men's business suit (especially when pink lingerie peeks through) as in the buff. And this Madonna is inspirational mother to those who cannot quite break out of the constricting roles culture prescribes for them.

When I last rented *Truth or Dare*, the salesclerk told me that she loves Madonna and has written at least fifty papers on her since fourth grade. I asked her why she loves her, and she responded that it was because Madonna's mother died when she was so young and she was raised by her father. She then told me her favorite video is *Oh Father* (1989c), which depicts the life of a girl whose mother dies and whose father (and later, lover) is abusive. In the song, Madonna attributes her low self-esteem to the father's treatment of her, repeating the refrain, in which she says she never felt so good about herself. At the song's end, the grown Madonna merges in shadow with her child self, walks away from the abuser, and sings the refrain in such a way as to suggest that she never felt so good about herself as she does now. This video and song, haunting and beautiful, could easily be the theme for Bradshaw's treatises on healing the child within.

Another song about abusive relationships, *Till Death Do Us Part* (Madonna 1989b), ends less happily, with the female stuck in an emotionally abusive love relationship. I believe that Madonna only increased her popularity by turning to confessional song-writing, and particularly by making it her project, evident in *Truth or Dare*, to blur the lines between her private and her public life. The public craves the regulating ideal of a person who has it all (together) as much as it craves a star who struggles with her fragments just like an ordinary person.

To conclude, I would like to challenge the myth of the individual, Madonna-style, which revolves primarily around her notion of control. To do so, I want to put Madonna in cultural and historical context. In 1985, Dave Marsh, an astute music critic, noted that, whereas Madonna seems to think that she is the product only of shrewd individual calculation, she is actually the product of a particular historical moment. His piece was written when *Material Girl* was a hit, and he sees the intersection of Madonna and history in the way she honestly spoke the materialism of the '80s, proclaiming a girl's right and wish to own things, and the way she legitimated a woman's sexual desire in a puritanical but sex-filled era.

Many have spoken of Madonna's capacity to set trends in fashion. But when you read Madonna's self-reinventions against the backdrop of Susan Faludi's *Backlash* (1991), what emerges is that Madonna, like you and me, is just as much the pawn of as the setter of trends: her switch from lace underwear to high glamour between 1985 and 1987 fits right into Faludi's description of the manipulations of the fashion industry. And the commentators in *The Famine Within* (Gilday 1990), a documentary about women's obsession with weight, would see Madonna as emblematic of a time in which women who experience increasing success and opportunities for greater autonomy find themselves increasingly obsessed with physical fitness and hatred of body fat. Was the aerobicized Madonna of 1990 another chosen self-reinvention, or was she a casualty of an autonomy conflict in a gender war?

Madonna's move to make her life her work can be seen as a postmodern refusal to maintain a rigid line between the self as artist and as woman, or it may be seen as part of the same confessional trend that Foucault (1980) argued marked modernity and that has secured the popularity of Oprah Winfrey and Sally Jessy Raphael.

And Madonna is also the unlikely spokesperson for a particular version of family values, hot topic of the present moment. *Truth or Dare* is structured by both Madonna's yearnings to be a mother and her cravings for her father's approval. The way she enacts these yearnings and cravings does not at all show a person in control of her image. She would like us to see her as maternal, and she makes it clear from the outset that she somehow unconsciously chose a tour entourage of emotional cripples whom she could mother. As portrayed in the film, however, her version of maternity is oddly devoid of love. Although Madonna's mothering at moments keeps the children from hurting each other, it is mostly marked by teasing and humiliation, sexual play with the children in and out of bed, buying the children goods at Chanel to make up for their deprived childhoods, and making them stars.

With regard to her relationship to her father, we find that Madonna's rebellious mode of asserting autonomy is conditioned by her longing for love. Her provocations towards her father and the way she performs them are products both of choice and of her place in a sadomasochistic relational dynamic over which she does not have control. She seems to need to shock her father in the same way she needs to shock us—with, for example, sexual provocativeness.

Truth or Dare ends the way the Blonde Ambition show ends, with Madonna's tribute to family values, *Keep It Together*. The song proclaims: "When I look back on all the misery/And all the heartache that they brought to me/I wouldn't change it for another chance/'Cause blood is thicker than any other circumstance." The song is performed in the manner and costume of *A Clockwork Orange* (Kubrick 1971), with more than a hint of mutual family torment. Here, as in her double attitude to materialism, femininity, and everything else, what marks Madonna is not that she is in control, but that she is open about the pros and cons of family life and obviously echoes the experience of many in our culture.

What is most ironic, as Daniel Harris (1992) points out, is that the very Lacanian, Foucaultian, and Baudrillardian academics who laud Madonna for challenging the fantasy of wholeness claimed by the rational, ego-centered bourgeois individual have made of her an *auteur*, sole generator of her image, songs, videos, and shows. These postmodernists have thus contributed at least as much as Madonna's biographers to her self-generated myth that she as individual is in control. For example, McClary (1990) writes as though Madonna is solely responsible for creating her music, which is not the case even for the two songs McClary analyzes. As the *Village Voice* music critic Robert Christgau (1991) points out, if McClary had looked at other contemporary pop musicians (he suggests Paula Abdul), she would have found that Madonna's chord changes are not all that extraordinary.

Nor do her lyrics, which Madonna does write, unequivocally exemplify postmodern positions on identity. In analyzing *Like A Prayer*, for example (co-written by Patrick Leonard), how could McClary miss the fact that the lyrics show longings for origin, for merger, and, as always, are marked by a mood of dominance and submission? Madonna cannot be claimed solely for postmodernism or solely for modernism; her contradictions show the complicated way that the two are intertwined.

Carla Freccero's (1992) analysis of *Like a Prayer* is one of the few Madonna analyses that capture the relationship between the two. Freccero writes that the video generates a vision of interracial harmony that goes against male-authored visions of interracial conflict (her example is Spike Lee). This is a world where "women are both heroic and omnipotent, where female agency can be effective" (p. 182). Yet, at the same time that Madonna sets up the black female choir leader as her double and the black male protagonist as a saint,[1] the vision serves a self-aggrandizing fantasy where black women "approve of white women's desires for the leading role in the narrative of African American salvation" (p. 182). Freccero points to the existence in Madonna's work of both an intersubjective, relational, egalitarian model of agency and an individualist, dominating, self-aggrandizing model that erases the subjectivity of others.

In a culture distinguished by black-and-white thinking, one rarely finds Madonna critics like Freccero, who can live with shades of gray. I will speculate in Chapter 5 on why many of Madonna's academic critics have chosen to look only at her triumphs and not at her pain; the pain and contradictions are clearly there and Madonna herself seems unafraid to reveal them, although she may not be aware of how much she reveals. And revealing them made her all the more popular ("Lucky me," she might say). In fact, my sense is that part of the reason that she has lost popularity is that the tension she was able to maintain between the relational and the

---

[1] It is important to note that very few white stars have videos in which black people are protagonists, a fact not lost on black Madonna fans (see, for example, Scott 1993).

individualist self has broken down. What we have seen since the release of *Sex* (1992b) is less the relational multiculturalist than the daughter of a patriarchal family rebelling against daddy–authorities with ever bolder sexual displays (the multiculturalism has been reduced to multicultural humping). It may be that the insistent assertion of white female sexual enjoyment of the bodies of men of color is in fact the most important challenge to the current sex-obsessed but punishing regime of white daddies; nonetheless, Madonna's way of doing it has a stuck, adolescent quality to it. She has always wanted her father's approval too much. Perhaps motherhood will open new possibilities for her work.

Thus it is that Madonna's two projects are contradictory and irreconcilable yet highly representative of contradictions with which most of us daily contend. In trying both to destabilize fixed identities and to be a spokesperson for the discrete, autonomous self of bourgeois ideology, Madonna mirrors the identity dilemmas of our culture. She herself tells us that the need to maintain the fantasy of control comes from unresolved pain, the kind of pain that marks most of us on both an individual and a cultural level. It is the bourgeois individual, not the postmodern proponent of multiplicity, who puts up a front of unity while desperately trying to control an identity-disordered, fragmented self. Madonna both mocks the bourgeois individual and incarnates her. And so, I answer the question "Who's That Girl?" with the suggestion that Madonna is the likely icon of a cultural moment in which progressive social movements (such as feminism, gay liberation, and civil rights) coexist with abusive families, violence, virulent racism and homophobia, and loss of community accompanied by compensatory rampant materialism—a moment with tensions that make us all wonder who we are.

5

Trauma, Gender Identity, and Sexuality: Discourses of Fragmentation*

If, as I have argued, Madonna is a darling of postmodern feminist critics, it is because she reveals that the self is constructed from a multitude of fragments and she celebrates those fragments. I also suggested that there are other ways to look at Madonna's fragments, ways explained by theories of self disturbance. Here, and in the next chapter, I will examine how different postmodern theories discuss fragmentation, and I want to compare these discussions with those that occur in Anglo-American psychoanalytic theories of self formation and self disorder. One of the major obstacles to productive conversations between postmodern theories and clinical practice is precisely the different ways that fragmentation, and, by implication, trauma are understood. If gender identity formation is traumatic, as both postmodern and relational feminist theories assert, and trauma produces fragmentation, then how do we distinguish those fragments that restrict possibilities for multiplicity from those that guarantee multiplicity?

---

*This chapter is adapted from Layton 1995 (copyright © 1995 by Johns Hopkins University Press and used by permission).

In the past several years, a number of discourses—among them cultural criticism, psychoanalytic theories of the self, trauma research, and avant-garde art—have arisen to discuss the fragmentation of the self, and these discourses are quite contradictory. In literature departments, Lacan's critique of the ego and his dictum that the self is essentially fragmented were taken over into culture criticism in the 1970s. Early on, in work such as that of *Screen* theorists, this criticism focused primarily on the pain of fragmentation. A core assertion of Laura Mulvey's (1975) groundbreaking Lacanian film criticism was that film and other apparatuses of culture conspire to allow a male subject to fantasize that he is not essentially fragmented, to allow him to take an imaginary unified ego for the whole of his being. While maintaining this fantasy guarantees that he will not have to face his pain, the price of his unity and sovereignty is paid by women and other Others, whose subjectivity goes unrecognized. Kaja Silverman, one of the best-known contemporary Lacanian film critics, continues to insist on the primacy of fragmentation. In *Male Subjectivity at the Margins* (1992), she writes, "The implicit starting point for virtually every formulation this book will propose is the assumption that lack of being is the irreducible condition of subjectivity. In acceding to language, the subject forfeits all existential reality, and foregoes any future possibility of 'wholeness'" (p. 4).

According to Silverman, subject formation itself is fragmenting and traumatic; the condition of entering the symbolic, of using language, is a condition of lack, a forfeiting of being for meaning. Feminist critics such as Silverman argue that in a patriarchal symbolic the condition of lack is denied and projected onto women (see also Ragland-Sullivan 1987). All the metaphors of both lack and fantasied unity will be male-defined. At the heart of what Silverman calls the dominant fiction is the way that various apparatuses of culture, especially the family, allow the male penis to take itself for the phallus, the condition of plenitude. The theory, which posits male narcissism as a societal norm, suggests that the only way to assure respect for difference and diversity is to acknowledge that we are fragmented beings, that no one has the phallus (Mitchell and Rose 1985, Silverman 1992). Acknowledgement of fragmentation becomes a strategy of resistance to patriarchy's dominant fiction.

More recently, other strains of poststructuralist thought (such as Derrida's and Barthes' notions of the free play of signifiers) have crossed with Lacanian theory or with British Cultural Studies to produce cultural criticism that celebrates diversity, ambiguity, and fragmentation. Theorists as different as Judith Butler, Constance Penley, E. Ann Kaplan, and Ellen G. Friedman posit the fragmentation of the subject as a strategy of resistance and/or a guarantee of indeterminacy, especially gender indeterminacy. Whereas Mulvey and Rose argue that the symbolic system violently fragments the female subject, in much recent cultural criticism the pain of this fragmented subject is forgotten or bracketed and she is rather figured as able to subvert the system by enjoying, rearranging, and playing with her fragments.

Teresa Ebert (1992–1993) has recently labeled the bulk of this work "ludic feminism," by which she means cultural criticism that "tends to focus on pleasure . . . as in and of itself . . . a form of resistance" (pp. 7–8). In celebrating difference, this criticism, she argues, glosses over how difference comes about within systems of exploitation, how differences are valorized unequally in the culture. Tania Modleski (1986b) has also criticized the pluralism inherent in many versions of British Cultural Studies. And, in later work (1991), she has pointed out that the separation of sex from gender in so much contemporary feminist cultural criticism leads to a celebration of diversity that does not take into account real power inequalities between men and women, gays and heterosexuals, blacks and whites (see also Martin 1996).[1]

---

[1]Kaplan (1987, 1993) and Penley (1992) would fall under Ebert's "ludic feminism" rubric (she also includes Donna Haraway and Jane Gallop). Ellen Friedman (1993), who associates fragmentation with women writers' refusal to constitute an identity in accord with patriarchy, is not a ludic feminist; I include her because her essay evaluates fragmented style as a strategy of resistance and shows little regard for the social and personal roots of the painful state of fragmentation that produces such a style, a style that reveals as much oppression as resistance. As I have noted several times in this book, Butler's work is so multiple itself that it is hard to categorize. But I would say that parts of Gender Trouble (Butler 1990a) are ludic, in that power inequalities between men and women are not addressed (in Chapter 9 I shall try to untangle some of Butler's theoretical shifts).

As we have seen, much of contemporary Anglo-American psychoanalytic theory focuses on self disorders (see, for example, Kohut and Kernberg). In psychology departments, too, people are discussing fragmentation (although, to my knowledge, they are not discussing Lacan). In these discussions, fragmentation is not posited as a feature of normal development, nor is language acquisition posited as traumatic. And the agent of fragmentation is neither metaphysical nor linguistic systems, but rather specific interactions with other people, primarily early caretakers.

In Kohut's work (1971, 1977), the self fragments when not properly mirrored or when traumatically disappointed by an idealized other. For Kernberg (1975), the self fragments when frustrated in its attempts to negotiate needs for independence and dependence, separateness and attachment. Kernberg, drawing on Klein, argues that the mechanism central to fragmentation is splitting, an early defense that operates to keep separate good and bad affects, good and bad self-representations, and good and bad object-representations. In an environment that is not too unpredictable or harsh, a child comes to be able to integrate good and bad experiences, to tolerate ambivalent feelings and cognitions, and to experience the self and the other as primarily good though at times disappointing. If the environment is harsh, particularly with regard to interactions around dependence and independence, the child continues splitting in order to preserve enough of a sense of a good object to keep developing. In this situation, the child's inner and outer world fragment, become black and white in all arenas. There are rigidly good and rigidly bad self-representations: the person oscillates between self-deprecation and grandiosity. There are rigidly good and rigidly bad object-representations: the person alternately idealizes and devalues the other. Cognitions tend to be black and white. Good moods alternate with very bad moods, and each seems to come out of the

---

I cite Ebert because the celebration of fragmentation and the celebration of diversity (internal and external), while not the same thing, stand in relation to one another, as the ensuing discussion will demonstrate.

blue. When in one state about the self or the other, the person can barely remember having ever felt differently.

High correlations have been found between diagnoses of self disorder and histories of abuse (Herman et al. 1989). The literature on those who have been repeatedly traumatized describes an internal world peopled by victims, abusers, and saviors, expectations of the world that can only echo what exists in the internal world, and a life marked by splitting and fragmentation. Judith Herman (1992) writes of victims of child abuse: "The child victim's inner representations of her primary caretakers, like her images of herself, remain contradictory and split," and, "under conditions of chronic childhood abuse, fragmentation becomes the central principle of personality organization" (pp. 106–107).

The focus of the work discussed above is the pain suffered and inflicted by those who do not feel cohesive, who feel always threatened by a loss of self. Repeated narcissistic and abusive modes of interaction are the designated causes of fragmentation. In this discourse, the norm posited as both desirable and possible is one of mutual interdependence, in which each person recognizes the other as a separate center of subjectivity (see, for example, Benjamin 1988, Mitchell 1988). Although Lacanian and Anglo-American psychoanalytic theories seem to have the same goal—to go beyond pathological narcissism—Lacanian theories propose that to do so the subject must come to grips with the lack at the core of being, while Anglo-American theories seek to promote a kind of cohesion of disparate and split-off parts of the self. Those postmodern theorists who celebrate fragmentation and indeterminacy, on the other hand, do not speak of narcissism. In fact, by suggesting that all options are possible, they participate in what could be seen as a narcissistic denial of limits. In this chapter, I address the trend in cultural criticism that celebrates fragmentation. I do not want to suggest, however, that it is impossible to have a cultural criticism mindful of the experience of fragmentation. Indeed, the cultural critics Patricia Williams (1991), Cindy Patton (1993), and, at times, Judith Butler (1993) do seem able to synthesize psychoanalytic and postmodern views of fragmentation, precisely because of their focus on the historical specificity of fragmentation and on the pain engendered by those cultural traumas that fragment the individual. These authors accommodate both the pain and the possible pleasures of marginality, and, in part, they are able to do so by holding cohesion and fragmentation in tension.

These exceptions notwithstanding, I find that often, after reading a brilliant piece of cultural criticism, my clinician self feels very uncomfortable with the way fragmentation has been figured. I will say more about my discomfort with Lacanian views in the next chapter. Here, I want to discuss and critique celebrations of fragmentation. In postmodern work that lauds indeterminacy, fragmentation is essentialized, universalized, and celebrated in a way that seems not to acknowledge what it feels like to experience it. As in the Lacanian frame, here, too, fragments do not derive from specific relational interactions or specific historical circumstances. But Lacanian theory situates the subject firmly within a patriarchal family structure, whereas the work on the play of fragments suggests that nothing constrains gender performances. As we saw in the chapter on Madonna, at the same time that these postmodern readings demean any notion of a unified self, any wish for an integration of fragments, they paradoxically leave the reader with the sense that their protagonists are in total control of their fragments, that they are *auteurs* who pick and choose how they wish to represent themselves at any given moment. In this work, the unconscious is evoked when it is convenient and ignored when it is not.

Often, the protagonists of these texts—the lesbian, the transvestite, the sadomasochist, the hermaphrodite—are made emblems of a third space, a space outside of various forms of cultural oppression. In this status, they perform an important cultural service: they challenge heterosexism, reified notions of gender identity, repressed forms of sexual expression, and the hypocrisies of a puritan yet violent culture. At the same time, when these figures become postmodern heroes and heroines, the pain of fragmentation, of marginality, of indeterminacy is often overlooked or glossed over. Discussions of the film *Paris is Burning* (Livingston 1991), a documentary about the gay men of color who frequent New York drag balls, are a case in point. While most critics were aware of the fascinating

way that the film's subjects made of their oppressed position a creative and celebratory experience, few critics spoke of the ways that
these creations were marked by pain and by the terms of the oppression (exceptions are hooks 1992 and Butler 1993). For example,
few wondered why people whose experience of family is so devastat-
ing would choose to form nuclear-style families, why they seek awards
for most convincing emulation of business executives and other
emblems of the white power structure, or why Venus Xtravaganza
could come up with no better fantasy than to be a white, middle-
class housewife. *Paris is Burning* clearly suggests that there is more to
parody than ironic distance and critique; there is also longing.

Similarly, critics who want to make of Madonna a postmodern
heroine simply omit all the textual evidence that shows her pain (for
example, Kaplan 1993 and Schwichtenberg 1993b). These critics laud
her continual reinvention of self, seeing in it her refusal to be bound
by cultural definitions of the feminine, and they are right to do so.
This is one of Madonna's cultural meanings, one way that she is read
by such varied groups as young girls and postmodern academic theorists. At the same time, her longings for unity, her abusiveness to
herself and others, and the pain that is everywhere in her work are
ignored. It is in fact the exclusion of her pain that makes celebration possible. If we were to acknowledge it, we would notice how
domination and submission inform everything she does; we would
wonder whether Madonna's continual reinvention of self is a product of joyful choice or of painful and driven necessity.

Writing about Foucault's study of the hermaphrodite Herculine,
Judith Butler (1990a) has also observed this tendency to gloss over
pain. She notes the way Foucault romanticizes Herculine's multiple
pleasures, all the while knowing that sexuality cannot lie in a safe
realm outside of power. Butler's own reading of Herculine compels
her to write: "In the place of univocity, we fail to discover multiplicity, as Foucault would have us do; instead, we confront a fatal ambivalence, produced by the prohibitive law, which for all its effects
of happy dispersal nevertheless culminates in Herculine's suicide"
(p. 99). Because power and sex are coextensive, because the law generates sex, there is no way that Herculine could be in a limbo of

heterogeneous pleasures.[2] What Butler locates in her critique of Foucault is the postmodern critic's wish, despite his/her knowledge, that the Other or the unconscious be the unproblematic antidote to our pain (see Rose 1986). As a clinician I find that these texts make me uncomfortable, because every day I sit face to face with people who experience fragmentation not as joyful but as tormenting.

Unlike the cultural criticism discussed above, pain is everywhere in such avant-garde texts as Kathy Acker's *Blood and Guts in High School* (1978), and the pain is avowedly a product of trauma. Acker's protagonist, Janey Smith, has been fucked by her father since early childhood, and the whole book is about how women are fucked and fucked over by men. Janey's fragmentation is rendered in the book's fragmented style. At first glance, this seems the very opposite of what I have been discussing. Acker's text in fact mirrors the way many of my clients experience their fragmentation: as divorced from affect, as irreconcilable, as inevitable, as sometimes their fault, sometimes someone else's, sometimes consensual, sometimes driven. But in texts such as Acker's, the pain of fragmentation is universalized and aestheticized in such a way that, before long, one either forgets that Janey is an incest victim or one assumes that all women in a materialist society are incest victims. By suggesting that Janey's pain is woman's condition, Acker blinds the reader to the fact that Janey's fragments and Janey's relational capacities are reified in certain distinct ways that result from her being an incest victim. Janey, for example, can figure her sexuality in only two ways, either as pure pain and exploitation or pure wildness and freedom. In this text, as in many of the texts of contemporary culture criticism, sexuality is depicted either as a mystical free space or a space of pure power

---

[2]Ebert focuses on pleasure as central to the "ludic feminism" she critiques; the heart of her criticism is the suggestion that only a class that does not have to worry about the body as a source of labor could so focus on the body as primarily a source of pleasure. Here I am arguing that this focus on pleasure entails not a safe haven from pain but a denial of it. That is, I assume that even the class position from which the ludic feminists speak must be marked by its own dialectic of pleasure and pain; for this reason, the omission of pain or labor is not just a sign of privilege but is in some way defensive.

struggle. In both discourses, fragmentation is universalized and essentialized in such a way that our choices boil down to complete despair or joyous celebration, *choices symptomatic of the black-and-white thinking that is a product of fragmentation.* If we compare Acker's text to another piece of experimental writing, Toni Morrison's *Beloved* (1987), we again see how different contemporary discourses on fragmentation can be, and we can also see the political stakes of the various discourses. For in *Beloved,* historically specific cultural traumas induce fragmentation and the text centers on selves as agents struggling to integrate their fragments without disavowing them. *Beloved* thus represents fragmentation and trauma somewhat similarly to the way it is represented in Anglo-American psychoanalytic discourse.

Thus various contemporary discussions of identity center on fragmentation, but they radically differ in how they talk about it. How and whether these disparate discourses on fragmentation can be brought into relation is the question I now want to raise. To begin, I want to look at how my clients describe their experience of fragmentation and what they and researchers say about the nature of the fragments. Although fragmentation can follow from many kinds of early childhood experiences, I want to focus on sexual abuse because its consequences stand in a distorted mirror relation to the gender indeterminacy and sex radicalism celebrated by culture critics. I will therefore draw on the case material of one of my clients, a woman who was sexually abused in childhood by multiple perpetrators and who feels she always had a fluid gender identity. I will call this client Sheila, protecting her privacy and the confidentiality I offer her. I speak about her with her knowledge and her permission. Her therapy has dramatically revealed both the pain and the promise of fragmentation.

At the very beginning of therapy, Sheila revealed that she had coded different parts of herself male and female. She identified her voice, size, tomboy activities, intellect, and hardness as masculine. She had not felt at all feminine until her first lesbian relationship and identified her femininity as a "marshmallow" aspect of herself, totally vulnerable and "weak." Early in treatment, she claimed that at a very early age she had rejected things feminine because of her proclivities (you can't be athletic in a dress and Mary Janes; Sheila never wore a dress after first grade) and because she wanted to be like her older brothers, who appeared to have all the family privileges. This "masculine" identification drew upon her the taunting and even violence of peers who clearly did not allow a space for gender indeterminacy.

Sheila claimed she consciously chose a masculine identity, but in an autobiographical novel that begins with the description of her first sexual abuse, she appears as a sexy, wild, long-haired, alluring 7-year-old girl. This, as well as many of her dreams, suggests that Sheila unconsciously came to associate a certain vision of femininity with something that provokes abuse. Her choice not to wear a dress at age 7 was thus in part a rejection of a femininity she deemed dangerous; the choice was clearly overdetermined. As Sheila grew older, she distanced herself from the vulnerable little girl and came to experience herself as rigidly gendered: she identified her intellectual self as male, her rageful, sadistic self as an abusive male, and all her vulnerability and compliance and pain as female. Her wish in therapy was to integrate her "masculine" and "feminine" selves.

According to researchers, Sheila's rigidly gendered identifications are typical of abuse victims. Margo Rivera (1989), a clinician who specializes in multiple personality, writes, "It is very common for their vulnerable child personalities and their seductive and/or compliant personalities to be female and their aggressive protector personalities to be male" (p. 27). The alter egos, she asserts, usually reflect extreme cultural stereotypes of masculinity and femininity.

Sheila's story illustrates that when the experienced trauma is sexual abuse or rape, splitting and fragmentation operate on gender identity. As the psychologist David Lisak (1991) has argued in his work on male victims of sexual abuse, the process of male gender-identity development itself is traumatic (pp. 244–246), itself enforces a process of splitting, and this is of course true of female identity development as well (see Brown 1991 on the traumas of "normal" female development). Lisak (1992) cites a story told by one of his subjects, who, as a young boy, was humiliated for crying when he saw a moth killed. Here was a case of one-trial learning: boys don't cry, at least not in front of others. I agree with Lisak that each gender undergoes a "self-mutilation," for, as he puts it, each is forced to extirpate from the self characteristics that are experienced as part of the self yet coded by the culture as belonging only to the other gender. The tomboy and the effeminate male are only the most obvious sufferers of the trauma of gender identity development. When sexual abuse is added to the first trauma, splitting is intensified, fragmentation guaranteed.

In cases of sexual abuse, gender identity fragments, and it does so in somewhat predictable ways. Sexually abused girls show significantly greater gender identity conflict than those who have not been abused (Aiosa-Karpas et al. 1991). Rather than the flexibility some postmodernists might see in a person whose gender identity is indeterminate, what I and other therapists and researchers see are fragments rigidly coded with cultural stereotypes of femininity and masculinity. Each identity is split between highly negative and highly positive traits; identifying with either is fraught with anxiety and pain because each has complex associations to the abuse and the gender of the abuser. In these cases, gender indeterminacy usually reflects severe conflict about taking on a gender identity.

For Sheila, femininity feels dangerous and dirty, though longed for and alluring. Masculinity is sadistic, ugly, and violent, though at times this identity makes her feel safe, smart, invulnerable to hurt. Sheila can go back and forth between the two gender identities, but each is so rigidly constructed that it gives rise to pain; she cannot flexibly interweave these identities, nor can she modulate the extreme way that she experiences their traits. Thus Sheila's problem lies not in missing masculine and feminine identifications but in the rigidity with which each is encoded, in the dangers that attend identification with any one of the fragments, in the incapacity to integrate the marshmallow woman and the man of steel. Further, some of her identifications, such as the young girl, are, against her conscious wishes, split off from what she calls herself, and others are kept at a distance because they are felt to be shameful. One task of therapy is thus to deconstruct the rigid masculine/feminine dichotomy.

Sexual abuse creates rigid binaries not only in its victims' gender identifications but in their relational style as well. Sheila, like all of us, developed her relational style within a particular matrix of relationships, and her conflicts and current relational patterns reflect, as Stephen Mitchell (1988) has put it, her commitment and deep allegiance to past modes of connection. A core experience for Sheila, both as an abuse victim and as the only daughter of her particular family, is that others find her unacceptable and try to coerce her to be different from what she is. Sheila's relationships are marked by her longings to be overpowered by an other who will teach her how to be acceptable. What usually occurs in these relationships is that she soon feels coerced, overrun, and misunderstood, and she then sadistically and self-destructively retaliates. Relational conflicts intensify feelings of fragmentation, and these play themselves out in conflicts about desire and about sexual orientation, in volatile moods, and in her split-off but frequently experienced rage.

The victim of repeated abuse tends to split the world into victims, abusers, and rescuers, who are locked in a dialectical dance. S/he enacts and reenacts relational patterns wherein s/he is sometimes the victim, sometimes the abuser, and sometimes the rescuer. Traumatization thus splits the experience of power and powerlessness, domination and submission in extremely marked ways. As recent research by Joan Liem (1992) and colleagues indicates, the literature on women sexually abused as children suggests that they are preoccupied with issues of power. In comparison with women who were not abused, the abused women exhibit a heightened desire or need for power as well as a need to see themselves as capable of exerting power. But, at the same time, they are frightened of power. In Liem's research, women construct stories from pictures on TAT cards (the TAT is a projective test consisting of pictures that are designed to pull for the story teller's unconscious conflicts about self and others). Preliminary results showed that women who had been abused created stories about unequal power relations significantly more often than did women who had not been abused. Liem and other researchers find that power becomes an organizing theme of the relationships that women with an abuse history enter into, and the need for and fear of power are central to how they engage in and provoke particular kinds of interactions.

Margo Rivera's (1989) work with multiple personalities shows that power/powerlessness is the axis along which alter egos congeal. She notes that for every personality that identifies with, for example, a compliant girl, there is one "who ferociously resists that position" (p. 27), such as the antisocial boy. Sheila's relational patterns, like her gender identity, are fragmented in these predictable ways because of her history of abuse. Power and powerlessness, domination and submission is the central axis around which her interactions occur, not only with lovers and parents, but with bosses, friends, and, of course, with me as her therapist. Sheila seeks powerful people to heal her; the tragedy is that those drawn to her usually have little capacity or desire to heal or understand but rather are drawn to her because they need to dominate.

The lack of historical and personal specificity in certain avant-garde and postmodern critical texts often makes it seem that all of us fragment our relations with others predominantly along the axis of domination and submission. While all of us certainly have experiences of helplessness and powerlessness, while all of us constantly negotiate and renegotiate our needs for dependence and independence, it is not evident to me that power and powerlessness are the primary organizing features either of most people's sexuality or of their relationships. The dramatic terms in which Sheila codes her fantasies and experiences are particular to people who have consistently been rendered powerless. Her core waking fantasy, where she is Joan of Arc saving hordes of innocents from sadistic rapists, is not in my experience a typical one. Nor are frequent feelings of rage the norm; rather, these intense feelings are generated, I think, from traumatic histories of power and powerlessness. Within our cultural matrix, which condemns the infliction of pain and humiliation yet habitually inflicts it, sadomasochistic desire will necessarily have conflictual multiple meanings, and these demand exploration rather than either facile celebration or condemnation. (Tania Modleski's [1991] "Lethal Bodies" discusses sadomasochism in a way that transcends simplistic pro and con positions.)

At one point in therapy, Sheila began to write the stories of her internal characters, and each story brings her closer to various gendered split-off parts of her self; each story not only makes these parts more known but makes them more acceptable to her. Sheila oscillates between a painful fragmentation in which she cannot recognize an overarching self that can claim the fragments and a kind of flexibility that brings pleasure and enrichment, wherein she can see herself in each identity and thus feel each is part of her. When clients such as Sheila or Jason (Chapter 7) talk about oscillation between fixed and fluid gender positions, they seem to be describing something that arises from their severe conflicts around gender. (For a perspective that suggests that such oscillation is normative, see Sweetnam 1996.) A goal of therapy is to create an atmosphere that erodes shame so that the fragments of self become available and less reified, and can be claimed as parts of the self. My recognition of her and all her parts as subjects allows the various parts to recognize and enter into dialogue with each other as subjects, which perhaps erodes the power/powerlessness, subject/object binary (see Benjamin 1988). Simultaneously, the act of writing itself seems to be providing Sheila a longed-for sense of consistency. At first startled to find that certain images keep repeating in her work, she has come to find this comforting, an antidote to her painful awareness of inconsistencies that plague both herself and those with whom she is involved. Sheila's longing to be consistent is a longing that nearly all postmodern theories pathologize and condemn as inherently oppressive.

Sheila's oscillation recalls for me Judith Butler's (1990c) sense that we need a "typology of fragmentations," so that we can distinguish between the kind of fragmentation caused by oppression—in Sheila's case, by sexual abuse, peer homophobia, and parental narcissism—and the kind of fragmentation celebrated in most postmodern theories, the kind that is meant to challenge the equally oppressive drive of Western culture towards silencing the diversity within us and around us. We must recognize, however, that even our experiences of diversity are rife with pain because there are so many external and internal attempts to silence them. The omission of that pain in postmodern theories that celebrate fragmentation is meaningful and needs to be explored.

Even Lacanian cultural criticism, which does not disregard pain, privileges the splitting of the subject in language and so makes it hard to appreciate the impact of historically specific forms of cultural and familial oppression. Lacanian feminism tends to explain all forms of oppression as a result of men's projection of lack onto others. In Silverman's (1992) study of masculinity, for example, historical traumas such as World War II become opportunities for men to recognize that they are castrated (that the penis is not the phallus). It is hoped that such recognition will shake the foundations of patriarchy. The black cultural critic Patricia Williams (1991), on the other hand, offers a personal experience that suggests to me that what people suffer from is neither alienation in the Lacanian mirror stage, where the ego is born as a fictive unity, nor a denial of fragmentation that may be the response to such alienation. Rather, people suffer from the fragmentation caused by specific historical forms of oppression sustained by power inequalities. The image of cohesiveness offered by the mirror helps Williams to survive and to resist the effects of racist oppression:

> There are moments in my life when I feel as though a part of me is missing. There are days when I feel so invisible that I can't remember what day of the week it is, when I feel so manipulated that I can't remember my own name, when I feel so lost and angry that I can't speak a civil word to the people who love me best. Those are the times when I catch sight of my reflection in store windows and am surprised to see a whole person looking back. . . . I have to close my eyes at such times and remember myself, draw an internal picture that is smooth and whole; when all else fails, I reach for a mirror and stare myself down until the features reassemble themselves, like lost sheep. [pp. 228–229]

This passage suggests to me that moves towards cohesion can be every bit as resistant to racism or patriarchy as awareness of fragmentation.

So I feel torn between commitment to a humanist paradigm of a cohesive, non-narcissistic self that functions as an agent and a postmodern paradigm of fragmentation (Flax 1990). In the best of cases, I imagine a dialectic in which we strive for coherence but find that we have failed to accommodate a contradictory part, that there is conflict, and that the conflict may come from contradictory desires or from external prohibitions on desire. I think that cohesion and fragmentation can be reconciled at some points or at least held in tension, and I want to conclude by looking at the work of two theorists concerned with a similar problematic, Joel Whitebook and Margo Rivera.

In "Reflections on the Autonomous Individual and the Decentered Subject" (1992), Whitebook argues that Freud saw the project of the scientific age to be not mastery over internal and external nature but rather the need to renounce omnipotence. Linking Freud's and Kant's notions of the maturity of the autonomous subject, Whitebook writes that the path to mature autonomy is one that requires decentering, or, one might say, the surpassing of a narcissistic position. Whitebook's concern is with the subject who frees himself from the dictates of the authoritarian other. As Jessica Benjamin (1988) has argued, however, domination and the subject–object dichotomy from which domination ensues are not incidental to the Western version of the autonomous subject but rather constitutive of it. In her intersubjective frame, the relinquishing of a narcissistic position requires recognition of and by an other experienced as a separate center of subjectivity—a relational event.

Whitebook criticizes Lacan for essentializing fragmentation, and he questions why the state of fragmentation that precedes development of the ego, the body in fragments, should be hypostatized into the true state, why the later developmental dimension that arises with the ego is dismissed as fictive and violent. Whitebook calls on Winnicott and Kohut, for whom "the integrating experience of the mother's smile, far from situating the child on an alienated trajectory, provides him with *hope* in a future when he would no longer suffer the pain and anxiety of infantile helplessness" (p. 103). Now Lacanians might argue back that mother smiles only when the child conforms to her, or to society's, wishes. But I agree with Whitebook's assessment because I feel that Lacan is not specific enough about what kinds of relational patterns constitute our fragments: he presumes falsely that our first relationship is narcissistic, and he privileges fragmentation over cohesion (I shall elaborate on all of this in the next chapter). Flax's (1990) argument, that Lacan describes not human development but narcissistic development, is compelling.

Margo Rivera (1989) has also wondered about the relation between the subject of postmodern theories, particularly the political feminist versions, and the question of, as she puts it, a central consciousness that integrates the fragments of the self. Rivera writes about severely abused people who become multiple personalities. Noting that about 90 percent of the multiple personalities clinicians see are women, Rivera calls attention to the cultural causes and sequelae of fragmentation, and primarily to gender inequality. As I noted above, Rivera writes that splitting for the trauma victim leaves not arbitrary fragments but fragments gendered in starkly stereotypical ways. Like Liem (1992), Rivera makes it clear that the fragments are organized around the axis of power and powerlessness.

Clinical data suggest that fragmentation is one moment in a dialectic that also must include integration. Rivera writes that clinicians have found that those patients with multiple personality who did not move toward integration, who continued "to guard their separations jealously, were much more likely to lapse into their earlier state of dysfunctional dividedness and acute suffering" (p. 28). She contrasts this to the poststructuralist imperative, where "concepts such as a unified self and a well-defined individual identity are not only not viewed as ideals but are considered to be dangerous ideological fictions used to erase the awareness of differences within and between human beings" (p. 28; see also Flax 1987 and Flax 1990, pp. 218–220). Now, again, a poststructuralist would probably argue that clinicians who value cohesion are merely patching clients up so they can fit into an oppressive and narcissistically structured world with less pain. But here is precisely where the discourses of fragmentation butt heads: critiques of cohesion presume that cohesion reinforces narcissism, whereas Anglo-American psychoanalytic theories of the self presume that non-defensive cohesion is an antidote to pathological narcissism.

I agree with Rivera that what is necessary is some way of recognizing the self in one's fragments, or, as she puts it, a growing ability to call each voice "I." What you call this "I" has all kinds of ramifications, but some experience of a cohesive "I," of something that recognizes itself even in its most disparate fragments, seems to be necessary to relieve suffering. This sense of unity that one identifies as a core self may be no more than a cultural artifact, but it is one that is necessary not only to good mental health but to ethical behavior. Whether it is because our culture forces us to constitute ourselves as agents if we are to be recognized at all, politically and personally, or because there could be no morality without a responsible subject (Greifinger 1995), or because the alternative to feeling cohesive is the painful state of psychosis or emptiness, a sense of identity and agency are crucial components of the ability to be good both to the self and to others. An error of postmodern theories is their assumption that the experience of a core self precludes the possibility that one experience this self as evolving and changing in its interactions with the world and with others. A core self is constructed and not necessarily stagnant; nor is it necessarily narcissistic.[3]

Rivera feels that we can learn a lot about development unimpeded by major trauma from looking at what happens to trauma victims. She sees those who have not been traumatized as "capable

---

[3]I am here extending to the experiential psychological level Amanda Anderson's political/ethical argument in "Cryptonormativism and Double Gestures" (1992). Anderson argues that, to maintain a feminist politics, postmodern political theorists have had to perform a double gesture, that is, to allow for essentialism or identity politics in practice while asserting what they consider to be a superior antifoundationalism and antihumanism in theory. Anderson presents an intersubjective ethical theory (based on Habermas) in which subjects are constituted not by dominating systems but by ongoing relations with others. In this view, the systemic informs intersubjective relations but does not define them, and domination is no more endemic to communication than is mutual respect. What I want to suggest here is that the same is true on the intrapsychic level. See Chapter 2 for my discussion of the relation between narcissistic and non-narcissistic constituents of the self.

of pretending to a unified, non-contradictory identity and denying our complex locations amid different positions of power and desire" (p. 28). Aiosa-Karpas and colleagues (1991) found that females who were sexually abused were more aware of the constructed and contextual nature of sex roles than those not abused. They write that the abused female adolescents in their study "acquired an expertise for modifying sex roles values and attributions according to the circumstances of the external environment. What is feminine in school is very different from what is feminine at home, and the sexually abused adolescent is acutely aware of the difference. It is this ability to present a variety of roles that helps maintain the secret of the victimization" (p. 270). The implication here is that a nonabused person who does not experience identity in a fragmented way may have a harder time seeing what there is to see about the social construction of gender, gender identity, and sexuality.

Is the trauma victim the person most able continually to reinvent the self? Is she the quintessential postmodern figure? Perhaps so, but the above study suggests a parallel between the problem facing the trauma victim and the problem I find with postmodern theories that celebrate fragmentation: yes, the trauma victims are aware of being socially constructed, but their enactment of a variety of roles is defensive and meant to keep the trauma secret. So the pain of fragmentation—its roots in trauma—is erased. In denying the unhappy moment of fragmentation, this particular kind of culture criticism sometimes reads like the high theory analogue of the Reagan–Bush happy years.

But what does it mean that those who have not been abused may be less aware of the constructed nature of identity? While these people may suffer less, postmodern critics point to the political ramifications of their blindness, for example compulsory heterosexuality; their blindness becomes part and parcel of the social reality that inflicts trauma. It is clear that cultural criticism that constructs marginalized people as victorious outsiders occupying a third space serves the important political function of challenging mainstream blindness and violence. But I also think it has the effect of healing trauma, and the way that it does so feels more modern than postmodern to me. This culture criticism, I think, accords people who are usually stuck with only the pain of marginality an avant-garde stature that brings pride and pleasure. The humanist moment lies in the paradox that to achieve this recognition the criticism performs the very unifying function of which it is skeptical, for it endows its subject with a sense of an essential "we" (e.g., the lesbian, the hermaphrodite) and suggests even more rigorously than bourgeois criticism that this subject is in control of how she represents herself.

Sheila is white and middle class; her trauma of sexual abuse fragmented her gender identity and sexuality. Recent research suggests that this level of trauma is not as rare as one might hope. For example, a demographic study of a random sample of young adults in Detroit showed that 39.1% were exposed to stressors at the level of post-traumatic stress disorder and 23.6% developed PTSD (Breslau et al. 1991). The authors concluded that PTSD is among the most common disorders of young adults, surpassed only by phobia, major depression, and alcohol and drug dependence. Trauma is thus quite prevalent in the culture.

As we have seen in Sheila's case, developmental traumas also arise from the abuses of a racist, sexist, heterosexist culture (Brown 1991). Feminist critics, such as Waugh (1989), have written about the decentered status of women and the strategies women adopt to deal with the fragmentation caused by oppression; Afro-American critics, such as Gates (1988), have written similarly about the signifying strategies of decentered Afro-American subjects. Some of the best postmodern criticism captures the specificity of cultural sources of fragmentation and the effect on an individual psyche. These demonstrate that the kind of fragmentation that is oppressive to the self and to others does not derive from defenses against *existential* lack; rather, the denial that one is lacking is a defense against relationally inflicted wounds, many of which are caused by inequalities of gender, race, and sexual orientation (see, for example, Williams 1991, 1995, Pratt 1984). What is lacking, then, is culturally constructed: a male defends against dependency because dependency is not consistent with the dictates of hegemonic masculinity; a black person in a culture of white racism defends against the humiliation of being found wanting (Fanon 1967). As one of my abused clients recognized, if the mirror of the world does not reflect your smile back to you but rather shatters at the sight of you, you, too, will shatter. The decentered subject of much of postmodern cultural criticism and art is a victim of culturally imposed trauma. These victims are agents, too, making meaning out of their traumas. Nonetheless, trauma restricts the possible domain of self-expression and relational expression and restricts them in particular ways.

Thus I conclude that theory must find some way of holding in tension a modernist focus on cohesion and a postmodern focus on fragmentation. The tendency in certain versions of postmodern theory to split off pain from pleasure enables the celebration of a fragmented subject. Alternately, the view that the price of subject formation is fragmentation enables a Lacanian theorist to claim the fragmented subject as the authentic, non-narcissistic subject. But fragmentation arises historically, from private and public developmental traumas. These traumas lend particular specificity to the fragments, which tend to be coded in rigid binaries, in stereotyped ways that are the opposite of the fluidity longed for by postmodern theorists. Therapy deconstructs these binaries. And, as Bromberg (1996) has suggested, it does so in part by helping the client move from dissociation to conflict. Parts of self that have been dissociated and called "not-me" are recognized eventually as parts that have been split off to avoid conflict with other parts. The capacity to tolerate conflict provides an important challenge to binary structures. The process of reclaiming fragments creates a sense of cohesion in the client that does not obliterate diversity and is not oppressive, but is instead liberating. Most important, a *different experience of the other*, one that is consistent and predictable and does not repeat the sadomasochistic or narcissistic dynamics of early development (or, if it does, subjects the event to analysis) enables the client to see the "self" in each of her parts and thus to undo the rigid boundaries between them. At this point, these parts can no longer be called fragments but rather multiple and contradictory parts of the self.

It seems to me that both therapists and cultural critics need not only to identify the fragments that make up identities but to exam-

ine their historically specific nature and origins. Therapists who fail
to do so will likely reinforce norms as "normal." Further, therapists
and critics alike need to be aware of both the defensive and the trans-
formative uses to which these fragments are put in various self-representations. More attention needs to be paid to the tension between
cohesion, which yields a sense of agency, and fragmentation, which
does not.[4] And, finally, many postmodern thinkers would do well
to question their assumption that relations between self and other,
self and systems are always narcissistic and grounded along an axis
of power/powerlessness, for this assumption perpetuates an ahistorical
way of figuring fragmentation and results in strategies of subversion
that can only be highly individualistic.[5] For it is indeed narcissistic
self-other relations that cause fragmentation, but, as I argued in
Chapter 2, such relations do not exhaust either political or individual
experience, and theories that presume that they do work within a
narrow and distorted range of human possibility.

---

[4]Butler (1992) argues that there is no necessary contradiction between the assumption of a socially constructed subject and the experience of agency: "We may be
tempted to think that to assume the subject in advance is necessary in order to
safeguard the agency of the subject. But to claim that the subject is constituted is
not to claim that it is determined; on the contrary, the constituted character of
the subject is the very precondition of its agency" (p. 12).

[5]The intersubjective stance (as opposed to the narcissistic subject–object stance)
obviates the need for what Anderson (Note 3 above) calls the double gesture. I
am arguing that a non-narcissistic subject experiences the self as continuous and
coherent but as constituted in and by its relations to others, others also conceived as separate centers of initiative. A breakdown in these relations is what
leads to the experience of the other and the self as primarily dominating or submissive (see Benjamin 1988). And it is in this situation of breakdown that agency
and cohesion (and thus ethics, politics, and so forth) become problematic.

6

Blue Velvet: A Parable of Male Development*

David Lynch's 1986 film *Blue Velvet* elaborates a narrative of male development that reveals the narcissistic origins and structure of hegemonic masculinity. The film has stirred up a number of critical controversies relevant both to contemporary feminist film criticism and to the relation between postmodern and Anglo-American theories of fragmentation: Is the film paradigmatic of postmodernism or stuck in the crudest of binaries? If it is postmodern, what version of postmodernism does it proffer? The one that decenters what Kaja Silverman (1992) has called the "dominant fiction" of phallic wholeness (see also Bundtzen 1988)? Or the one that is the psychological and moral equivalent of contemporary capitalist relations of production (see Harvey 1989, Jameson 1983), the one that Jane Shattuc (1992) calls the new patriarchal dominant of commercial postmodernism? Does the film's style deconstruct the narrative's logic or mime it? Is the film an enactment of an oedipal scenario?[1] Or is Shattuc

---

*This chapter is adapted from Layton 1994a (copyright © 1994 by Oxford University sity Press and used by permission).
[1]Most critics who discuss the film use Freudian categories, such as the Oedipus complex, the primal scene, the forces of the id (as represented by Frank). See, for example, Biga (1987), Bundtzen (1988), and Maxfield (1989).

right to argue that Freudian categories are incapable of describing what goes on in the film?[2]

The analyses occasioned by *Blue Velvet*'s stylistic and content confusions reveal some of the contradictions in the critical vocabularies of contemporary film theory and relational feminist psychoanalytic theory, particularly in their views of masculinity and male dominance. Male dominance perpetuates itself via a variety of overlapping discourses—medicine, science, religion—as well as via the structure and relational patterns of the white heterosexual family, the workplace, government, and so forth. What I called normative or hegemonic masculinity in earlier chapters is psychically produced and reproduced in accord with particular narratives of male dominance, for example, the Oedipus complex. As Chodorow's (1978) theory made clear, oedipal and preoedipal narratives are lived in such relational events as the greater separateness between mother and son than between mother and daughter in the white middle-class family. White men's narcissistic wounds differ from women's, and we can understand narratives that serve male dominance only when we understand the particularity of the wounds against which these narratives defend.

In recent years, psychologists in the relational feminist paradigm have looked at hegemonic white male development and focused on two of the systemic wounds that contribute to male gender identity and male dominance: the traumatic, too early abrogation of the mother–son holding environment (Pollack 1995a,b) and the absence of nurturant fathering (Kaftal 1991, Lisak 1991). Concurrently, prominent feminist culture critics in postmodern paradigms have been using Freudian and Lacanian categories to examine male development (see, for example, Adams 1988, Silverman 1988, Smith 1988b). In Silverman's terms, the differences between the requirements of a phallic, hegemonic masculinity and the instabilities of individual male identificatory dynamics reveal many disjunctions between the phallus (the fantasy of completeness) and the penis: while

---

[2]Simon (1986) and Pellow (1990) agree with Shattuc's ultimate conclusion that the film makes neither psychological nor narrative sense.

most men strive to fulfill the masculine ideal because it promises freedom from pain, no one can in fact fulfill it. The clash between how a male lives his subjectivity and the masculine ideal can be quite painful, as we will see in Chapter 7. But even those who approximate the masculine ideal suffer pain (see the discussion of hardboiled detective fiction in Chapter 3). The editors of *Camera Obscura* called their special issue on the contradictions of masculinity *Male Trouble* (Penley and Willis 1988).

As feminist film theory and relational analytic feminism ponder male development, and as Anglo-American psychoanalytic theory deconstructs the drives and the oedipal story, *Blue Velvet* seems to be worth looking at again. For its view of male development sheds light on the interplay between oedipal and preoedipal fantasies and fixations in our particular historical moment, and thus sheds light on contemporary gender relations. My analysis of the film will entail a deconstruction of the oedipal/preoedipal binary. And because feminist film theory has turned to the preoedipal as a possible place of resistance to hegemonic, phallic masculinity, I would like to look first at recent figurations of the preoedipal in this theory.

MALE TROUBLE

In moving from Laura Mulvey's (1975) focus on the way film works to enable a male spectator to secure his sense of solidity and dominance to a focus on "male trouble," feminist film theory has shifted its interest from oedipal to preoedipal dynamics. Male trouble includes those aspects of male development that challenge the reign of the phallus and the masculine and feminine positions it prescribes (for example, see Adams's [1988] discussion of the male's preoedipal oscillation in gender identifications, or Silverman's [1988] notion of imaginary as opposed to symbolic identifications). In Adams's and Silverman's work (as well as in Smith's [1988b] "Vas"), the preoedipal is figured as resistant to the phallic "dominant fiction" and thus is seen as potentially subversive (in the same way that hysteria has been seen as a subversive protest against dominant versions of femininity). While these critics aim to challenge the supremacy of the Oedipus complex, they nonetheless remain within the confines of Freudian categories, interpreting the preoedipal, as Freud does, backwards from the vantage point of what is supposed to happen in the Oedipus. Thus they allow Freud's story of male and female development to obscure other possible developmental scenarios. As DiPiero (1991) argued in his response to the above articles, there is a problem in granting such legitimacy to Freud's story: if you posit castration and sexual difference as the central organizers of culture, you cannot escape hegemonic masculinity, even if you envision a preoedipal realm that works in opposition to the oedipal; the exception merely proves the rule.

Gaylyn Studlar (1985), who is not a Lacanian, is one of the few film critics to have let preoedipal categories stand on their own terms. Opposing Mulvey's view of a sadistic, voyeuristic filmic apparatus, Studlar offers a masochistic aesthetic that, for example, reinterprets the mother as complete rather than lacking, and the fetish as a transitional object promoting self-cohesion rather than a stand-in for the missing phallus. The Lacanian response to her work was quite critical; for example, Kaja Silverman (1988) dismissed Studlar's work in a footnote, calling it biological and apolitical and arguing that to focus an argument solely at the level of the preoedipal is to participate in a disavowal of the Lacanian Law. Silverman's criticism, however, sustains binary categories by assuming that the preoedipal mother is a phallic mother, which presupposes that what is disavowed at the preoedipal level is castration, the actuality of fragmentation. But this fantasy of a phallic mother also reads development backwards from the oedipal: indeed, the phallic mother is a phallic fantasy/defense that is every bit as violent towards women as its complement, the view that women are deficient.

The question, however, is: Where do these binary fantasies of completeness and deficiency come from? Several analysts have offered preoedipal interpretations that go beyond a Freudian framework. Chasseguet-Smirgel (1986), for example, has argued that the preoedipal mother's power comes from the child's dependence on her. The child experiences such helpless dependency as a narcissistic wound and defensively flees it, with boys and girls showing different defensive styles. In such a view, the fantasy of merger with a phallic mother would be interpreted not as a stage of development, nor as a denial of primary lack, but rather as one of many defenses against dependency.

Dependency is, in fact, a category Freud's rhetoric consistently evades. For example, in his papers on sexual difference and female development (1925, 1931, 1933), he lists the many reasons that the child feels hostile towards the mother, the first three of which he labels "rationalizations": another child comes to take the first child's place; the mother does not have enough milk; the mother does not love the child enough; the mother forbids masturbation; because it is the first and most intense love, the love for the mother is ambivalent. In "Femininity" (1933), however, Freud finds none of these sufficient to explain the girl's hostility, because all of these complaints are true for the boy as well (and he presumes girls are more hostile than boys towards their mothers!). He has not yet studied the pre-Oedipus of the boy, he asserts, so he really cannot explain why boys are less hostile to the mother (1931). As for the girl, he finds the determining reason that she turns from the mother just, as he says, where he expected to find it: in the castration complex, or, more precisely, in the mother's lack of a penis. The leap from explanations based in relational slights and vulnerability to an explanation based on visual evidence of inferior and superior organs appears as a theoretical *non sequitur* and betrays Freud's discomfort with dependence. Chasseguet-Smirgel concludes that Oedipal theory and the "sexual phallic monism" at the core of Freud's theory of male and female development are, in part, defensive strategies to manage the power of the mother and the state of helpless dependency (see also Sprengnether's [1990] discussion of the defensive denial of dependence on his mother that structures Freud's theorizing of the Oedipus complex).

Freudian theory tends to cover over dependency not only by phallicizing it but also by eroticizing it, which, in fact, is a fairly typical male defense against experiencing dependency. As Dinnerstein (1976), Chodorow (1978), and Benjamin (1988) have shown, the fact that women are responsible for child care—and thus become culturally associated with dependency, nurturance, and preverbal sexuality—makes the preoedipal every bit as political as the oedipal. Indeed, because that fact plays a large role in reproducing the heterosexual family and male dominance, it is pointless to insist on a clear opposition between the preoedipal and the oedipal. As I argued in Chapter 2, stage theories do not capture the fact that negotiations of attachment and differentiation, conditioned by cultural norms, are lifelong developmental processes.

While Studlar's work, and Silverman's earlier work on the pleasures of passivity (1980), are important challenges to Mulvey's focus on the desire for mastery, each errs in trying to set in place a single aesthetic by which film operates (and one psychology by which spectators operate). What I will argue here is that films such as *Blue Velvet* (and most of Lynch's other films) enact both the masochistic and the sadistic dynamics put forward by Mulvey and Studlar, but that the best way to understand these dynamics is by starting with male trouble on the preoedipal level, working forward to male trouble on the oedipal level, and historicizing both of them. Jeffrey Beaumont, the hero of *Blue Velvet*, seeks knowledge of things that he knows are there but have always been hidden. The big secrets in dominant male discourse are male dependency, desire for a nonrivalrous and nurturant father, and female agency: *Blue Velvet* enacts the struggle between keeping and breaking these secrets.

BLUE VELVET

While the "secret" is one of Lynch's favorite tropes, it is by now no secret that abuse and the abuse victim are central to his aesthetic (and indeed central to much postmodern art). From one of his earliest films, *The Grandmother* (1970), in which a boy abused by his parents grows a benevolent grandmother from seeds, to *Twin Peaks. Fire Walk with Me* (1992), in which Laura Palmer discovers that her long-time secret abuser is her father, David Lynch has consistently chronicled the horrors of social and family life. In Lynch's world, parents are completely unreliable, if not abusive. And it is important to note that his victims are not always female and his perpetra-

tors not always male: the Elephant Man (*The Elephant Man* 1980),
for example, is abused by his male "owner" and, Lynch suggests, by
his more benevolent medical patron; the mother in *Wild at Heart*
(1990) is the abuser.

But in *Blue Velvet*, Lynch offers a psychology of the abuser/
abused and a psychology of male development that begin to map a
patriarchal dominant marked by the kind of defenses characteristic
of narcissistic and borderline personality disorders: splitting and fragmentation, primitive idealization, projection, denial, omnipotence
and devaluation, identity diffusion (including diffusion of gender
identity), and rage about dependency. In Lynch's world, and in our
own perhaps, the particular oedipal possibilities that follow are two:
the lobotomized Mr. Happy Face and his flip side, the rageful, violent but impotent sociopath.

Much of the early criticism of *Blue Velvet* noted Lynch's dichotomous world view. Critics spoke of a "startling mixture of naiveté and
kinkiness" (Ansen 1986, p. 69), "candy sweet scenes of picture postcard America" against "scenes of horrific sexual violence" (Shattuc
1992, p. 73), the stark contrast between Frank's obscene language
and Sandy's syrupy sentimentality.[3] While some applauded the dis-
junction between Sandy's world of robins and love and Frank's world
of sadomasochistic evil (largely those who saw the sentimentality as
ironic commentary on the more real evil), others called Lynch and
his film immature, a vision with no middle ground (see Jaehne 1987
and Powers 1987). Interviews, as well as Lynch's other films, bear out
the conviction that Lynch sees the world as split between innocence
and naiveté on the one hand, sickness and horror on the other,[4] or,

---

[3]Jeffrey Beaumont is the male protagonist of *Blue Velvet* and Sandy, daughter of
the police chief, is his girlfriend. Frank is the older male villain, who has kidnapped
the husband and child of Dorothy, a singer who is the subject of a police investigation and whom Sandy and Jeffrey decide to investigate on their own. Frank is
forcing Dorothy to do his sexual bidding.

[4]Lynch said in an interview, "This is all the way America is to me. There's a very
innocent, naive quality to my life, and there's a horror and a sickness as well"
(cited in Berry 1988, p. 82). Laura Dern, the actress who plays the female leads in
Blue Velvet and *Wild at Heart*, said of Lynch, "Here's this guy who's so weird and

in Karen Jaehne's film history terms, between Frank Capra and *film noir* (Lynch's split world is also discussed in Berry 1988, Bundtzen 1988, Maxfield 1989, Pellow 1990, and Powers 1987). In *Eraserhead* (1977), Henry, the beleaguered father of the deformed, controlling infant he finally kills, unites with The Lady in the Radiator, who sings that in heaven everything is fine. Laura Palmer, in *Twin Peaks. Fire Walk with Me*, unites with Agent Cooper and meets the angel she had to erase from the picture on her bedroom wall once she realized her abuser was her father. Sailor and Lula, in *Wild at Heart*, find a space safe from Lula's wicked witch mother, her nightmare flashbacks of abuse, and Sailor's lack of "parental guidance." And the Elephant Man holds fast to the pictures of his benevolent mother and his benefactress after a life of abuse from his "owner," the rabble, and medical science. Do Lynch's films overcome these splits? Do they reveal splitting as a mechanism arising from the problems he explores? Or does he formally enact the splitting that is at the center of the content of his films?

Feminist film criticism has always focused on the endemic splitting enacted against women in Hollywood films. Women who write about *Blue Velvet* have been most concerned with the way Lynch treats women in the film and have disagreed about the function of his propensity towards splitting. Early reviews on Lynch and women were quite critical, although Biga (1987), drawing on relational feminist theory and on Kaplan's (1983) question about whether women want to possess the gaze, argues tentatively that Sandy represents an alternative gaze of affirmation and affiliation. Bundtzen's "'Don't look at me!': Woman's Body, Woman's Voice in *Blue Velvet*" is one of the few articles that tries to rescue Lynch from charges of misogyny. She performs this feat by suggesting that Lynch's postmodern style subverts the classic relations of looking embodied in the film. Her sense is that while one could easily see the film through the lens of Mulvey's theory, Lynch takes away the viewer's pleasure in looking at Dorothy by filming her naked body in nonerotic ways and

---

does things that are so terrifying to the psyche. And yet there's this purity in him and this belief in love that is almost cartoonlike and childlike" (cited in Kaleta 1993, p. 166).

by making the viewer feel the hero's shame at looking, his shame at expressing his sadistic impulses on the female body. She argues that Dorothy remains a mystery through to the end, which "undermines an audience's confidence in Lynch's images and frustrates its desire to know and understand his world" (p. 192). Bundtzen interprets the final scene, in which Dorothy embraces her son, Donny, in a sunlit park, as evidence that Dorothy escapes the representations imposed upon her:

> Underneath, Dorothy is maternal plenitude, the good mother, a figure of love and care, and all of her representations are fantasies imposed on the maternal to enact childish aggressions toward her. In this, Lynch as director plays a role for his audience like the one Frank claims in relation to Jeffrey: he is "a candy-colored clown they call the Sandman" and Blue Velvet is his dream of total possession of the mother: "In dreams you're mine, all of the time." Lynch presents a waking dream, however, forcing us to see the cloying "candy-colored" nature of his illusion, and the result is a nightmare like Jeffrey's where the mother is shamefully cannibalized . . . . [p. 192]

Indeed, the film's final image evokes Dorothy with the object of her desire, her son. But has Dorothy here escaped a male representational economy? Whose fantasy is the fantasy of maternal plenitude? And why do so few critics note how deeply woven together are violence and impotence in this film? To answer these questions, one needs to go beyond Freudian categories (see Layton and Schapiro 1986).

While less certain than Bundtzen that the film's style subverts its message, I agree wholeheartedly that the dream at the center of the film is one of total possession of the mother. But here, as elsewhere in male popular culture, the emotional intensity of the film seems less focused on women, or on the relationship between women and men, than on men and their relations with each other. As Bundtzen's title suggests, "Don't look at me!," which Frank yells repeatedly at Dorothy, is precisely the emotional point; it literalizes the breakdown in male–female mutuality of which Benjamin's intersubjective theory speaks. What Bundtzen does not comment upon, however, is the moment when the injunction reverses to "Look at me!" Frank speaks this to Jeffrey at the climax of Jeffrey's initiation rite into manhood, the scene where Frank "fucks with" Jeffrey. How and why does this shift from female to male centrality occur?

The film suggests that the mother's gaze stirs reminders of dependency and reminders that the mother has agency and thus can leave. So the dream must strip woman of her capacity to desire. Yet the only woman who could fulfill Frank's desire is the one who wants him all the time, the one whose desire is focused solely on him. If he desires her, but her desire is not solely for him, his dependency and fear of abandonment are revealed. To avoid revelation of these secrets—female agency and male dependence—woman's desire is rendered irrelevant, dependency is projected onto her, and what is left is a world that tries to function solely around the various looks between men. But the "castration" of female agency leaves the men violent and impotent, desperately searching for something from each other, but not knowing what. Lynch dramatizes this primal scene of our culture by making his film a parable of male development, a parable in which one grows from power as a male baby, rid of the father and in possession of the mother, to impotence as a man.

THE PARABLE

In the first scenes of *Blue Velvet,* an elderly man suffers a stroke while watering his suburban lawn. We next see him in the hospital, hooked up to machines and weeping because he cannot speak to his son, Jeffrey Beaumont, the film's protagonist. On his way home from the hospital, Jeffrey finds an ear in a field and takes it to the police station. Detective Williams, father of Jeffrey's love-interest-to-be, Sandy, warns Jeffrey away from the dangers of life. But Detective Williams cannot solve the crime, indeed does not even know that one of his top men is involved in it. The benevolent town fathers are impotent; Jeffrey cannot depend on them to protect him or to reveal to him the secrets of life. The first lesson of oedipal masculinity is that fathers cannot help you become a man; what you do, you must do alone (even though Sandy offers help, her attempts never quite work out). The film suggests, however, that once you are a man, you are useless.

Jeffrey is investigating the mystery of the severed ear, the mystery of the castrated, impotent father. His investigation leads to Dorothy, the enigmatic woman, but his real mission is to discover the mystery of masculinity. The film begins with the mention of losses and underscores the hero's isolation; Jeffrey has not only lost a connection to his father, but his mother barely looks up from the television when he enters a room, and he mournfully tells Sandy that all his friends are gone from the town.

Those critics who see the film as an oedipal drama argue that Dorothy and Frank, the man who kidnaps Dorothy's husband and son and makes her his sexual prisoner, become Jeffrey's surrogate parents, Dorothy initiating Jeffrey into sexuality, Frank teaching him what beer to drink and how to be polite on the family trip to Pussy Heaven, the pivotal scene of the film. Dorothy and Frank, totally unpredictable parents, make Jeffrey aware of the drives and of sex and aggression, and finally lead him to accept, with his new self-knowledge, the law of civilization. Indeed, critics also see Lynch's film as a kind of "Civilization and its Discontents" (Freud 1930), in which Frank represents the id—sex and aggression—lying just beneath a surface of civilization. Lynch's camera, however, focuses as frequently on signifiers of Frank's impotence as on signifiers of his power, subverting any easy equation of Frank with the id and returning us to the preoedipal and to male trouble.

On his second trip to Dorothy's apartment, Jeffrey searches each of her rooms, but the camera singles out and pauses in closeup on only one object, a child's hat. Hiding behind the closet, Jeffrey hears Dorothy talking on the telephone, asking Don (her husband) whether little Donny is all right. The camera comes close up to Dorothy as she says, "Mommy loves you." The object of Dorothy's desire is revealed to be her kidnapped son (although it is unclear whether it is Donny or "baby" Frank on the line; Frank, indeed, longs to take the place of her baby). Jeffrey later tells Sandy that Dorothy wants to die, that Frank has kidnapped her son and husband as bait to keep her alive. When she hangs up the phone, Dorothy reaches under the couch and looks at a hidden picture; Jeffrey's last act before leaving the apartment is to look at the picture, which is of Don and Donny (in his hat), and then at the marriage certificate behind it. "Oh my God, the hat," he says. "She's married. Don." Solving the mystery would appear to have something to do with tracking the sources of Dorothy's desire.

Before Jeffrey discovers the picture and leaves the apartment, Dorothy discovers Jeffrey in the closet and simultaneously humiliates and stimulates him. In this scene, too, when Dorothy calls Jeffrey "Don," we get a clue that Dorothy's desire is elsewhere. Then Frank enters. Jeffrey's first (and, at the film's end, his last) view of Frank is from Dorothy's closet and what he sees is no primal scene but a scene shot through with the cultural dynamics of preoedipally fixated male–female relationships. Bundtzen well describes the infantile aggression played out against the mother as Frank calls himself alternately baby and daddy, smacks Dorothy if she looks at him, and puts the blue velvet from her robe into his mouth and hers, simulating, as Bundtzen writes, an umbilical cord. But then Bundtzen calls the velvet a fetish (pp. 195–196), a code word in feminist film criticism that immediately returns the theorist to the Freudian categories, such as castration, that deny dependence on the mother in order to establish male dominance. In the Freudian framework, the fetish stands in for the mother's penis. What happened to the umbilical cord (also a key image in *Eraserhead*)?

For the past twenty years psychoanalytic theorists have been questioning the phallic interpretation of the fetish (see, for example, Person and Ovesey 1978), arguing instead that fetishes are used to self-soothe, to replace dependency on an outside source of soothing and nurturance so that the subject does not fragment when the soothing other is absent (in Kohut's terms, a selfobject). While a few critics have noted that Frank has enormous trouble getting it up, it is odd that few have made his impotence central to their interpretation of the film. Frank needs drugs, alcohol, the right atmosphere, a fist, the blue velvet selfobject, and the banning of his partner's gaze to be able even briefly to have intercourse ("impersonating male orgasm," as Bundtzen well puts it [p. 193]). It is no accident that Frank wants Ben (the proprietor of Pussy Heaven) to toast not his health, but his fuck, because, although *fuck* is every other word out of his mouth, the word represents precisely what he has so much difficulty doing.

Lynch plays hide and seek with revealing the nature and source of Frank's impotence and rage. The key to interpretation, I think, lies in the film's central songs, *Blue Velvet* (Wayne and Morris 1963) and *In Dreams* (Orbison 1963). The mystery begins to unravel in the film's climactic scene at Pussy Heaven. Although "Pussy Heaven" suggests a world of girls, girls, girls, all we actually find at Pussy Heaven are relations between men. The film answers the riddle of how to be a man via such things as beer preferences: Jeffrey likes Heineken, Sandy's father drinks Budweiser, the king of beers, and Frank will allow Jeffrey to drink nothing but Pabst Blue Ribbon. Frank's men continuously circle and gaze at Jeffrey, teasing him and threatening him with a knife, and Frank himself has eyes only for Ben, proprietor of Pussy Heaven, who later sings him a song of love and loss. Frank's homosexual desire is clearly one of the mysteries that Jeffrey always knew were there but that had remained hidden. Both Frank and Ben "nurture" Jeffrey with physical violence: Frank proudly tells Ben he can make Jeffrey do whatever he wants.

At Pussy Heaven, Frank holds in his hand another of his fetish/selfobjects, the tape of Roy Orbison's *In Dreams*. He allows Dorothy to visit her son ("Let tits see her kid"), she lights up with joy, and, with the camera on the closed door, we hear her try to reassure Donny that mommy loves him, which is the perfect introduction to *In Dreams*. Frank puts on the tape and Ben, "one suave fucker," lipsyncs. The camera focuses on Frank's face, and we see what we saw through Jeffrey's eyes when Dorothy sang *Blue Velvet* in the Slow Club: a rapt expression of vulnerable longing. Here, Frank gazes beyond Ben as he gazed beyond Dorothy in the Slow Club; his desire, in both scenes, is for something in the lyrics. In both songs, there is a golden moment, a moment of plenitude in which the singer possesses someone entirely. In *Blue Velvet*, that moment was in the past. In *In Dreams*, the moment is ushered in by a man, the sandman, a good father who reassures that everything is going to be all right. This is a moment that repeats every night, a moment when the singer has a nurturant father and is the sole object of his love's desire; but it is a moment that does not last. In the middle of Orbison's song, Frank's look changes to one of disturbance, pain, and then, finally, rage, at which point he shuts off the tape and yells that it is time to go for a joyride. The interpretation of the film, of Lynch's view of male development, hinges on how one interprets that rage. And the interpretation can be made only after the song is played a second time.

When he clicks off *In Dreams*, unable to tolerate its ending, Frank begins to yell, "Let's fuck. I'll fuck anything that moves." He tries to make his pain disappear by eroticizing it. The next scene, Jeffrey's final initiation rite into masculinity, reveals the way that oedipal and preoedipal damage are interwoven. Frank herds everyone into the car for a ride. At their destination, he uses his inhaler and begins to paw at Dorothy's breasts ("Baby wants to pinch them"). Frank has identified Jeffrey as like him, as having the same psychic structure. Jeffrey tells him not to touch Dorothy and hits him; now Frank's rage is fueled by jealousy: in a common reversal of Freud's version of the oedipal story, the father discovers that the son has the power, and he becomes violent toward the son (which is in fact the original story of Oedipus, a story in which fathers are not nurturers, but hostile rivals; see Ross 1994 on the Laius complex).

Frank has Jeffrey removed from the car and has his men prepare him for the rite to follow. Then Frank smears his own mouth with lipstick, inhales, calls Jeffrey "pretty, pretty," and kisses him. He asks to have *Candy Colored Clown* played, and the tape begins. As the song starts, with its father–son bedtime reassurances that everything will be all right, Frank tells Jeffrey he is fucking lucky to be alive. At that moment, he commands Jeffrey to look at him. This is a marked moment because he has so many times become infuriated when Dorothy, and once Jeffrey, has looked at him. With Jeffrey's gaze on him, he gives Jeffrey the oedipal lecture: stay away from Dorothy. Frank yells that if Jeffrey doesn't leave her alone, he'll send him a love letter. "Do you know what a love letter is? It's a bullet from a fucking gun. You receive a love letter from me, you're fucked forever." Then Frank speaks the lines of the song's moment of plenitude to Jeffrey, telling him that in dreams the beloved is with him at all times, in all activities, forever. The beloved is his, eternally present, eternally under his control. Frank then gently wipes the lipstick from Jeffrey's mouth with the blue velvet, for a moment a nurturant father. But as the song turns to the part that Frank had switched off, we finally discover the source of Frank's rage. Orbison cries out plaintively that when he awakens from his dream, the beloved is gone. And at that moment, the moment that reminds him of absence and loss, Frank turns violent. He tells Jeffrey to feel his muscles and asks whether he likes it, marking the shift from nurturant to phallic masculinity (and reminding the viewer of the sexual scene when Dorothy asked him whether he liked the feel of her breast). At this point we hear the singer confess that when he wakes up to find the beloved gone, he can't do anything but cry. Frank asks his men to hold Jeffrey tightly for him, and he begins to beat him as the song, at higher volume, repeatedly wails that the beloved is only his in dreams.

The pain Frank expresses in the scene at Pussy Heaven is explained when we hear the end of the song: it is the pain of abandonment, loss, powerlessness, dependency. This pain evokes Frank's rage, which is highly eroticized. Frank's desire, both heterosexual and homosexual, is inextricably fused with rage and violence, which are aroused at the moment he feels abandoned by both a male and a female intimate.[5] In both Freudian theory and Frank's psychology, dependency is eroticized, and the rage it engenders eliminates female agency and male nurturance while celebrating a (missing) phallic power; this is one aspect of what we have come erroneously to call the oedipal. Stuck in the moment of narcissistic rage, Frank fragments and displays the gender, age (baby/daddy), and identity indeterminacies characteristic of self disorder. Phallocentrism thus rests

[5]For a discussion of the violence and shaming rituals evoked by male–male desire in film, see Neale (1983). See also Kaleta (1993), who argues that homosexual desire evokes Frank's disturbance and rage in this scene and the one with Ben.

not on a denial of fragmentation or castration but on a denial of dependency and loss, a denial of female agency, and a desire for a nurturant father. More specifically, it rests on an inability to mourn early losses and disappointments in one's parents: that mothers are primary caretakers but they come and go, that fathers are absent, that parents are not involved enough or too involved. Thus are the failures of the oedipal incomprehensible without an understanding of the failures of the preoedipal; the way the male oedipal script plays out bears the marks not only of loss, as Lacan suggests, but of rage at dependency and abandonment, split off and projected onto the female although experienced in relation to both father and mother.

This is male trouble. After Jeffrey is beaten senseless by Frank, a candle glows, a hellish sound returns, the screen fades to black, and Jeffrey wakes, a man. Lynch, master of sound, immediately provides his association to what it means to be a man. Jeffrey wakes to a sound, then a sight, of hoses, the very sound/image that in the opening scene accompanied his father's collapse into impotence. Dorothy is punished and figured as the abandoner, but the film's other secret is father abandonment, which Lynch reveals ragefully not just by making the fathers absent, but by making them impotent or evil.[6]

When Jeffrey wakes up he knows all he needs to know about the mysteries of masculinity. He sits on his bed thinking. He sees Dorothy's mouth saying, "Hit me." He cries. He sees himself hit her. He cries more. Then he sees an image of Donny's hat. He cries even more. He pictures the closed door at Pussy Heaven and hears Dorothy say, "No, no, Donny, momma loves you," her attempt to reassure her son that she has not abandoned him. He sees himself hitting her again, and his crying continues. Why is Jeffrey crying? What, according to Lynch, do men want? It seems to me that both Frank and Jeffrey want to be Dorothy's baby. Dorothy's voice-off in

---

[6]Lisak (1991) found that males with abusive attitudes towards women had more difficult relationships with their fathers than with their mothers. In a recent undergraduate thesis on domestic violence, Ou (1996) found that authoritarianism predicts male violence against women better than sexism, which again suggests that male–male hierarchical relations may be the source of the kind of male trouble that results in violence toward women.

Pussy Heaven does not establish the power of the mother (Bundtzen argues that it does); the film, like the culture of which it is a part, and like Freudian theory, denies this possibility. Rather, the offscene reunion of mother and son establishes the power of the son—he who is reassured that he has the mother's desire (indeed, Dorothy's husband is mysteriously absent in this scene). What is denied in this slippage from mother to son is female agency, that one depends on a female whose desire is not just for the son, not even just for the husband, but is also elsewhere.

Donny's power is established via the recurring image of his hat, which, in Jeffrey's visual imagination, seems to evoke Jeffrey's sense of his own innocence before his detective work reveals to him the baser impulses of this vision of masculinity. Jeffrey is seen playing with the hat in the scene immediately following the one in which he hits Dorothy. After he hits her, they make love, and we hear animal sounds reminiscent of the sounds in *Elephant Man* that accompany the mother's rape by elephants. The sight and sound of hellfire recur, the screen fades to black, and we next hear Dorothy say, "I have your disease in me." Then we hear child's music and see Jeffrey playing with the hat. When Dorothy hears the musical hat, she runs down the hall and quickly grabs it, holding it to her like a sacred object. She says, "He used to make me laugh" (something we never see Dorothy do). In Lynch's world of dichotomies, of naiveté and innocence as opposed to sickness and horror, the male adult and his sexuality are diseased, and the child holds the power. At some point abandoned by mommy and daddy (if not actually abused by them, as in Lynch's other films; even here, Dorothy pushes Jeffrey and hits him first), the trajectory of manhood shifts from innocence and power to degradation and impotence. Whether they result from parental abuse or from unmourned inevitable parental failures, Lynch dramatizes a narcissistic solution to narcissistic blows.

Jeffrey comes downstairs to breakfast, and when his aunt asks about his bruises, he tells her he does not want to talk about it and lightly says that if she keeps asking she's going to get it. Masculinity is now inextricably linked with the threat of violence, and it is distinguished clearly from femininity; Aunt Barbara suggests that Jeffrey should talk about his problems, that marriages are saved by talking. Jeffrey has stopped talking. He no longer confides his knowledge to Sandy, protecting her from his harsh insights into the world and masculinity, making of her an object to his subject.

Jeffrey wants to turn the case over to the town fathers now and bond with Sandy at the hop. But the town fathers are impotent, and Jeffrey is not allowed to escape the consequences of masculinity so easily: in the film's oedipal moment, he has to kill Frank and repudiate a now not-so-sexy Dorothy. In the final scenes, however, the alternatives for oedipal manhood become clear. With Frank gone, we return via Jeffrey's ear to the world of family life in the suburbs. Jeffrey's dad is fine, and he and Detective Williams, garden tool in hand, chatter on the lawn, while the "girls" are inside either gossiping over tea or cooking. The robins have come, and even if the robin has a worm in its mouth, the music and everything else suggest that Jeffrey has joined the world of Sandy's dream, the world of the impotent fathers.

In these closing moments the too-vibrant, too-peaceful images of the opening, with the music of love and reconciliation, are repeated, but this time they end with Dorothy smiling at her son in the park. Wearing his trademark hat of innocence and power, Donny runs to her in slow motion and she happily holds him. She then looks off in the distance and hears herself sing the final line of *Blue Velvet*, a line that suggests she is still in touch with the pain of the past (in the opening rendition by Bobby Vinton, the line had been cut off, keeping the pain in the song hidden until we first see it on Frank's face). Perhaps Dorothy is the only figure allowed to be in touch with both the world of innocence and the world of horror at the end. But the very splitting of the world in this way is a problem bound up with the psychology of the film.

Where I disagree with Bundtzen is in her suggestion that Lynch finally allows Dorothy her desire. Although it could be argued that before she was violated by Frank, Dorothy must have had the kind of agency that allowed her not only to be a mother and wife but also a sexy singer in a nightclub, it was the sexy singing that led to the ripping away of her agency. The film's ending evokes Freud's own deconstruction of his oedipal theory, the poignant moment of his essay "Femininity" (1933), where he sadly acknowledges that the oedipal promise to the male actually does not quite work out, for while the adult male's desire is for his wife, her desire is for the penis, incarnated in her male child. (Freud writes: "How often it happens, however, that it is only his son who obtains what he himself aspired to! One gets an impression that a man's love and a woman's are a phase apart psychologically" [p. 134].) But this piece of theorizing, too, is a male fantasy, the fantasy of preoedipal life, which conjures a lost moment of plenitude in order to avoid acknowledging the child's dependency on a powerful female whose subjectivity cannot be reduced to the maternal. Dorothy, before Frank, was precisely the female subject that the dependent child/preoedipal adult cannot tolerate. On Lynch's screen, however, the powerless, helpless Dorothy—Dorothy after Frank—predominates. *The film must be read as incarnating rage against her agency, not against her lack.*

Thus the masculine dichotomy drawn by Lynch is either rage and impotence or blandness and impotence, a vision that has certain resonances with the Reagan–Bush years, when bland smiles and homilies hid rageful acts of violence. In Lynch's films, these may be represented by different characters, as in *Blue Velvet*, or by the same character, such as Laura Palmer's father, Leland, in *Twin Peaks. Fire Walk With Me.* Jeffrey's insight into masculinity is precisely a vision of Leland Palmer, good bourgeois father on the surface, raging abuser underneath.

THE POLITICS OF MALE RAGE

Where does the psychology of the film meet the political reality of the contemporary United States? I shall conclude by taking up the challenge posed by Jane Shattuc (1992), the challenge for feminist theorists to begin to map the patriarchal dominant of our time. Shattuc is disturbed by the moral ambiguity, in Lynch's work, that does not allow the viewer to make ethical determinations about the unprecedented level of violence against women in films such as *Blue*

Velvet and *Twin Peaks*.[7] I agree with her that Freudian categories do not help to understand this rage. Discussing the mix of historical periods in the film, Shattuc writes, "*Blue Velvet* extends this blurring of history to an image of generalized masculine rage which has no source. Why does Frank brutalize women? Frank's obsession appears to originate from a fragmented and contradictory Freudian problem—a drug-induced Oedipal fixation—that ultimately makes no sense" (p. 30). As I have argued, Lynch's world does make psychological sense in the split world of self disorder. The fact that Frank's narcissistic rage has become a staple of contemporary mainstream and avant-garde filmmaking suggests that these dynamics operate on the cultural as well as the individual level.

The film within a film, *Dangerous Game*, by the U.S. independent filmmaker Abel Ferrara (1993), provides an interesting example of this phenomenon, because Ferrara does not hide what I have called the secret of male dependence and rage at female agency. For much of the film, we watch a director (Harvey Keitel) try to get his male protagonist (James Russo) in touch with feelings of abandonment stemming from rejection by his wife (Madonna). Keitel tries to get Russo to show more pain, a pain that is the director's own, but what the audience largely sees is the violent abuse Russo plays out against his wife as he gets in touch with that pain. While Keitel assures Madonna that her character has power, the power of her new spirituality, he directs her to submit to Russo's violence. Only at the point at which Russo threatens to kill her is she to try to stop him, which

---

[7]Shattuc is disturbed when she overhears someone at a film conference call Laura Palmer the town slut. Shattuc "gasped: 'Laura Palmer was no slut, but the victim of a perverse sex crime'" (p. 73). From here, Shattuc questions her memory and focuses her critique on the moral ambiguity that she takes to be a postmodern moment in Lynch's work, one that ultimately condones violence against women. While I agree that violence against women is the problem, I would argue that Laura Palmer was indeed both a victim of a perverse sex crime and the town slut, and that such a characterization is not psychologically false nor a sign of postmodern decadence. Part of the violence of sexual abuse is that it damages the psyche of the victim; feminism needs to deal with the fact that abuse victims often have internal worlds split between victims, abusers, and rescuers, worlds not so different from the one Lynch repeatedly presents.

she does—ineffectually—by questioning his manliness. Ferrara hides few of his film techniques and clearly means for us to see filmmaking as the dangerous game, violent toward its actors, its audience, and even toward the emotional life of the director. Nonetheless, what we see for much of the film is continuous and escalating violence toward the woman, a violence that the film implies is real, not just acted.

Shattuc challenges us to understand what this filmic rage at women tells us about contemporary gender relations. I have argued that Lynch presents a particular vision of male development, in which a powerful child, innocent and in full possession of the mother's desire, grows to bland impotence and/or rageful impotence. The secrets in the film are male dependence, female agency, and the desire for a nurturant father. But another secret that remains hidden in Blue Velvet and in writings about it is the secret of recent history: Shattuc writes that none of the eighteen reviews of the film she read "sought to explain the film's central sadomasochistic relationship between Dorothy and Frank in the context of contemporary sociopolitical circumstances" (pp. 77–78). Lynch mixes images of the 1950s with images of the 1980s, one of the main attributes that impel critics to call his work postmodern (by which they seem to mean "confusing"). But a possible political interpretation arises from the fact that the 1950s and the 1980s mark the period of development of our real hero, David Lynch. Blue Velvet is thus a historicized parable of male development.

Chodorow's The Reproduction of Mothering (1978) is an attempt to understand how the patterns of childrearing in the 1950s led to a situation in which heterosexual men and women, by virtue of their self structure, could not fulfill each other's needs. Her story, located in the suburban, middle-class United States, where Jeffrey Beaumont's story also takes place, features overinvolved mothers deprived of outlets for their desire other than their children, and largely absent fathers. The psychological consequences of preoedipal development are different for the male and female children of these families. Drawing on the work of Robert Stoller, Chodorow argues that because the primary caretaker of boys and girls is a woman, a woman becomes the first object of identification. Nurture, caretaking, emotion, and dependence all become associated with females. Father absence prevents the boy from identifying with these attributes in a male, which, as I have argued, leads to an oedipal theory and reality that center on competition and hostility rather than connection and care. The road to male gender identification involves disidentifying not only from the mother but from everything that has been associated with her. This, Chodorow argues, is the characteristic psychic constellation of the heterosexual middle-class white male who comes of age in the 1960s and 1970s. Kaftal (1991) adds that the lack of a nurturant father and the projection of the boy's dependency and need for nurturance onto the female lead to misogynistic envy of women, rivalry and hostility towards men, and driven, repeated enactments of (failed) separation via acts that require heroic isolation.[8] Thus the psychic constellation involves a lack of fathering and the eroticization of dependency needs, as well as the expectation that mother has no other interest but her children. The pain caused by the absence of a nurturant father (in *Blue Velvet*, the Sandman) is disavowed, and mother is blamed for all wounds.

As Fredric Jameson (1989) has noted, what is absent from nostalgia films like *Blue Velvet* is the 1960s (and, I would add, the 1970s). What happened during the 1960s and 1970s that was so threatening to masculinity that the decades have become a secret? I would suggest that films such as *Blue Velvet* simultaneously reveal and hide the secret of white, heterosexual masculinity in crisis. The crises come from many sources; they stir up the vulnerability, emotionality, and dependency that phallic masculinity wishes away: the consequence is shame and helpless rage. One such crisis was the women's movement, which has made it hard to continue to fantasize that a woman's desire is only for husband and child. Woman's desire is equally likely to be elsewhere: in a career, in a woman's group, in other autonomous pursuits.

---

[8]On a somewhat lighter note, Ann Murphy has suggested that if women were writing the psychiatric diagnostic manuals, they would add a male disorder titled something like "Excessive Autonomy Syndrome" (personal correspondence).

A second crisis is the challenge that gay and lesbian movements pose to the dominance of heterosexuality. Homosexual desire now makes its appearance on screen, but also evokes rage and violence in heterosexist films. Third is the challenge posed to white dominance, first by the civil rights movement, then by Vietnam and other "Third World" liberation struggles, and now by the demands of multiculturalism. While the only nonwhite actors in *Blue Velvet* are somewhat peripheral to the plot (Jeffrey's father's black employees, who clearly know how to run the store without help from the white master, even though one is blind), an astute critic points out that one of Lynch's many dichotomies is the contrast between "a blond, apple-pie-American sweetheart" and "a dark, sick, European-accented one" (Simon 1986, p. 56). The rage against the dark European might also reflect a fourth crisis, the decline of the U.S.A. as an economic power and the rise of countries like Germany, with the threat of a united Europe. The threat of a dependent U.S.A. unites symbolically with the threat of the displaced, dependent male to suggest that the current rage against women is historically, as well as psychologically, motivated.

There are many other variables contributing to the increased visibility of fractures in the fantasy of phallic wholeness. The economics of the 1980s interrupted the fantasy of male classlessness. In good economic times, men can bond as men and deny class differences. In bad times, when the rift between poor and rich becomes more palpable, lower-class and displaced middle-class males lose a group identity that gives them a sense of phallic power: they are all thereby made painfully aware of their place. (Popular magazines run feature articles on white male anxiety about every few months. See, for example, Gates [1993].) Finally, paving the way for the public to hear and believe stories of parent–child abuse were Vietnam and Watergate, which together put many nails in the coffin of belief in reliable and benign male authority. The loss of this belief has also never been mourned.

If the postmodern has something to do with threats to white heterosexual male hegemony, then perhaps the level of violence against women we see not only on the screen but in real life is a reaction to postmodernity. In Massachusetts in 1994, a woman was

killed by a partner or ex-partner about every nine days. Often, as in
the scenario of *Dangerous Game*, these murders occur at the moment
a chronically abused woman abandons the abuser. This has provided
the clue to those who study domestic violence (Goldner 1991) that
male dependency is the underside of these displays of male violent
power. In stirring up male trouble, these crises put men in the position of both abuser and abused, and evoke the defenses of the fragmenting self: splitting, projection, insecure attachment and immense
sensitivity to abandonment, and narcissistic rage against anything
perceived as a physically, racially, or culturally less powerful other.
Such rage is not the manifestation of an aggressive drive, but the
response by narcissistically vulnerable psyches to perceived threats
to security. As Mitchell (1993) writes, "If there is aggression, there
is, by definition, threat" (p. 166).

Lynch's film enacts narcissistic defenses on the level of both content and form. The critic Karen Jaehne (1987), looking at the psychology of *Blue Velvet*, calls Frank and his men "sadomasochists
teetering between childhood and manhood" (p. 38). Criticizing Lynch
as a binary thinker, she writes:

> What *Blue Velvet* effectively does is to scare us into a panic or
> cynicism over lost ideals. It should not make us think that the
> only alternative to naiveté is humiliation into abuse, with the
> only solace the sound of a Sixties' song. Innocence is not lost; it
> is transformed. American dreams encounter their greatest chal-
> lenge not in preserving innocence, but rather in maturing—an
> observation beyond Lynch at this point. [p. 40]

One might include in that indictment most U.S. cultural production and much of U.S. politics. Indeed, John Powers (1987) makes
what I consider the same point as Jaehne's, raised to the political
level, when he argues that Lynch scares us into sticking to the safe
side of lobotomized *bourgeoisement* by picturing the only alternative
as horrific. Powers speaks of a breed of films he calls the New American Gothic, films that challenge the bland pap of most Hollywood
offerings that "flicker across the screen with the practiced, comforting banality of a presidential smile" (p. 51). He says of Lynch's film:

Such a dichotomy is typical. All the New American Gothic movies share a taste for extremes, but when it comes time to show anything in between, the credits begin to roll. *Blue Velvet* finds no mid-range of experience between Jeffrey's daylight world and Frank's murderous "love letters" in the dark. . . . In fact, these films exude the Manichaean, middle-class paranoia that infects countless recent movies . . . all of which imply that once you leave bourgeois life, you're immediately prey to crime, madness, squalor, poverty.

Now it would be wrong to criticize *Blue Velvet* and the others for not dramatizing the excluded middle, for not finding alternatives to the extremes of good and evil that give them their spark. Literary gothicism is distinguished by similar stylization; it goes with the territory. Nevertheless, one suspects that these films don't dramatize alternatives because they can't imagine alternatives. [p. 51]

Perhaps the patriarchal dominant is the psychology and politics of this split world, a world with no alternatives to black-and-white thinking because so much vulnerability is kept secret. As anxiety heightens, splitting intensifies. Lynch's psychology of male development mirrors the fantasy of the U.S. that it has fallen from a '50s innocence into a '90s violent nightmare. Such a fantasy results in political "solutions" like the Gulf War, solutions that are as dangerous and aggressive as the kind of personal solutions Lynch shows.

A look at the imagery of contemporary male popular culture suggests that those of Jeffrey Beaumont's generation do not feel overly mothered but rather feel either abused or abandoned by both their parents and by cultural authority figures.[9] Lynch's films capture this psychological reality as well (for example, neither of Jeffrey's parents

---

[9]The testosterone-saturated action films of summer 1996 all feature anger at traitorous, lying male government officials: *Mission Impossible* (de Palma 1996), *The Rock* (Bay 1996), *Independence Day* (Emmerich 1996). In both *Mission Impossible* and *Eraser* (Russell 1996), the heroes are betrayed and set up for murder by their male mentors; in *The Rock*, Ed Harris can no longer tolerate colluding with the government's abandonment of its sons who have died for the U.S. in secret missions.

is involved with him and Donny is kidnapped). These films suggest, however, that if we fail to mourn our losses on both the individual and the political level, we repeatedly enact narcissistic relations and solutions. The narcissistic nightmare in Lynch's parable of male development—the wish to dominate an omnipotent/impotent mother and merge with an omnipotent/impotent father—is symptomatic of an inability to mourn the loss of those who have inflicted narcissistic blows. Lynch's alternative, equally narcissistic and disingenuous (and thoroughly American), is to claim the position of an innocent baby.

Lynch's films, focused so heavily on trauma and abuse, enact the dynamics of splitting on the level of both form and content. These dynamics, I would argue, are central to mapping a patriarchal dominant. The anxiety that Lynch is such a master at generating with images and sounds very much reflects the heightened anxieties experienced by many men at this historical moment. It is in part an anxiety about gender identity and gender roles, about threats to the traditional ways that attributes such as dependency and autonomy have been split between the genders. Lynch captures the essence of the Reagan–Bush years in his vision of a world of robins and love facing off against a world that rages against female agency and violent or ineffective male authorities.

CONCLUSION

Blue Velvet, a parable of male development for our time, sheds light on some of the problems of contemporary feminist film criticism, particularly as the latter turns its attention to male trouble. Just as Freudian categories are not able to explain the dynamics of *Blue Velvet* and other films that feature the interplay of impotence and rage, so they are inadequate to an understanding of male trouble. The Freudian oedipal/preoedipal is an instance of splitting that mirrors the kind of splits we see in Lynch's world, and it is hard to go beyond these splits if we remain in a Freudian framework. If aggression is a drive rather than a response to a threat to an endangered sense of self, if castration anxiety is bedrock, it is difficult adequately to historicize increased violence against women. As Doane indicates in *The Desire to Desire* (1987), the danger of using Freudian and Lacanian categories to interpret gender relations in film is that film and classical psychoanalytic theory are built from the same phallic categories.

Freudian theory and feminist film criticism too often have kept the secret of male dependence and female agency by focusing their energies on such categories as originary fragmentation, castrated women, oedipal dynamics, merger with the screen, and so on. Whether castrating or phallicizing the mother, the developmental theory offered not only by Lynch, but by Freud and Lacanian film critics, describes and enacts a moment in the development not of men, but of narcissistic men. In proposing that relational theory be used to deconstruct the oedipal/preoedipal binary, I am suggesting that this theory is perhaps more postmodern than Lacanian film theory can be.[10] It seems to me that we must look beyond classical psychoanalytic categories to categories of self disorder, trauma, to experiences of shame and humiliation, and to narcissistic defenses if we are to understand the contemporary psychic and social world. Why this is so is perhaps the biggest current challenge to theory.

---

[10]I refer the interested reader to Benjamin (1995), who insists that dyadic relations are not necessarily regressive but in fact potentially deconstruct oedipal relations. Benjamin argues that in the dyad a form of symbolization emerges that differentiates self from other. While I disagree with the distinction she makes between oedipal polarities and preoedipal fluidities, I agree with her (and Winnicott) that mother and child can co-create the potential space that enables differentiation. I disagree with the implication in Lacanian theory that dyadic relations are narcissistic, and, unless broken by a third term, lead inevitably to psychosis.

7

What Is a Man?
Postmodern Challenges
to Clinical Practice

Blue Velvet, I argued in the previous chapter, is a parable of normative male development. In this chapter, I want to look at versions of
masculinity that lie outside the hegemonic masculine/feminine gender binary but are nonetheless marked by it. Drawing on the work
that I have engaged in with two of my clients, I hope to convey how
harmful it can be not to question their and our concepts of masculinity and femininity as rigorously as we question any other certainty
presented to us by our clients (see May 1986).

As I have been suggesting all along, hegemonic masculinity does
not exhaust the playing field of possible identity positions. Indeed,
class differences, race differences, age differences, the challenges of
such social movements as feminism and gay liberation, and changes
in capitalism have all produced competing versions of masculinity,
all of which operate in relation to one another and to versions of
femininity (see Connell 1987, 1995, Rutherford 1988, Segal 1990).
Connell (1995) has proposed that we understand masculinities as
configurations of practice. Rejecting essentialist, positivist, normative,
and semiotic definitions, he defines masculinity as follows: "*Masculinity*, to the extent the term can be briefly defined at all, is simultaneously a place in gender relations, the practices through which men

and women engage that place in gender, and the effects of these practices in bodily experience, personality, and culture" (p. 61). In Connell's study of masculinities, he looks at various male subcultures that each operate in relation to hegemonic masculinity: some as resistant to it, some as complicit, some as subordinated or marginalized.

At least since Stoller (1965, 1968, 1976b), clinicians and theorists have seemed to agree that males are more likely than females to experience difficulty solidifying a gender identity. Many different etiologies for this difficulty have been proposed: (1) Presuming that a child needs to consolidate a gender identity by identifying with the same-sexed parent, Stoller argued that when a female is the primary caretaker, the primary identification of both sexes will be "protofeminine"; separation from the mother and identification with the father are difficult but necessary to establish a male gender identity; (2) Chodorow (1978) added that, because of father absence, boys do not identify with a male person but rather with cultural constructions of masculinity, which roots masculinity in an abstraction rather than in a relationship (see Kaftal 1991, for further elaboration of the negative effects on male development of a missing preoedipal nurturant father); (3) Pollack (1995a,b) and Benjamin (1988) have talked about the boy's pseudo-separation from mother, Benjamin referring to it as a cognitive rather than an emotional event, Pollack calling the cultural pressures that dictate that a boy separate abruptly from his mother a traumatic abrogation of the holding environment. Postmodern theories emphasize the instability of all gender identities, the impossibility (and undesirability) of incarnating the norm. And postcolonial and British Cultural theorists focus on the social and psychic differences that follow from where one is located in a social system and what gender, race, and class power differentials are operative there.

To understand the masculinity of my clients in cultural context, I want to continue to interrogate a psychoanalytic tradition that seeks the source of psychic conflict only in the individual and his or her family. As Brenkman (1993) has pointed out, Western theories, including psychoanalysis, have consistently deflected narratives of community onto narratives of family and have thus obscured the social context of the production of individuals. Postmodern theorists (cf. Brenkman 1993, Connell 1987) have studied the evolution of the institutions and discourses that have produced the hegemonic modern male subject. Their work alerts us to the fact that at any given historical moment, cultures, through the various discourses and social practices that sustain them, legislate what counts as a "normal" or legitimate subject. Psychoanalysis itself is inevitably such a discourse, but different versions of psychoanalysis are more or less complicit in replicating the status quo. A critical psychoanalysis must understand a client's conflicts as stemming both from the accidents of the individual's history and from the cultural forces in which they are embedded. As we shall see in the case material, if we fail to contextualize conflict in this way, we collude with the most psychically harmful aspects of the West's most powerful ideology, individualism.

How do we as clinicians participate in producing subjects who reproduce the status quo? Let me give one possible example. A 35-year-old single female client says she wants to have a baby. I would guess that not many clinicians would ask her why. But what if this same woman says she does not want to have a baby? I think most of us would ask why. This innocent question that we would ask as part of our job in fact suggests the deviance of her wish; one might argue that in psychoanalysis everything is worth asking about, but the fact is that not everything is questioned. When put together with our tendency not to ask in the former case, we can see how therapeutic practice cites the norm, creates deviance, and thus participates in the formation of particular kinds of subjects.

The clients that I will talk about here suffer in part from the reified masculine/feminine binary that supports traditional gender arrangements, compulsory heterosexuality, and a toxic model of individualist autonomy. Thus their pain must be understood not only in the context of their particular parents' pathology but in the context of the pathology of their cultural surround. The strict enforcement of a binary in gender identification—which we see not only in the culture but in most psychoanalytic theory—is part of the pro-

cess of "subjection" that Derridian, Foucaultian, and Lacanian feminist critics see as basic to the formation of the (troubled) subject.
Butler (1993), for example, urges that we vigilantly take account of
the fact that identifications are always implicated in what they exclude, that they are based as much on disidentifications as on identifications. What is repudiated, disavowed, always returns to threaten
the boundaries of the subject. Being a man or a woman, Butler argues, is always an unstable state of affairs, always beset by ambivalence, because there is a cost in every set of identifications: the loss
of some other set of identifications.[1] Butler emphasizes that the oedipal scenario disallows two particular identifications, which she refers to as "abject," an identification with a feminized masculinity and
an identification with a phallic femininity. While a multitude of possible identifications exist, she argues that the abjection of the fag and
the dyke keep a heterosexual system stable.

As a clinician, I would like to take up Butler's challenge to seek
out the ways that identifications, particularly those that are built on
disidentifications, include what they seem to exclude. To illustrate
the way in which Butler's and other postmodern theories have been
helpful to me, I will present moments from the treatment of two of
my clients, two middle- to upper-middle-class white heterosexual men
in their thirties. I have titled this chapter, "What is a Man?," which
unfortunately imposes a false unity on the multiplicity of masculinities
discussed above. Each race, class, ethnicity, age cohort, religion, and
so forth has its own assumptions about masculinity and femininity,
so what I say here about the men I work with is in no way univer-
sally applicable. Further, the ideologies that have constructed the
white middle-class men whom I will talk about have meaning only
in relation to what *they* exclude: ideologies of white middle-class femininity, black middle-class masculinity, white working-class masculin-

---

[1] I differ from Butler in my contention that the costs incurred by having to conform to oppressive gender norms are of a very different order from costs incurred
from the fact that one cannot be everything. While all identifications *exclude* other
identifications, they do not all *disavow* the identifications they exclude (see Chapter 9).

ity, black working-class femininity, and the like. A multiple-person psychology (see Goldner 1991) is an extraordinary challenge.

As chance would have it, I began treatment at about the same time with clients I shall call Bob and Jason—I speak about them with their permission—whose presenting problem was an urge to cross-dress and fantasies of being those females whose look they admired.[2] While the transvestism literature clearly finds the source of the symptom in separation–individuation struggles with the mother (see Person and Ovesey 1978), the histories of both of these men present an opposite and a much more complicated picture. In each case, the evident source is a conflicted relationship with father, particularly with the versions of masculinity he represents and holds out as ideal, the versions he repudiates, and the vision he has of the relation between masculinity and femininity. Less evident but equally powerful sources are in the rigidly-held, stereotypical gender relations of the parents. Each of my clients feels that what he suffers from—and also, in some way, what makes him special—is his identification with femininity. Because masculinity and femininity are co-implicated, however, it soon became clear that Bob and Jason also suffered from a difficulty identifying with men, because the particular version of masculinity offered them for identification was noxious to them. Their sense of who they were bore little relation to their ideas of what it means to be a man.

We are all well aware that there are cultural norms and constraints that suggest what it is in our culture to be a white middle-class man. There are traditional ways that have been deemed appropriate for how such a man relates to a woman or to other men. There are generally agreed upon cultural norms for what this man should wear, what kinds of careers he should choose, what kinds of emotional responses are appropriate and inappropriate, what kinds of behaviors are acceptable and unacceptable. When you think about

---

[2]Although I realize that in mentioning cross-dressing, I arouse interest in the symptom, in this chapter I am less focused on what these men presented as a symptom than in their acquisition and management of untenable gender identifications. For an interesting study of cross-dressing in cultural perspective, see Garber 1992.

the narrow band of options, it almost seems inevitable that constriction would be a prevalent psychic outcome. In Chapter 5 I mentioned Lisak's (1992) discussion of the traumatic one-trial learning one of his male patients experienced when he cried at the killing of a moth in first grade. The humiliation he suffered for crying taught him that boys don't cry; that's for girls and babies. Indeed, humiliation, or fear of it, is probably one of the most powerful tools operative in the creation of all gender identities, the tool that enforces which identifications are acceptable and which are "abject." To what degree is the threat of feminization precisely what makes a man? Jason and Bob certainly came to experience their identifications as abject because of the humiliations inflicted on them by their fathers. Instead of knuckling under to their fathers' threat of feminization, Jason and Bob eroticized it.

For Jason and Bob, as for many of us, masculinity and femininity were internalized as mutually exclusive sets of attributes bound up in a clear hierarchy that dictates which attributes are superior. In their histories, many experiences were interpreted via the gender binary, whether they had anything to do with gender or not. Their stories begin with the ways their parents, especially their fathers, set about creating "men" out of the raw material that was their sons, a contradictory process in which the fathers both repudiated femininity yet obviously desired and perhaps envied females.

Bob is the elder of two sons in a family where his father was also the elder of two sons. Father's mother appears to have groomed her other son to be the "man" and groomed Bob's father to be a not-so-successful nice guy. He in turn performed the same drama with his own sons; Bob's brother was the designated man and his manhood was built on Bob's back. What is meant in this family by "man"? Masculinity is nearly coincident with phallic or hegemonic masculinity: in cultural terms, macho. Bob's uncle is a successful corporate lawyer, whom Bob describes as only out for himself, a bully with little compassion. Bob's father has gone from job to job and has never felt he made enough money, clearly an important component to him of the definition of a real man. So Bob's father made Bob's brother an egotist with little compassion, whereas Bob has, until recently, considered himself the nice guy who all too often gets used as a doormat and doesn't make much money. Money figures prominently in mother's psyche as well; she has always expected men to provide for her and is quite adept at manipulating situations to get taken care of.

Jason's father is highly successful in a very male-dominated field, a field considered macho and emotionless, which is the way Jason describes his father. Jason is the fourth of five sons and has been told by his mother that his father really would have liked to have had all girls. Nonetheless, Jason has always been aware of his father's very denigrating attitude towards women. Jason describes his mother as always yielding to his father and others. All three of Jason's older brothers were excellent athletes; Jason played but did not excel at football, the sport around which the rest of the males in the family bonded. Jason always felt his father's disappointment with him was that he wasn't an athlete, but Jason's memories suggest that the real disappointment, for both father and mother, was that Jason was not a girl.

In both Jason's and Bob's histories, their fathers explicitly humiliated them by feminizing them, by projecting their own repudiated femininity onto their sons. Bob's father, for example, occasionally called him Barbie. Jason found a position in the family as the one who made people laugh, which was in part a tool to dissipate tension between his parents. But at least on a few occasions, father expressed his annoyance at Jason's giggling by threatening to dress him up like a girl.

Siblings played a role in reinforcing the fathers' humiliation tactics. Because he wasn't a good athlete, Jason's brothers made him feel he couldn't do anything right. Father yelled at him for not being aggressive enough on the field, and throughout his life, Jason's father and brothers disapproved of the kinds of things Jason liked to do (for example, art), equating them to this day with the despised feminine. Uncertainties about competence and agency became interwoven with gender identity; Jason always feels as though he is not the right kind of man, not doing "it" the right way. His dad and his brothers are the right kind of man, and fitting into this fairly close-knit family requires either being the right kind of man or accepting a position as the beloved butt of jokes.

Conflicts with dress were reinforced by the Catholic school that required Jason to wear a uniform he associated with his father's right way of being a man. Jason reports hating to wear that uniform every single day. Every single day cultural and familial forces colluded to break Jason's will, and often when he experienced his will being overrun, he experienced himself as feminine. The legacy is not just gender confusion but confusion on all fronts. Indecision plagues Jason, evident in relations with women, in choices of career, and in gender identity. Whenever a family member disagrees with one of Jason's choices, he is thrown into uncertainty, becomes self-deprecating, and experiences his own choice as the unmanly, girl choice. The topic for decision may have nothing to do with gender, but the experience of choice becomes gendered because of Jason's history.

Bob's sense of agency, too, was weakened and entangled in the creation of his gender identity. When Bob disobeyed, his father would try to insure his compliance by giving his brother the very thing Bob longed for. Father, who had suffered the same indignities at the hand of his mother, had clearly not simply become a nice guy. He is in fact an alcoholic who was verbally and at times physically abusive when drinking. The legacy for Bob is that he shuns an identification with his father's preferred and enacted form of masculinity. Ironically, Bob's father played the macho male at home but never felt the macho male in the world, which suggests the complicated way that different versions of masculinity appear in the same person and how context-dependent these versions can be. As a child, the macho male was the only male Bob could see, and since the culture celebrates this male, he did not have to look far to see it. Nor did Jason.

Because the parents conveyed gender in its most reified binary form, and because the version of masculinity endorsed by the fathers was so alien and nasty, Bob and Jason repudiated an identification with macho men, which they generalized to a repudiation of masculinity. At the same time, each still wished, if ambivalently, to be the object of his father's love. One incident in Bob's life well illustrates the complexity of his gender identifications and how they were woven together with love choices: when Bob was about 10 his father humiliated him in front of one of his friends and he ran away. His parents took him to a therapist, and he told the therapist that he had run away because he was expected to do too much work. Although this was not the reason he ran away, it is not untrue. His parents had divorced before this incident, and Bob feels that his mother, performing the only gender roles she knew, did indeed turn to him to be the provider. When Bob talks about his wishes to be a woman, he expresses a longing to be taken care of and to have less responsibility. But he also despises his mother's expectations to be provided for. Gender indecision is perhaps safer than making identifications either as his father's woman or his mother's man. Therapists should note, however, that Bob chose a patriarchal "mother-blaming" narrative to give the male therapist, protecting his father and positioning himself as the beleaguered male provider, not the feminized male.

Both Bob and Jason entered treatment feeling a lot of shame about what men are like; both disliked their bodies and felt generally unattractive. Yet they both clearly longed to make it as a man. In fact, a feeling of not quite making it as a man is often what precipitates their urge to be a woman; they can experience such a feeling when sexually rejected by a desired woman; when manipulated, humiliated, or overrun by a male or female; and when feeling unsuccessful at work. Indeed, both men entered treatment at a time of career crisis, which was not coincidental, for work is so central to the definition of a man in the culture and again marks the intersection of gender and agency. Jason chose a field favored by his father and practiced by a brother, but he never felt his heart was in it and never quite completed the training. About a year into treatment, he told me he had really always wanted to be a sociologist, his undergraduate major, a field that his father definitely saw as feminine. He made inquiries about this for several months, but conversations with the family always made him lose his resolve. Over time, Jason has shifted decisions on four different careers, variants either of his father's choice or of his own. Recently, he told his father that he wanted to get an MSW; he reports that his father looked at him as though he'd just told him he was "a queer" (here, he imitates his father's speech).

As Butler says, the identification with feminized masculinity is "abject" because it threatens heterosexuality. Clearly, either the father relays his feelings about many neutral areas in gendered terms that are meant to have implications regarding sexual orientation, or Jason receives them so, or both. I understand Jason's difficulty in making decisions to be his way of dealing with his father's tendency to overrun his son's will. Gender conflict becomes a defense against choosing, because one choice seems to entail the loss of his father's acceptance and the other entails loss of the kind of person Jason feels he is. Further, the indecision keeps him from being rageful toward his father. Were he to experience rage, he would not only threaten whatever bond there is between them, but he would also *be* aggressive like his father, an identification he has repudiated. What makes it all even more complicated is the uncertainty about what father really wants. Father consciously seems to want Jason to make the masculine choice but unconsciously seems to need him to make what father considers the feminine choice.

In the course of treatment, Bob became more clear that he wanted to change his career, which was in the arts. About two years into therapy, he met some people who stirred up excitement about a much more entrepreneurial career. A few months later, he began exercising a lot, and within a month or so he spoke of liking his body more. All the while, Bob was becoming more and more comfortable asserting himself; a turning point had been an incident with his mother where he refused to sacrifice what he'd wanted in order to take care of her. Soon he began to talk about the female fantasies abating. Because Bob had felt sexually rejected by his wife, which he experienced as emasculating, he thought that these new positive feelings about himself as a man had to do with a concurrent loss of desire for his wife. On the contrary, I thought that, after much discussion in therapy, he had finally begun confronting her with his discontents, which, to my mind, had to do with her own gender identification uncertainties. Uncomfortable with her role as unemployed, primary caretaker of their children, she had no energy for much of an intimate relationship with Bob and it seemed that it was a blow to her self-esteem that, though not working, she often felt overwhelmed by the tasks of motherhood. She asked Bob for a lot of help and rejected suggestions of hiring help because she felt she ought to be able to do it. Meanwhile, her requests for help interrupted Bob's attempts to get work done. Indeed, in the period in which I worked with Bob, he did quite a bit of primary childcare, which he enjoys, but which conflicts with his work demands and those of everyone else in that position: this, too, is an oppressive by-product of traditional gender relations. There is no way to pursue career success in this culture and also devote yourself to your children (Goldin 1995).[3]

If Bob is correct that it was his loss of sexual desire that consolidated a less conflicted gender identity, I'd argue that that is much too big a price to pay! Bob has always felt that his difficulty setting limits and being assertive had to do with his feminine fantasies, about which he felt ashamed and which made him feel unworthy of asserting himself. Not surprisingly, his wish was that treatment would make this part of his life evaporate. Nonetheless, the fantasies were most present at the point of treatment just preceding the career change, and part of what was going on then was that he felt more comfortable exploring and enacting parts of the fantasies; he talked about them more openly to his wife, and she tentatively allowed him to talk about this and even experiment with it. My guess is that his wife's recognition, and the consolidation of his capacity to be assertive without fear of abandonment, humiliation, or destruction, have made him able to find a version of masculinity that he can live with. In this version, Bob delights in his capacity to perform not only tasks he considers feminine but also tasks he considers masculine. He is less concerned about his fantasies and, even though he still has fantasies of being female, he is less likely to feel that this prohibits him

---

[3]Goldin found that 24–33 percent of women college graduates of 1972 have a career (which she distinguishes operationally from a job). Of that group, only 13–17 percent had combined a career with having children by age 40. Fifty percent were childless.

from being assertive. Indeed, he is less likely to label attributes and behaviors either masculine or feminine. Bob's new comfort with being a man enabled him to make a career choice he could never have made when he felt flawed by gender confusion. Indeed, the new career, in which he has been quite successful, is one that our culture values as a macho profession.

Before discussing where Jason is currently, I want to say a bit about the kinds of feelings these men have toward women. Consciously both men have nothing but positive feelings about women. In fact, as you might imagine, both men experience envy of what women are able to do, and for some good reasons. Each has said things that show how and why traditional gender identifications are oppressive and why they produce desire for the very things they prohibit. For example, each wishes he could get up in the morning and choose, depending on how he felt, whether he was going to wear pants or a dress. Indeed, I have that choice; why shouldn't they?

Envy is rarely present without anger. Jason often conveys his sense of the power of the beautiful woman to get what she wants—and to arouse him whether he wants to be aroused or not.[4] But his identification with the powerless aspect of women makes him hate men whose actions are motivated predominantly by their sexual needs, which he thinks is true of all the men he knows, even his closest friends. These paradoxical feelings about women's power/powerlessness find expression in the cross-dressing: at one point Jason recognized that cross-dressing enabled him to control the entire process of arousal, desire, and sex by himself. Since he felt too awful when he found himself lusting after women, a by-product of his Catholicism and his defenses against aggression (see Stoller 1975),

---

[4]Bordo (1993) discusses men's feelings of powerlessness vis-à-vis women's power to control male sexuality. Most of the heterosexual men I have seen in treatment have expressed this feeling. See also Frosh (1994), who argues that because men split off feelings of dependence, and sexuality is built around dependence, men feel most dependent and least sufficient in sexual relations. Frosh says that sexuality poses the greatest challenge to the male model of autonomy; I would say that love relations, in general, pose the challenge.

he could use cross-dressing to control how a woman looks and have the woman he wanted without offending her with his masculine desires—he could determine the height of her heel, the length of her skirt, how seductive she would look. In cross-dressing, he enacts identification with both parents, the passive mother and the active father, as well as with their mode of relating to each other.

During one phase of treatment, I began questioning what was so shameful about lusting after women. As he began to feel it was okay to find a woman beautiful and desire her, that desiring her wasn't the same thing as harrassing her and wouldn't lead irrevocably to domestic violence, Jason was able to make some tentative identifications with men and was able to tolerate some degree of aggression. Indeed, Jason was initially disdainful but subsequently delighted to realize that his wish to control the woman's look made him similar to other men. He is not always delighted, however, when he discovers in himself his father's way of splitting the world into good macho/bad effeminate male. He despises the macho male, but his fantasy is that this is the male who is adored and has everything, particularly the women Jason desires. Women he is attracted to often greatly value his friendship but are sexually attracted to men who treat them poorly. Jason says that much of the time he accepts himself as fluidly gendered, but he will often catch himself imposing his father's rigid gender categories on himself. This oscillation between rigidity and fluidity seems to represent Jason's conflict: perhaps a conflict of allegiance between his father's way of viewing the world and mine, perhaps a conflict, as I said above, between hating himself for being other than what will gain him his father's acceptance as opposed to being comfortable with the full range of his desires and longings.

Dean (1993) offers a Lacanian understanding of transsexual identification, where the refusal to line up on one or the other side of the phallus is a disavowal of difference, a denial of lack, a sustaining of the fantasy of completeness (see also McDougall [1980], who argues that in the perversions sexual difference fails to become symbolized). In my view, Jason acutely feels he is lacking something that would make him the right kind of male, and in this way he does sustain a fantasy of completeness. He does indeed deny loss, but what loss is he denying? Is it the loss of all gender possibilities? I think not. It is the loss of his father's love and approval that he has not yet been able to mourn, in part because there are mixed messages about what his father wants. For Jason, cross-dressing is not used solely in the service of a fantasy of completeness, of being both genders. When his feelings of defectiveness are stirred up, he will often cross-dress to soothe anxiety. But when he began in therapy to feel less shame about cross-dressing, he was wont to do it when he felt most at peace with himself. Cross-dressing is not simply or primarily a denial of difference. In fact, the developmental requirements of hegemonic femininity and masculinity reveal that what needs to be problematized is the way difference is established in the culture: it is as damaging to fall in line with the norm as not to do so (see Chodorow 1994).

One of the greatest resistances that we have come up against is Jason's denial of women's aggression. There are several female figures in his history who were cruel and abusive, and, while he is aware of this, he has not incorporated it at all into his view that women are hapless victims of male boorishness and cruelty. He is likely to assume his inferiority to women, especially with regard to their capacity to endure poor treatment at the hands of men without retaliating (as his mother did). Thus, in identifying with hegemonic femininity and disidentifying with hegemonic masculinity, Jason sustains rather than finds his way out of the gender binary, denying men's vulnerability and women's aggression.

As it happens, Jason's father, who has always been a good Catholic husband when it comes to sexual fidelity, has also always had a weakness for beautiful women and has adopted several financially disadvantaged women to take care of. In Jason's view, only beautiful women and athletic men have the power to make father do anything for them. So, for Jason, a woman's power also has a triadic element: if he were a beautiful woman he would have the power not only to seduce those he desires but to win his father's love away from his brothers and from other beautiful women. Interestingly, however, Jason was first able to see a disparity between his father and ideal masculinity when he realized that his father makes a fool of himself for beautiful women. The capacity to see that disparity, to be angry at his father for "screwing up" and for trying to make Jason feel bad about himself, has been part of a developing ability to escape from the strict masculine/feminine binary in which he has lived. For, if his father is not the ideal male, maybe the ideal male does not exist, or isn't all that ideal. This disillusionment has paved the way for Jason to endorse his own version of masculinity.

Jason's rapid shifts in ideas about a career have lately been background music to lyrics about masculinity and cross-dressing. He had not cross-dressed for about four months and was finding he had little interest in doing more than fantasizing about it; simultaneously he seemed to feel much less shame about either of these activities. This was largely a function of therapy, but was also aided by a very recent shift in the culture toward a much greater visibility of and permissiveness towards cross-dressing. We have come across articles in women's magazines that normalize male cross-dressing, articles in the local paper about the Tiffany Club, a group of heterosexual men who cross-dress, movies such as *The Crying Game* (Jordan 1992), a local museum show on cross-dressing, appearances by male grunge rockers in skirts, and changes in men's clothing. In the fall, Jason happily reported a shopping trip where, for the first time, he found men's clothes he could wear to work that felt like him. Moved by the quote "Nothing human is alien to me," Jason spoke of accepting his sexuality and feeling less shame about it. He also began talking about TV men he identified with, men who were admirable but not macho. As we examined these identifications, we found that he was becoming free to explore new models of masculinity that were circulating in the culture, ones that fit more with who he felt he was.

A turning point in Jason's therapy was when I realized that, although I had aspired to take a totally accepting stance towards his desires to cross-dress, towards his feminine identifications, and towards who he felt he was, I was yet going along with him in labeling many of his desires as "feminine." He and I were continuing to conflate particular attributes and gender identifications—wearing a skirt is feminine; giggling is feminine—precisely what Jason's father had done to cause gender trouble in the first place. This prevented us both from seeing that he was finding new ways of being a man, ways that could include both his skill at carpentry and his pleasure in wearing a skirt.

I'd like to conclude this section on Jason with some dreams that have dramatized his struggle against the masculine/feminine binary in establishing a gender identity. About two and a half years into treatment, Jason reported two dreams that he said were different from recurring dreams he'd had about cross-dressing. In the first, he was in a store buying a skirt and blouse for a woman. The saleswoman, who bore some resemblance to me, asked whether he wouldn't like to try a larger size, assuming that the clothes were for him. She and another saleslady just started bringing him things, nicer and nicer things. At the end, he walked out of the store in the clothes, feeling happy and feeling as though he looked right. This dream was remarkable to him, he said, because it was the first dream he had ever had in which he had gotten the look right. Was his recent comfort with cross-dressing a result of what he felt was my acceptance? Or was he complying with something he thought I wanted of him?

The second dream followed one that he had reported the previous week, in which he had gone to a big football game, realized when he got there that his clothes weren't right, and had to change. Relating the second dream, Jason became quite excited when he realized that in the dream he was watching the game, which is much different from playing. When he played as a child, his father would yell at him that he wasn't aggressive enough. The anxiety raised by the anticipated humiliation made him so focused on himself that, as he put it, he was unable to see the whole field. And that's what you need to do to play well. He was feeling so good about himself, recently getting a lot of praise for his skill in sculpting, that he thought he could now play the game and see the whole field.

After he reported the clothing dream, I wondered with him whether getting the look right wasn't a metaphor for getting it right in other areas of his life; I recalled for him the dream about seeing the field, about being an artist in a family that thinks his sculptures are "cool" but is just as likely to make fun of him for it. He then excitedly remembered an "amazing dream." He was in a football game, and he could see the field, and he scored several touchdowns, and it just felt so great. Dad was the coach and one of his brothers was there, too. Then Jason went to the locker room and put on clothes that weren't like anyone else's; they were more like Jimi Hendrix's clothes. He was definitely dressed differently from anyone else, but he figured he could get away with it because he had just done so well in the game and thus had already gotten acceptance. He then spoke of his intense anger at his father for not accepting him as he is.

The dreams are remarkable in many ways. Just as for Bob, acceptance for Jason is central. Jason's fantasy includes a woman who allows him to dress like a woman, who encourages him and, in other dreams, even lets him dress as she does. Jason's images so poignantly describe the way that narcissistic wounding limits him to a focus on the self and robs him of being able to see the whole field. As was true for Bob, Jason's dream suggests that only when he is feeling competent in a field *he* considers masculine can he allow himself to wear a skirt and enjoy it. As we saw in Chapter 5, if core gender identity is refused via disidentification or disavowal, the resulting fluidity is not pleasurable. Some kind of core identity seems to be a necessary prerequisite for the capacity to play freely with alternate identities (see Flax 1990, Rivera 1989).

The masculine/feminine binary manifests itself in more subtle ways as well, which require us to look beyond mere content to process and to our clients' modes of relating to us and to their world. In Bob's case, the rigid masculine/feminine binary that narrowed his options is not only operative in the expression of sexuality, sexual fantasy, love, and work, but also oddly shapes his world view and way of relating. From the beginning of treatment, Bob has complained that all that he does he does alone. At the point that he entered treatment, he was both the breadwinner and doing a lot of domestic tasks and child care—too much work! He feels that no one has ever been there to help him emotionally, and he generally anticipates disappointments. In fact, while he did not identify with those attributes of his father that he considered macho, he did find common ground with his father's sense that the world sucks and, in hard times, you've got to make your way alone. While this world view of rugged individualism has been evident to me for awhile, the fact that Bob sought treatment and was going through his struggle with me somehow kept me from exploring this paradox until a few years into treatment. Although Bob repudiated an identification with authoritarian macho masculinity, he nonetheless identified with his father's masculine model of autonomy, in which the individual is a monad that defensively denies its deep connections to other people and contexts. In the early part of treatment, what I noticed was that he doggedly tried to restrict any problems in his life to his own person; *he* lacks motivation, *he* lacks drive, *he* never sees something through to the end: perfect fodder for the traditional therapy mill. In this phase, I tried to point out, however, that his wife's rejecting behavior played a role in many of the conflicts he described. He resisted this analysis, although very occasionally he would confront his wife with his discontents.

At times, he has lambasted himself for not being in the league of the world's most successful 30-year-old men; he feels he has the ability, so something must be wrong with his drive. At these moments, he completely forgets that he has made choices to spend time with family that preclude the kind of life necessary to be that successful—and the magazine stories that feature the most successful men never talk about the personal costs. To explore Bob's motivation issues here would be to collude with his decontextualization of the problem.

What became clear later in the treatment is that going it alone is a way Bob preserves a sense of specialness, even though it also requires taking on all the responsibility and even though it is very lonely. Going it alone requires foregoing peers, but it also protects from disappointment and from experiencing neediness and dependency. This model of autonomy is central to the masculine/feminine binary that structures our culture, a model so oppressive that Bob's childhood way out took the form of a wish to be female, which he connected with less responsibility and work. Bob's difficulty contextualizing his conflicts, I would argue, is a problem for thera-

pists and for Western psychology itself. If we fail to place our clients
in the context of their relationships and cultural constraints, we play
our role in reproducing the lonely individual of Western ideology.
Thus a very important part of individual therapy, I think, is for the
therapist to resist the pull to decontextualize; on the contrary, the
therapist needs to explore, deepen, and complicate understandings
of the multiple contexts within which individual acts, feelings, and
thoughts occur.

This problem also arises in Jason's therapy but more directly
between him and me. From time to time he recognizes that he thinks
like his father, and one thing that his father thinks is that therapy
is for the weak, for girls. At these times, Jason feels he ought to be
able to do it alone, that he will have to stop coming to therapy before
he can really move on. Therapists are often confronted with such a
reified and gendered dependence/independence binary, where, as
elsewhere in the culture, independence is narrowly defined as pull-
ing yourself up by your bootstraps, going it alone. I find this to be
a central struggle in many therapies, and when I encounter it I propose a Fairbairnian (Fairbairn 1954) notion of mutual interdependence to help clients cognitively get beyond this strong/weak dualism.

In fact, if I were to hypothesize some of the factors that have
led to change for these two men, I would suggest an increasing comfort with dependence as one. And even this has come about through
the mediation of gender, because dependence and independence are
gendered in the culture and in their families. For example, Jason recently noticed that I see a male client before him; he'd thought he
was the only male I see. While this made him wonder about whether
or not he was special to me, it also made it permissible to be a male
in therapy. Clearly, gender identifications continue throughout life
and can facilitate change as well as impede it.

What seems to be curative for both Jason and Bob is a mix of
a few things: giving permission to hold onto whatever identifications
they have already made and enjoy, working with the shame around
what has made them experience certain identifications as "abject";
continuously challenging any exclusive associations they make between gender and a human attribute (for example, it's feminine to

do ceramics); and continuously questioning their devaluing and idealizing associations to femininity and masculinity. However, these men have become less conflicted about their so-called feminine identifications only as they have been able to take more pleasure in being men and in having male bodies. Each has grown to find himself more attractive as a man. Jason has recently had fantasies of being penetrated by a man, which not only reflects more awareness of homosexual desire but also has made him understand for the first time why a woman might desire a man's body. This has made him appreciate his body in new ways. Jason and Bob are defining for themselves ways of being a man that differ from both hegemonic masculinity and hegemonic femininity.

In conclusion, I would like to return to the thorny problem of gender acquisition in our cultural context and what postmodern theories have to offer us as clinicians. Postmodern theories, like feminist relational psychoanalytic theories, propose a trauma model of gender acquisition, that is, they argue that the "normal" path to gender acquisition involves enacting and/or internalizing the norms of compulsory heterosexuality/heterosexism as well as the norms of gender inequality. These theories account for cultural and familial power inequalities in a way that many other psychoanalytic versions of gender acquisition do not. As we know from our work with self disorders and post-traumatic stress disorders, trauma induces splitting and other dissociative behaviors, and I have been making the case throughout this book that the masculine/feminine binary on which our culture rests (in terms of both identity and coupling) is a culturally sanctioned instance of splitting, especially in the reified form in which we witness it in Bob and Jason. In their cases, humiliation was the active tool of coercion that irrevocably marked their identifications and that tied power and gender, gender and agency, gender and relationship, inextricably together. Their parents, whose stereotypically traditional gender arrangements displayed the worst aspects of compulsory heterosexuality, were faced with boys whose temperaments, interests, and desires were in part formed by the unconscious desires of their fathers but also came into conflict with what the fathers perceived a man ought to be, regardless of whether or not the fathers themselves incarnated that norm. The fathers took it upon themselves to punish these deviations from the norm. But in each case the punishments were guided not only by their own histories of gender acquisition but by cultural norms of what a man needs to be. Both of these fathers expressed overtly and covertly their conviction that the worlds of business, intimacy, and sociality require a certain kind of male individual (see Brenkman 1993). And because there is cultural consensus on such requirements, it is easy to imagine a clinician retraumatizing a client, although, to be sure, in more subtle ways.

If Jason and Bob had not gotten stuck in their fathers' gender binds, they would not have chosen to disidentify with masculinity, nor would they have been ashamed of their gender. This put them at a disadvantage. But I feel they also had a distinct advantage over those who have allegedly acquired a male gender identity in the traditional way: by disidentifying with femininity. For they did not repudiate their identifications with women (although, at moments, the version of femininity identified with was as oppressive as the companion version of masculinity that was repudiated). They feel comfortable with women; they like women and women like them; they treat women as subjects; they identify with attributes associated with women in the culture, such as nurturance; and they feel they have more in common with women than with men. The capacity to enjoy being a man *without repudiating identifications with women* seems to lead to something new, something that is not dominant in the culture and that the term *androgyny* does not quite capture. Androgyny theory suggests that one identify as human and forgo gender identity. But as postmodern theorists have demonstrated, power relations reduce identification with the human to identification with the white, upper-class male, and this is one reason for the postmodern rejection of humanism. These theorists want a culture where difference is not only valued but valued on its own terms, that is, not subjected to a normative matrix wherein it is at best tolerated as an interesting or exotic deviation.

As I have argued here, our culture forbids one to identify as both male and female; the culture, and most psychoanalytic theory, makes these two identities mutually exclusive. Only if the culture were to change could one achieve what Jason and Bob are in the process of achieving, without having to go through the horrible pain they experienced to get there. To capture the newness of what Jason and Bob represent, I would like to borrow the concept of hybridity from the postcolonial theorist Homi K. Bhabha. Bhabha (1990, 1994) suggests there is a third, hybrid space which goes beyond the binary's prior manifestations and cannot be understood solely by tracing the history of these prior manifestations—that is, it is something new. While Bhabha speaks of cultural identities, I believe we can translate his theory to gender identities as well.

Jason and I spent a few sessions discussing an incident with one of his uncles. The uncle was having a late-life crisis of meaning and told Jason that he sees him as a new soul, as someone who is not still working through old problems, not still stuck in the past. He labeled himself and all Jason's brothers old souls. Jason heard this in gendered terms and thought his uncle was saying he wasn't really a man. I heard it in gendered terms as well, but I thought his uncle was saying he was a new kind of man, not stuck in some of the painful limitations he and Jason's brothers were stuck in. Jason tentatively took on this identification with the new soul.

What is the new soul? Following Bhabha, I would say it emerges from a process of inhabiting a sexed body and identifying with men and women in such a way as to displace timeworn histories of hegemonic masculinity and femininity, one element of which is the imperative to attain a masculine gender identity by disidentifying with women. Thus the new soul cannot be traced back to originary moments of masculinity and femininity, each with its separate set of attributes and its prohibition on certain identifications. Bhabha captures both the coercive and the facilitating aspects of identification in his notion that all processes of identification are ambivalent. Because the subject identifies with something other, and otherness is both same and different (see Benjamin 1995), intrusive and compelling, the process that yields hybridity "gives rise to something different, something new and unrecognizable, a new area of negotiation of meaning and representation"; this "'third space' ... enables other positions to emerge . . . and sets up new structures of authority, new political initiatives, which are inadequately understood through received wisdom" (1990, p. 211).

But someone has to recognize and validate the newness of the new soul. The challenge for clinicians is to reject a psychoanalysis that, in Butler's (1990a) terms, merely cites the norm, that labels it pathological to go a different route from the oedipus. We must be able to recognize a client's reworkings or rejections of the norm. The challenge is great, because often our clients look to us to enforce the norm, to make them fit. Those who have gone a different route, as have Bob and Jason, often suffer for having done so and at times wish more than anything that the accidents of their fate had not created for them a different path. The clinician walks the fine line between acknowledging the suffering and keeping open for the client a sense that the route he or she has taken may not be pathological, that there is, on the contrary, a pathological constraining quality to the norm. As Adam Phillips (1993) writes, perhaps the aim of psychoanalysis is not to cure people but to show them that there is nothing wrong with them.

Jason and Bob made what the culture considers "abject" identifications, but in so doing they reveal the instabilities and oppressive constraints of the norm; they reveal what the norm tries to hide: its own history and preconditions, its constructedness. They also reveal the intricate ways that gender gets entwined with agency, relationship, and power. We as clinicians must be aware of the way power circulates in culture, of the oppressive elements of norms, of *whose* needs a particular ideal of the individual serves. And we must be aware of the ways in which the questions we choose to ask or not ask, the categories we enforce or question, might participate in citing an oppressive norm.

8

A Deconstruction of
Kohut's Concept of Self*

In this and the final chapter, I want to look at the way gender is figured in key concepts of two theorists whose work informs much of this book: Judith Butler's theory of performativity (to be discussed in Chapter 9) and Heinz Kohut's (1971, 1977) theory of the self. In the chapter on Butler, I try to integrate her postmodern gender theory with a relational psychoanalysis. Kohut's project has little resonance with postmodern theories and has little to say explicitly about gender. His self psychology is rife with questionable binary assumptions, and his central tenet—anathema to a postmodern critique of unity—is that healthy people strive, from birth, for a cohesive self. But it was Kohut's writings on narcissism that enabled U.S. clinicians to hear and understand patients' postmodern symptoms of fragmentation, emptiness, and deadness.[1] In fact, in clearly dis-

---

*This chapter is adapted from Layton 1990a (copyright © 1990 by the William Alanson White Institute and used by permission).

[1]Kohut does not credit his sources, but much of what he has to say about the clinical features of narcissism had been adumbrated in the theories of British Object Relations theorists. Fairbairn (1954) and Guntrip (1961), for example, described similar states of deadness and fragmentation in what they called their "schizoid" clients. There is a real difference, however, between Kohut's focus on the ongoing

tinguishing healthy longings for cohesion from narcissistic longings
for merger or plenitude, Kohut's discussion of narcissistic transferences provides an interesting challenge to some tenets of Lacanian
theory.

Kohut's self psychology indisputably opened many clinical doors
that had seemed to remain shut in drive and oedipal theory. His
elaboration of selfobject functions and narcissistic transferences (the
use of another primarily to shore up a fragmenting self), of the role
of empathy and empathic breaks in the formation of the self and
the treatment of self disorders, of the clinical value of remaining in
tune with the experience-near, of the difficulties contemporary U.S.
clients have with the regulation of self-esteem and the many kinds
of selfobjects (drugs, food) they use temporarily to restore a fragile
sense of self—all of this work on narcissism enabled those of us clinicians who feel that this theory fits some of what we see to refor-
mulate our descriptions of pathology and our methods of treatment.
Yet, despite these contributions and despite Kohut's insistence that
health requires the capacity to experience both self and other as independent centers of initiative, his is not an intersubjective theory
in the sense elaborated by Benjamin (1988). In this chapter, I want
to focus on what I consider major shortcomings of Kohut's theory,
specifically the notions of two separate lines of development (narcissism and object love) and of the bipolar self that is a developmental
culmination of the line of narcissism. Here I want to use both relational theory and the postmodern questioning of binaries to examine the gendered and sexist underpinnings of central parts of Kohut's
theory.

In the '50s and '60s, Kohut began to elaborate a theory of narcissism, now termed self psychology by his followers. He returned
to Freud's distinction between narcissism and object love, with the
project of rescuing narcissism from the prevailing view that, in health,
primary narcissism gives way to object love. In "On Narcissism"
(1914), Freud used the term *ego* interchangeably with *self* and postu-

---

importance of the developmental line of narcissism and British Object Relations
theorists' assumption that humans are primarily object seeking.

lated two interrelated types of libido, one cathecting the self (ego libido) and one the object (object libido). Originally, only cathexes of the self exist; later, some ego libido is given off to objects, but ego cathexes persist. In Introductory Lecture 26 (1916), Freud wrote that "it is probable that this narcissism is the universal and original state of things, from which object love is only later developed, without the narcissism necessarily disappearing on that account" (p. 416). Freud's notion was that the more libido expended on objects, the less available for the self and vice versa.

In Kohut's earlier writings, he, too, spoke of narcissistic libido as separate from object libido. He later dropped the notion of two kinds of libido but persisted with the claim that there are two separate lines of development. In Kohut's view, empathic parenting transforms archaic narcissism—examples of which are untamed grandiosity and the infant's inability to self-soothe—into mature forms of narcissism, which include creativity, the capacity for empathy, the capacity for humor, the capacity to contemplate our own transience, and the attainment of a wisdom that is accepting of limitations. This line of development is autonomous from the vicissitudes of object love.

Kohut's notion of *self* comes from Hartmann's (1950) distinction between the ego, subject of ego psychology, and the self. In Kohut's early work, he spoke of id, ego, and superego, but these terms were gradually replaced with what he called *the self* as a supraordinate concept. In a 1978 paper co-authored with Ernest Wolf, Kohut defined the self as follows: "The patterns of ambitions, skills, and goals, the tensions between them, the program of action that they create, and the activities that strive towards the realization of this program are all experienced as continuous in space and time—they are the self, an independent center of initiative, an independent recipient of impressions" (p. 44).

While claiming only to be a theory of the self and thus different from object relations theories, self psychology yet seems to contain several elements of a relational theory. Central is the concept of empathic resonance between people. The theory's developmental perspective holds that the self grows from relationships with early objects, and Kohut first differentiated his field of study from that of

Freud on the basis of the kinds of transference relationships that unfold in analyzing those with narcissistic disturbances. Despite appearances and to the detriment of the theory, however, Kohut's formulations downplay the importance of relationships, and they do so by setting up a framework of false dichotomies—such as work and love, objects and selfobjects—and then privileging one side of the dichotomy while devaluing the other. In fact, a symptomatic reading of Kohut's texts reveals that the privileging of work in his theories of the self and of two separate lines of development is accomplished primarily by ignoring material that pertains to the analysands' relationships.

In *The Analysis of the Self* (1971), Kohut theorizes that the self structure grows from relationships with archaic selfobjects, more particularly with an empathic, mirroring selfobject who affirms and gradually tames archaic grandiosity, and with an idealized selfobject, who allows the subject to feel, as Kohut puts it, "You are perfect and I am part of you" (p. 25). The early selfobjects are not experienced as separate from the subject, and self structure comes about by internalizing the soothing, mirroring, and idealizing functions that the selfobjects originally perform. Thus, as Kohut describes it, the self is born from relationship but not from relationships with others experienced as separate and distinct centers of initiative (in Benjamin's 1988 terms, as subjects). Rather, these relationships are with others experienced as coexistent with the subject and under the subject's control. In health, these selfobject relationships do not disappear, do not cede to object love, according to Kohut, but continue to exist in a mature form. Kohut again and again likens the need for mature selfobjects to the need for oxygen, something we do not really notice but which we need to live. In the words of his collaborator, Wolf (1980):

> one may compare the need for the continuous presence of a psychologically nourishing self-object milieu with the continuing physiological need for an environment containing oxygen. . . . As long as a person is securely embedded in a social matrix that provides him with a field in which he can find the needed mir-

roring responses and the needed availability of idealizable values, he will feel comfortably affirmed in his total self with its ambitions and goals. In short, he will feel himself strong and, paradoxically, relatively self-reliant, self-sufficient, and autonomous. [p. 128]

Kohut's definition of the structure that grows from these relationships, the bipolar self, ironically bears no trace of any kind of relationship at all: one pole of the bipolar self is defined by skills and ambitions, the other by goals and ideals. The poles are said to be connected by a tension arc, the talents and skills "needed for realization of the patterns of the basic ambitions and basic ideals that were laid down in the two polar areas" (1977, p. 49). Kohut presents several cases in *The Analysis of the Self* to illustrate his theory, and he argues forcefully and repeatedly that deficits in the line of development of narcissism are independent of whatever goes on in the realm of object love. If, as a result of therapy, there are therapeutic gains in object love, Kohut argues that they are secondary, and he even goes as far as to assert that before treatment, his patient Mr. K., who had severe narcissistic deficits, "had attained a considerable depth and breadth of his object investments" (1971, p. 258). As with his other cases, Kohut insists that Mr. K.'s pathology "lay not in the area of his capacity for love and in his interpersonal relationships but in his ability to devote himself consistently to his work and to commit himself to worthwhile and absorbing long-term goals" (p. 258). Thus Kohut argues that the two lines of development are independent, that one can love well but work poorly and vice versa.

If we give credence to feminist theories that argue that, for women, self-esteem, morality, and knowledge are all based in relationship (Chodorow 1978, Gilligan 1982, Miller et al. 1991), we might wonder whether Kohut, like so many other theorists, arrived at his theory of the self and of development by excluding females from his data collection. As fifteen of the seventeen cases in *The Analysis of the Self* are men, this is indeed a possibility. But Kohut sees the same dynamics at work in both males and females with narcissistic disturbance and applies the same theory, so I think we need to look elsewhere to discover how and why he arrives at a theory of self that excludes relationship and a theory of relationship that is primarily narcissistic.

One clue to resolving this mystery is found in Arnold Goldberg's *The Psychology of the Self. A Casebook* (1978). This book presents extended case studies of four of the patients from which Kohut's theory in *The Analysis of the Self* was drawn, those of Mr. E., Mr. I., Mr. B., and Mr. M., not all of whom were treated by Kohut. Although most of the analysts who treated these patients formulate things in the same way Kohut does, the chance to examine the texts enables one outside the frame of self psychology to see that certain elements of the cases have been highlighted to support Kohut's theory and other elements have been minimized. What has most dramatically been minimized is the significance of the patients' relationships.

Looking at these cases, we find first that, while Kohut and the other analysts insist that work problems are the central element of the patients' pathology, all of the patients entered therapy because of problems with relationships as well as with work. In fact, many of them complained primarily of relationship problems. As one might expect, they all had the same kinds of archaic selfobject relationships with lovers, children, and parents that they developed with their analysts; there is absolutely no evidence in these cases that deficits in the realm of narcissism are independent of deficits in the realm of object love. Indeed, Mr. I.'s analyst acknowledges the similarities in the vicissitudes of Mr. I.'s relationship with his girlfriend and with the analyst. In this case, as in the others, the patient is gradually able not only to work better but to love better, and there is no clue given as to why the changes in the way Mr. I. relates should be considered subordinate to the changes in the way he works. In fact, the point is made that when Mr. I. feels he is getting enough from his analyst, he is able to give more both to his girlfriend and to his work.

Kohut (1977) begins his argument in *The Restoration of the Self* with the case of Mr. M. He spends many pages stating that it was not necessary to analyze the primary deficit in Mr. M.'s self, the deficit caused by failures in mother's empathic mirroring and by his early months in foster care. Rather, Kohut argues, the analysis can be considered complete when Mr. M.'s compensatory structures have been firmed—structures derived from the relation with the idealized father, a man who valued the verbal skills Mr. M. used in his career as a writer. Indeed, Kohut chooses to work in the realm of the paternally-created idealized pole in all three cases discussed in Chapter 1 of *Restoration* (despite occasional disclaimers, he consistently equates the idealized parent with the father, the empathic parent with the mother). The question Kohut deals with in Chapter 1 is: When is an analysis complete? I think his choice to work on the idealized pole again betrays his bias toward firming the self's ability to work well at the expense of its ability to love well. By choosing not to analyze the primary deficit, the analyst runs the risk of creating more contented and more productive narcissists who begin and remain nonrelational.

One of the most frequently used words in Kohut's case discussions is *overstimulation*. He uses it, for example, when he speaks of Mr. M.'s difficulty engaging in his writing. Early in *Restoration*, Kohut argues that adult self-esteem is based in work:

> With regard to his work as a writer—and it must again be stressed that his work should have made the greatest contribution to the enhancement of his adult self-esteem and should have provided the most important outlet for transformed grandiose-exhibitionistic narcissistic tensions through creativity—the structural defect caused by the failure of the maternal mirroring functions led to experiences of frightening and paralyzing overstimulation. He did not possess sufficient structures to curb and neutralize the grandiosity and exhibitionism that became activated when his imagination was mobilized. He therefore often became tense and excited when he was writing and then either had to suppress his imagination—to the detriment of the originality and vitality of the product—or cease working altogether. [p. 10]

When we turn to Mr. M.'s case in the casebook, we find that Mr. M. himself uses similar words to describe the feeling of closeness he had with his female analyst and the feeling he had when writing. In both cases he feared disintegration. In other words, he felt "overstimulated" both when he loved and when he wrote.

As in the case of Mr. I., the issue of most concern to the patient (as opposed to the analyst) is not work inhibitions but the regulation of closeness and distance, the oscillation between dangerous merger and dangerous isolation. While Kohut writes as though merger with empathically attuned archaic selfobjects is a non-conflictual need for the narcissistically disturbed patient, the cases in fact reveal a constant sense of overstimulation when the patient feels that the analyst gets too close. Mr. B., for example, clearly finds empathic gratification as frightening as the empathic breaks. Overstimulation is given a relational meaning as his analyst writes: "He feels revitalized, comforted, and reintegrated by the closeness with his new girl, and yet he must separate himself regularly from her too" because "any threat of feelings that are too intense or unmanageable utterly destroys his sense that there is reliability in the situation" (p. 407). This is one of the only cases where the analyst seems to recognize that what happens in the sphere of love is the same thing that happens in the sphere of work: "His tendency is to get buried in current experience, like teaching, the way he gets buried in his love relationships. He still must struggle to develop any degree of useful detachment . . ." (p. 415).

Mr. I. also expresses a conflict regarding merger experiences: "'Closeness and distance. Close, but not too close—in terms of verbal communication, not sex; once you feel understood and that need is gratified, for me it's a happy medium, a balance. Too much understood is as uncomfortable as not being understood'" (p. 63). Mr. I. becomes disorganized both when he has merger fantasies and when he withdraws too much from the intimate other. His fear, as the analyst tells us, is that if he moves too far away, becomes a separate self, he will lose closeness completely. The analyst, however, focuses only on the dangers of being separate and not on the dangers of being merged. One could argue that the fear of merger might inhibit both work performance and closeness in relationships, for, in one as in the other, some loss of control, some loosening of boundaries, must be tolerated.

Finally, Mr. M., too, makes distance regulation, not work inhibitions, the central issue. Of the analyst, he says, "She should be there, available, but not intrude with her presence so that he would feel obliged to consider her and to please her. . . . You are the coach [he said to the analyst], but I want to keep you on the bench. I am not a sportsman, but this image helps. I must keep you on the bench, otherwise the team [that is, he himself] will disintegrate" (p. 156). Again, this issue has the same manifestation in the realm of work as in relationship. The analyst tells us that the patient bought an expensive instrument just as he was giving up playing: "The musical instrument served a special purpose which he no longer needed; it was to test his ability to freely abandon himself to the rhythm of the music without becoming overstimulated" (p. 158). "Overstimulated" is thus really a code word for what one feels when one comes closer than one can tolerate, either to work or to lovers. Although the analyst in this case insists that the patient's changes in the realm of object love were nonspecific, it is not at all clear in reading the case how the ability to love would stem from a different source from the ability to work.

In *Restoration*, Kohut points to three events that signalled Mr. M.'s readiness to terminate. He bought the expensive violin, he formed a fatherly, non-erotic bond with a 14-year-old boy whose independence he admired and whom he saw as separate from himself, and, his greatest achievement (according to Kohut), he began a writing school. Kohut does not even mention that he also became involved in an enduring love relationship with a young woman at the same time he connected with the boy; the analyst of the case mentions it briefly at the end of the case. Why is this an event so unimportant as to be omitted completely by Kohut? Why does the analyst here describe the relationship changes as "non-specific"? In my view, this is evidence of a very selective attention to the facts and a clear bias against object relationship. Were we to expand the definition of the self to include object relationship, it would be clear that in both the realm of work and the realm of love what occurs is a greater flexibility of boundaries, an ability to come close without fear of annihilation and to separate without fear of loss or isolation.

In this final section, I would like to entertain some hypotheses as to why Kohut might not have seen all that there was to see in these cases. If we look first at the tradition within which Kohut writes, I think we find that the origin of his theoretical error—the error in the narrow sense—lies in his acceptance of the dichotomous framework of narcissism and object love initiated by Freudian theory. Further, Freud's nearly exclusive concern with the erotic and aggressive dimensions of object love seems to have set the stage for a rebellion that, in Kohut's generation of U.S. theorists, would take the form of a nearly exclusive concern with work and mastery. Kohut thus rebels but always remains locked within the same framework. In this view, Kohut's work, like Erikson's (1950, 1968), must be seen as lying along the same line of theoretical development as ego psychology. Both Kohut and Erikson make object love and intimacy something separate from and dependent on the establishment of the self and of identity, constructs that, in these theories, do not depend on relationship.

Kohut's theory of the self and his line of development of narcissism are constructs that must be understood as challenges to Freud's Oedipus complex and his focus on object love (and certainly to British Object Relations theory as well). Kohut is pushed into a one-sided theorizing by the one-sidedness of Freud, whose discussion of object love often seems to exclude such dimensions of relationship as intimacy. In Kohut, this one-sidedness results in such incomprehensible arguments as that in which mature selfobject relationships are said to be something qualitatively different from object love. What could it possibly mean to call the empathic resonance between two healthy people a selfobject relationship, as Kohut (1984) does in How Does Analysis Cure? Following Guntrip (1961), who argues that Freud's pleasure-seeking libido is an example of schizoid theorizing, I would suggest that this is an example of narcissistic theorizing. The capacity for empathy—as J. V. Jordan (1984) has eloquently argued—requires boundaries that enable both a oneness with and a separateness from the other, and thus it is absurd to assign empathy to a realm of selfobject relations that is sharply differentiated from the realm of object love. In other words, for a healthy adult, relationships with others undoubtedly include both what Kohut describes as selfobject functions and what Freud describes as object functions, but the two mix in ways that make them inseparable and, I think, they are falsely and incompletely understood if looked at separately. A healthy love relationship probably involves experiencing the other as a separate center of initiative who, at the same time, is a soothing, mirroring, empathic or idealized presence, but not one that is under the subject's control. To need an other solely as a selfobject is as much a sign of pathology as to need an other solely as an erotic object. The exclusive use of the other as a selfobject and the exclusive use as an oedipal object are probably both manifestations of self disturbance; to theorize them as separate kinds of relationship rather than as some of the many dimensions of the whole love object is to normalize something pathological.

Kohut's error in the supraordinate sense I think lies in his taking appearances as essences and theorizing the given as the healthy (see Cushman 1990). The core disturbance of the patients in the casebook is a severe tension between autonomy and attachment caused by failures in the earliest relationships (this is in fact better captured, I believe, in the theories of the British Object Relations theorists Fairbairn and Guntrip than in the theory of Kohut). What we have discovered is that the same kind of boundary problems that prevent a full engagement with the world prevent a full engagement with others. In these cases, relationships with the parents were able to be maintained only at the cost of autonomy, so the patient oscillated between sacrificing relationship to a disturbed autonomy and sacrificing autonomy to a disturbed relationship. Thus, in these severe cases of narcissistic disturbance, where patients cannot be both related and autonomous at the same time, we see what looks like two separate lines of development.

What further enables Kohut's theory to appear legitimate is that, in our culture, hegemonic masculinity and its version of self-esteem are in fact based in what have been called agentic behaviors, maintaining a separatist form of autonomy, whereas hegemonic femininity and its version of self-esteem are based in communal behaviors, maintaining relationship. Stone Center researchers are thus correct to propose a one-line development theory, the self-in-relation (Surrey 1985). They suggest that, ideally, individuation and attachment proceed together, as one process, but that our culture encourages the development of communal behaviors and the suppression of agentic behaviors in women whereas it encourages the development of agentic behaviors and the suppression of communal behaviors in men. I believe that our culture does a disservice to individuals of both sexes by fostering this deviant and one-sided development. Indeed, as I noted in Chapter 2, these socialization practices probably create narcissistic disturbances of two different kinds. To further complicate matters, the culture not only fosters this deviant development but then places a much greater value on agentic behavior than on communal behavior, and it is this that makes it possible for theorists to equate autonomy with the self and with good self-esteem.

I would argue, then, that the oppressive socialization practices of a culture biased toward a particular kind of agency result in the *appearance* of two separate lines of development, each of which, according to Kohut, offers a continuum that runs from pathology to health, and one of which he has privileged by calling it *the self*. Benjamin (1988) and Kernberg (1975, 1976, 1980), as well as Stone Center theorists, while differing on their views of separateness, would yet agree that the above-described *appearance* is already a sign of pathology; in the ideal case of development, the two lines would be either so intertwined as to make a theorist unable to speak of them as separate (Kernberg) or the two lines would resolve themselves into one. In both cases, any definition of *self* would have to be expanded to include relationship.

Thus it is my suggestion that Kohut, rather than being a theorist of "the self," has legitimized in his theory the distortions in development that a patriarchal, western culture, dominated still by the Protestant Ethic, has brought forth and called normal. The bipolar self values positively only the male version of this distortion; as is so often the case in western theory, the female version is erased or devalued as only the male version gains access to the status of the human self. Kohut argues eloquently that the sexual and aggressive symptoms of Freud's patients are not evidence of innate drives but rather are breakdown products of disturbances in the self. I am suggesting here that the same argument can be used against Kohut's theory: that the two lines of development he discovers are "breakdown products" of culturally-mediated failures in development. The cases in the casebook make it clear despite the analysts' intentions that working well and loving well, autonomy and relationship, are not independent and stem from the same relational source. Primitive modes of autonomy correlate highly with primitive modes of relating (see Fast 1995). Those who love their work primarily for its own sake rather than primarily for the status, wealth, or parental approval it brings them tend also to be able to perceive and love others as separate subjects (see Layton 1988). Thus I would conclude by suggesting that, rather than continuing to dichotomize and devalue, what we should look for as we attempt to define and theorize subjectivity are the broader capacities that underlie both the ability to love and the ability to work.

9

Performance Theory, Act 3: The Doer Behind the Deed Gets Depressed*

In *Gender Trouble* (1990a), Judith Butler elaborated a performative theory of gender and subjectivity that has since profoundly shaped academic discussions of gender, sexuality, and the project of feminism. Butler's discussion of performativity was not only the cornerstone of that text but also the core of what made her theory postmodern (in her terms, poststructuralist). Although *Gender Trouble* was highly engaged with critiquing French psychoanalytic theories, and is thus of great interest to clinicians, I want to argue that Butler's view of gender performativity as stated in that text was essentially unpsychoanalytic, unreconcilable with either a dynamic unconscious or an internal relational world. With each new publication, however, Butler has reworked her theory of performativity, and each reworking has brought her closer to an object relational psychoanalysis. Indeed, her most recent discussion of performativity (1995a) resonates with several feminist psychoanalytic relational accounts that envision normative femininity and masculinity as symptomatic and as produced and sustained by processes of splitting (Benjamin 1988,

---

*This chapter is adapted from Layton 1997 (copyright © 1997 by International Universities Press and used by permission).

Chodorow 1978, Dimen 1991, Goldner 1991, Kaftal 1991). In this
more psychoanalytic vein of her work, Butler complicates feminist
relational arguments by asserting that normative femininity and
masculinity are symptomatic not only because they split off whatever attributes are culturally defined as their "other," but also
because each is marked by the splitting off and ungrieved loss of same-
sex love.

To sketch how Butler's work has become psychoanalytic, and,
more specifically, how it has increasingly rejected tenets of the
Lacanian tradition and moved in the direction of object relations
theory, I would like to look closely at the evolution of her concept
of performativity. While Butler now occupies more common ground
with relational psychoanalytic feminist theorists than she did before,
her theory still is not a relational theory in the sense elaborated by
Mitchell (1988) or Benjamin (1988). This is both a flaw in Butler's
work and an obstacle for clinicians who, appreciative of the challenges she has posed to psychoanalytic theory, may yet find it difficult to incorporate some of her insights on subjectivity, gender, and
sexuality into their work.

It is not an easy task to trace the evolution of Butler's thought
because, when she responds to her critics, she often does not simply
clarify her position, as she claims to be doing, but rather changes it
in more or less significant ways. This is certainly true of her positions on agency, which I will discuss below; on the plasticity of the
symbolic (see 1994, where her focus on a dynamic symbolic and on
social practices sounds far more like Teresa de Lauretis [1984, 1987,
1991] than like early Butler); on the identificatory processes that form
the subject; and on the place of the psyche within her theory (see
below). With regard to performativity, however, she herself (1995a)
states that she has revised her theory because of a greater understanding of the psychic processes of disavowal.

As a clinician, I look to Butler because she is trying to forge a
non-reductive theory of the links between the individual psyche and
the workings of culture. Her theoretical twists and turns are thus
always worth following. In the latter part of this essay, I want to
suggest a few ways that some of the later incarnations of Butler's
theory of performativity might inform culturally conscious clinical

practice. As I read it, Butler's second delineation of performativity—
in *Bodies that Matter* (1993)—resonates not only with relational analytic theory but with some of the work of British Cultural Studies,
which, like Butler's work, is a counter-hegemonic discourse on subjectivity, identity, gender, race, agency, collectivity, and the relations
among these. Because British Cultural Studies offers a more relational
vision of the link between the psyche and the social world than that
found in much of Butler's work, it might provide the bridge necessary for clinicians to make use of performativity.

    Gender Trouble, I will argue, is two disparate texts, one a
nonpsychoanalytic meditation on performativity, the other a brief
psychoanalytic discussion of gender's roots in unmourned losses. In
her more recent writings, however, Butler works at linking the two.
The rich connections she has recently made between performativity
and melancholia have focused my attention on other clinical phenomena, in particular, dysthymia, that reveal mediations between
individual subject formation and cultural instances of subjectivity.

    In the clinical world today, much attention and interest has
been focused on abuse and trauma, making up for the relative lack
of interest shown them in the past. While a few of my clients have
abuse histories, many more of them are dysthymic, suffering from
low-grade depressions that result largely from ongoing hurtful relational patterns that are quite difficult for the client to identify. These
depressions are marked by particularly negative and conservative
ways of seeing both self and world, by a strong sense that nothing
can change; they are highly ego-syntonic and thus quite resistant to
analysis.[1] At the end of this chapter, I want to expand upon Butler's
understanding of the relation between performance and melancho-

---

[1] In the *Diagnostic and Statistical Manual of Mental Disorders, Fourth Edition* (1994),
associated features of dysthymia include "feelings of inadequacy; generalized loss
of interest or pleasure; social withdrawal; feelings of guilt or brooding about the
past; subjective feelings of irritability or excessive anger; and decreased activity,
effectiveness, or productivity" (p. 346). The client is in this state most of the time
and so takes it as "normal." Often, treatment is first sought when a major depression is superimposed upon this everyday depression. I will elaborate a more
psychodynamic notion of dysthymia in the last section of this chapter.

lia with case vignettes of clients who have such depressions, and I hope to show that a more relational psychoanalytic perspective might provide some of the links necessary to make clinical use of Butler's work on gender, subjectivity, and culture.

THE EVOLUTION OF THE
CONCEPT OF PERFORMATIVITY

In *Gender Trouble*, Butler theorized that gender identities are not internal essences. Rather, repeated performances of gender norms that include certain ways of behaving, dressing, gesturing, and speaking create an illusion of essence, an illusion that there is something inner called femininity or masculinity that we—females and males— express in such actions. Butler refers to this commonsense way of conceptualizing the relation between subjects and attributes as the expressive mode. The sentence, "She put on a dress today," evokes the sense that there is an essential, coherent female self that expresses her femininity in what she wears.

Gender identity is figured in *Gender Trouble* as what Butler will later call a simple performative, examples of which include "I now pronounce you man and wife" and "Let there be light." These are statements that bring into existence, or materialize, what they state in the moment that they state it. When a woman puts on a dress, she cites a gender norm, and, in so doing, she performs a gender identity, unaware that the citation of the norm and not a core gender identity is what brings a female gender identity into existence.

Butler is at pains to argue that core gender identity (a staple of object relations feminism) is an illusion, and she counters the expressive mode with the performative. The fact that gender norms constrain choice and bring forth particular performances of gender is displaced or kept hidden, she asserts. What emerges in place of consciousness of constraining gender norms is the psychological feeling Stoller (1968, 1976b) called core gender identity: we falsely come not only to believe, but to *feel* that it is that core that accounts for a woman's "choice" to wear a dress. Butler's critique of core gender identity suggests that most if not all of what feels internal to the psyche is not internal but rather an effect of enacting particular cultural norms.

What is Butler's stake in repudiating core gender identity? Her project throughout all her texts is to deconstruct how our grammar and our ways of thinking and feeling about ourselves are based in a logic that presupposes a precultural subject with attributes that express its inner core. The core is figured as immutable and coherent, and the attributes appear to be naturally and necessarily connected to that core. For example, if the "she" in "she put on a dress" is a biological (natural) essence and not constructed in the very act of putting on the dress, if her femaleness precedes what she does, then femaleness is static, not open to multiple constructions that might include whatever counts as maleness or as something in between. When attributes such as "putting on a dress" are interpreted as expressing a female core, then links are made between sex and gender that appear natural; "femininity" is legislated as that which most females express. In such a way, certain actions come to be denoted feminine, others not feminine, and a feminine gender identity is considered "normal" only when it is embodied in a female actor.[2]

Butler's interest in deconstructing the expressive logic in which attributes adhere to essences is not an academic exercise; the political stake is to reveal the workings of compulsory heterosexuality. In her view, the primary cultural constraint on gender performances is the demand to maintain the binary frames of both sex (male and female) and gender (masculine and feminine). Butler criticizes the second-wave feminist separation of sex and gender for having left the male/female binary undissected. From her perspective, it is the division of people into male and female that dictates binary gender identities and heterosexual desire and forges seemingly natural links between them (e.g., that normal females are feminine and desire men), and all of this serves to maintain compulsory heterosexuality. Citing the work of Wittig and Foucault, she (1995b) writes: "The

---

[2]It is clear then, that Butler would be quite opposed to the work of those analysts who derive female psychology, including unconscious conflicts, from female anatomy, for example, Kestenberg (1968) and Mayer (1995).

category of sex imposes a duality and a uniformity on bodies in order to maintain reproductive sexuality as a compulsory order" (p.
52). To reframe gender and sex as performative is to challenge the
imposition of these dualities: "The distinction between expression and
performativeness is quite crucial, for if gender attributes and acts,
the various ways in which a body shows or produces its cultural sig-
nification, are performative, then there is no preexisting identity by
which an act or attribute might be measured; there would be no true
or false, real or distorted acts of gender, and the postulation of a
true gender identity would be revealed as a regulatory fiction" (1990b,
p. 279).

In the performative mode, wearing a dress does not express femaleness and should be no more a signifier of femininity than eat-
ing a piece of pie or hanging from monkey bars—or being relational.
Butler's project is to undermine one-norm logics, whether the one-
norm logic of how to be a woman, or the one-norm logic of how to
be a lesbian. And this is a project that ought to guide clinical work
as well. Butler (1990c) accuses psychoanalytic narratives, be they
Lacanian or object relations, of pathologizing what lies outside of
cultural norms. In her view, these narratives unify "certain legitimate
sexual subjects and [exclude] from intelligibility sexual identities and
discontinuities which challenge the narrative beginnings and closures
offered by these competing psychoanalytic explanations" (p. 329).
Same-sex desire, multiple ways of being female and male, instances
where gender identity does not neatly line up with anatomical sex
or where genitalia defy categorization into male or female—these are
a few examples of what many psychoanalytic theorists and clinicians
past and present have pathologized.

When Butler argues in *Gender Trouble* that there is no doer behind the deed of gender performance, she does not mean that there
is no person putting on the dress. Rather, she means that the nature of the doer does not precede the deed. Her argument is that
normative femininity and a certain version of personhood (a coherent subject that fancies itself an agent with free will, fully in control
of and separable from its actions) go together ideologically; the illusion of an ego-centered subject and its core gender identity are si-

multaneously created both in the act of putting on the dress and in the way the sentence enunciates that act. Butler's criticism of the ego-centered subject is indebted to Lacan's (1977) critique of ego psychology. But, as we shall see, Butler is critical of Lacan's view that sexual difference, the division into male and female, is a *sine qua non* of subject formation. (Lacan asserts that to become a subject one must take up a position of either having or not having the phallus; Butler responds that this "must" serves the one-norm logic of compulsory heterosexuality.)

Before discussing critical responses to *Gender Trouble* and the further evolution of the concept of performativity that those criticisms compelled, I would like to underscore that, thus far, Butler's view of gender performativity is distinctly non- or even anti-psychoanalytic. To be sure, the constantly mutating subject of the performative mode seems quite compatible with the subject of many contemporary relational psychoanalytic theories (and with contemporary developmental theories as well, for example, that of Stern [1985]). Analysis, I would argue, is premised on the performative, for it presumes that "The subject is that which must be constituted again and again, [which] implies that it is open to formations that are not fully constrained in advance" (Butler [1995c] defining the relation between performativity and agency, p. 135). It seems to me that performativity's focus on acts as opposed to essences and Butler's critique of the way stage theories create substances that are prior to later acquired attributes are somewhat reconcilable with Stern's developmental vision. Butler's (1990b) sense that "one might try to reconceive the gendered body as the legacy of sedimented acts rather than a predetermined or foreclosed structure, essence, or fact, whether natural, cultural, or linguistic" (p. 274) calls to my mind Stern's baby, so as long as one adds to Butler's system an internal world of remembered and patterned interactions as well as the role of constitutional factors such as temperament. On the other hand, Butler would be critical of Stern's obliviousness to the effects of gender inequality, gendering, and other cultural determinants of the way the baby's capacities unfold in relationship. She would also contest his view that those capacities are "hard-wired."

Butler's contention that interiority is illusory, however, is not compatible with psychoanalytic theory. She suggests no internal reasons that might motivate the citing of norms, and her focus is on what seem to be only external normative constraints on performances. Further, she assumes that gender is reducible to that which is performed. But as I suggested earlier, the book itself is contradictory, for Butler sketches in a later section of this same text her theory that gender identity is a melancholy construct, a precipitate of ungrieved same-sex love. The melancholy gender argument rests on the theory of identification Freud (1917) expounded in "Mourning and Melancholia," which, interestingly, is often appealed to as a founding text of object relations because it posits an internal world of loved and lost objects. Thus *Gender Trouble* puts forth two irreconcilable versions of subject formation and of the status of subjectivity. Jessica Benjamin (1994b) has argued that Butler conflates the subject as a position in discourse with the experiencing subject, which is definitely a problem in Butler's work, as we shall see. But this problem occurs in part, I think, because Butler presents *both* a notion of gender identity built from internalizations of lost objects and *another* notion that gender exists only in the performative citing of norms, without commenting on how the two phenomena might or might not connect with one another.

Ironically, *Gender Trouble*, particularly the idea that gender is performative, has been criticized from two entirely contradictory directions. Some people read performativity as an extreme form of voluntarism, consumerism, individualism, role playing, as an argument suggesting that one freely selects and constructs one's gender identity.[3] This reading spawned a great deal of culture criticism that interprets any version of gender indeterminacy as subversive (see Chapter 5); it also contributed to a version of queer theory that posits

---

[3]In an essay published in *inside/out*, Butler (1991) distances herself from those who understood her discussion of the performative as something akin to role playing. Here, she insists on the intransigency of the psyche, noting that she cannot take radical distance from her performance of lesbianism: "for this is deep-seated play, psychically entrenched play, *and this 'I' does not play its lesbianism as a role*" (p. 18, emphasis in original).

itself as transcending gender.[4] At the other extreme, many critics read performativity as leaving no space at all for agency; these critics focused on Butler's vision of the coercive and determinant nature of the norm and on her adoption of Foucault's concept of power, a concept in which oppressive forces are not merely visited upon the subject from the outside but enter into the very formation of the subject (see, for example, Benhabib's [1995] reading).

The charge of voluntarism stemmed from the way many people interpreted Butler's discussion of drag, which comes at the end of the book in a section titled "Subversive Bodily Acts." Butler sees drag as a gender performance that denaturalizes the norm and thus reveals that gender identity is always a miming of norms, not an essence. When a man dresses up as a woman, he does not imitate an original "femininity"; rather, the capacity to put on femininity reveals that there is no such thing as an original, that femininity and masculinity are constructed by those particular ways of looking, acting, and speaking that she identified as what makes gender identity performative. Drag reveals that gender does not follow from sex and that gender identities themselves are imitations. Since the norm hides its contingency behind the psychological feeling of a core gender identity, anything that reveals the contingency of the norm is subversive.

The nonpsychoanalytic core of *Gender Trouble* is the very reason one can read it as voluntarist. For, if there is nothing internal to the self, if self and act occur simultaneously, if there is an arbitrary relation between each performative act (or even a relation based only in an external norm) rather than a relation informed by the history of the doer, it seems that one would be free to re-create oneself in each act despite the constraints of gender norms. A psychoanalytic vision provides at least two reasons why this is impossible, and each reason entails some notion of a substantive core. First, we all

_____

[4]Butler's critique of the version of queer theory that pretends to transcend gender—and that reads her work as providing a framework for doing so—is found in "Against Proper Objects" (1994). Other similar critiques have been offered by Martin (1994, 1996), Bersani (1995), and Walters (1996).

have psychic histories that do in some sense precede our acts. The version of "prior" or "core" that I have in mind does not negate the fact that every act or performance more or less subtly alters both self and gender; nor is it one that presupposes a substance that is a seamless unity (see Flax [1990] for a useful distinction between "core" and "unitary"; see Stern [1985] for a developmental model that suggests an ongoing interaction between substance and performance). Rather, it is a version that claims for the subject a history of contradictory but repeated and internalized relational patterns, the repetition of which provides a sense of continuity over time and allows one to read one's history as a coherent narrative, even as each new act might subtly change what was there before. Butler is right to critique an originary essence or an interiority that precedes any engagement with the world, and she is right to critique hegemonic cultural attempts to fix the flux of identity in seamless unities, but there is no place in her *Gender Trouble* for the multiple and conflictual internalizations that make up an actor's history.

Secondly, genders, too have their histories. Rosemary Hennessy (1995) calls attention to the histories of genders and sexualities and the inequalities that exist between men and women, heterosexuals and homosexuals. She charges that those versions of poststructuralism that focus only on the continuous slippage of the signifier, on the fluidity of gender and sexuality, ignore to their own peril "the insistence of the signified in the symbolic order" (p. 152)—and, I would add, in the psyche.[5] The origins of core gender identity do lie in the norms of compulsory heterosexuality, but the fact that we are sexed male or female by cultural fiat produces a conflictually gendered self that is indeed in some sense prior to its acts, in some sense "core."

This is what makes the nonpsychoanalytic piece of Butler's work problematic for clinicians. I stated earlier that clinicians ought to be guided by Butler's resistance to one-norm logics and thus to regard

---

[5]Hennessy's case in point is the physical violence inflicted upon those perceived as gay. Again, Butler (1994) herself was later to take up this same charge in her critique of those queer theorists who, in separating the analysis of sexuality from the study of kinship, perhaps reveal a "desire to desire beyond the psyche, beyond the traces of kinship that psyches bear" (p. 15).

subjects not as substances but as actors constituted in and by their acts. A performative logic, for example, would not regard women as "relational" and clinicians ought not do so either. But if femininity is dominantly defined in a culture as relational, and if the relational is further dominantly defined as self-effacing, requiring the splitting off of other desires and capacities, then most females will have some kind of psychic tie to the normative demand to be relational and will struggle with that demand.

When I first read *Gender Trouble* it raised my consciousness precisely about the ways that gender is "put on." I became aware of why I would choose certain clothes to wear on some days or in some contexts, what kind of gender identity I experienced when I would bat my eyelashes, shake hands in a certain way, wear pants, wear flowing skirts, wear dangly earrings. Gendered behaviors began to feel like the context-dependent set of ritualized repetitions that Butler's performance theory claimed them to be; I understood what Butler meant when she suggested that we are all always in drag. But this did not feel constraining; rather, I, too, read performativity as voluntaristic, feeling that it expanded my options to choose how I would express my gender identity on a given day or in a given context. This was clearly a misreading; what I missed, as the well-constructed American free agent that I allegedly fantasize I am, was Butler's critique of the ego-centered subject.

Because of such misreadings, Butler was at pains in her next book, *Bodies that Matter* (1993), to clarify that performative citings of the norm are compelled and constrained by norms (particularly by a heterosexual matrix), and it is precisely because these norms become displaced onto a psychological feeling that I experience myself as a free agent able to pick and choose how I enact a gender identity. But I am only partially apologetic about my misreading, because I do not fully subscribe to Butler's Lacanian argument on subject formation and thus do not see gender identity or a sense of agency as illusory.

I mentioned earlier that Jessica Benjamin (1994b) argues that Butler (and most postmodernists) conflate discursive subject positions with the psyche of the experiencing self, which has ramifications not

only for the description of the subject but for any theory of the relation between subjects:

> Butler collapses self and subject, as if political, epistemological
> positions, such as the "identity" of women as a unified political
> subject, fully correspond to the psychological concept of the self.
> To the extent that she defines emancipation as liberation from
> identity she also finds the problem of the other less interesting
> than the problem of identity. This tendency, perhaps endemic
> to critiques of identity, may perpetuate an elision between the
> other whom we create through our own identifications and the
> concrete outside other. [p. 233]

One way of understanding this comment is that postmodernism and
relational theory are talking about two different levels of experience
and identity, postmodernism about the way a subject is formed in
discourse and relational theory about the way a person experiences
him- or herself (see also Chodorow 1995). But I think that Benjamin
here also indicts Butler for restricting subjectivity to a narcissistic
elision of otherness (see Flax's 1990 similar critique of Lacan). Butler, Benjamin claims, conflates the two levels and thus reduces *self*
to *narcissistic self*. (Butler's criticism of identity politics presumes that
narcissism always dominates on the political level as well.)

The problem here, as I see it, is that Butler is uncertain about
what she wants to take and what discard from Lacan. She wrangles
with Lacanian theory in much of her work, and I think her "Lacan
trouble" starts with an unexamined adoption of Lacan's critique of
ego psychology. What appears to me to be the case is that Butler
too quickly reduces the "she" in "she put on a dress" to the fictive
ego of Lacanian theory, a part of the self made of identifications with
images of self and others that takes itself to be unitary, stable, and
unconflicted. Wherever *identity* appears in Butler's work, it appears
not as the conflicted, contradictory construct that it is in most psychoanalytic theory and in all people but rather as the falsely stabi-
lizing, homogeneous construct that we know as bourgeois individualism (and Lacan saw ego psychology as a celebration of that
construct). Butler's narrow view of both the experiencing self and the

discursive subject as "bourgeois individual" is part of what makes it difficult for her to put forth a convincing argument that her theory of performativity is reconcilable with some version of agency.

In a similar vein, Butler's view of subject formation imposes a pathogenic reading on a process that is not necessarily pathogenic. Butler (1995b) argues that identities are always built on exclusions of other identities: "for it is important to remember that subjects are constituted through exclusion, that is, through the creation of a domain of deauthorized subjects, presubjects, figures of abjection, populations erased from view" (p. 47; see also several essays in *Bodies that Matter*). As Nancy Fraser (1995) points out in the same volume, Butler presents this vision of subject formation as a conceptual necessity, as something like a developmental theory, when in fact it is better understood as a historical contingency. Fraser writes: "the view that subjectivation necessarily entails subjection precludes normative distinctions between better and worse subjectivating practices. . . . [T]he view that foundationalist theories of subjectivity are inherently oppressive is historically disconfirmed, and it is conceptually incompatible with a contextualist theory of meaning" (p. 69). Butler's (1995c) reply alters her original claim significantly:

> It might be clarifying . . . to consider that whereas every subject is formed through a process of differentiation . . . there are better and worse forms of differentiation, and that the worse kinds tend to abject and degrade those from whom the "I" is distinguished. . . . My call, then, is for the development of forms of differentiation which lead to fundamentally more capacious, generous, and "unthreatened" bearings of the self in the midst of community. That an "I" is differentiated from another does not mean that the other becomes unthinkable in its difference." [pp. 139–140]

This restatement, in which Butler distinguishes differentiation from defensively claimed difference, recalls Chodorow's thesis in "Gender, Relation, and Difference in Psychoanalytic Perspective" (1989; note that this essay was originally published in 1979).

Further, finding the other less interesting than the problem of identity is not a feature unique to Butler's work but rather an element in much of postmodern theorizing and yet another real stumbling block for a relational clinician drawn to Butler's work. Not only is narcissism an object of postmodern study, but, it seems, this object of study is itself often formulated from a narcissistic position, one in which the other is either coercive or irrelevant. In some postmodernisms, subjects seem peculiarly freed from embeddedness in relationships, particularly familial ones. They create and reinvent themselves anew in each moment, unfettered by conflict and relational bonds/binds. In other postmodernisms, the view of the other seems to have its roots in Hegel's master/slave dialectic and Sartre's assertion that other people are hell. Lacanian discussions of interpellation (Smith 1988a, Butler 1993), for example, suggest that any other that is external to the subject is coercive (which makes one question, as Benjamin does, how external this other actually is); all other others are imaginary projections of the subject, projections that might also be coercive. By contrast, in the relational school, relational experience motivates performances of varying kinds. People have narcissistic, coercive relational experiences, which polarize identity options into binaries. But they also have non-narcissistic experiences of mutual recognition, which potentially allow a multiplicity of positions to flourish (a multiplicity distinguishable from the fragmentation induced by splitting).

In several of her works (1993, 1995b,c), Butler responds to the criticism that there is no place for agency in her theory. She argues that to see the subject as constructed is not the same as to see the subject as fully determined. When she writes about agency, she wants to make it clear that agency, too, is constructed, that there are many versions of agency and each version has a history to be interrogated. As I have argued throughout this book, for example, a dominant version of agency is connected with the history of the separate and autonomous bourgeois subject, and this version has been thoroughly critiqued by feminist theorists. Butler (1995b) echoes Chodorow and Benjamin when she writes that "autonomy is the logical consequence of a disavowed dependency" (p. 46). She wants those who use the term *agency* to be aware that at any given time the political field legislates the very possibilities of what counts as a subject and what counts as agency. The challenge this stance poses to clinicians is great: (1) it suggests that clinicians in fact contribute to determining and bringing forth what counts as a subject and what counts as agentic; and (2) it suggests that what we hear clients say is conditioned by what, at any given time, it is possible to say and possible to hear (and that what is possible to say and hear is conditioned by gender, race, age, class, and other norms).

To further understand Butler's view of agency, we have to take a look at her criticism of the Lacanian law of subject and gender formation. In Lacan, the oedipal law of the father dictates that the paternal function wrest the child out of the Imaginary and into the Symbolic. Castration (lack), or loss of the maternal object (which are hardly synonymous but pass as such in the Lacanian system), is the price of subject formation. At the very moment of subject formation, the law dictates that subjects assume one of two gender identities, each of which is a position in relation to the phallus, signifier of difference and of lack in the Symbolic. In the Symbolic, no one has the phallus; both males and females are constituted by lack. But gender identity is a structure of the Imaginary (as is the ego). Masculinity, assumed largely by males, is the fantasy of having the phallus; femininity, assumed largely by females, is the fantasy of being the phallus. In the Imaginary, where most love relations take place, males and females hold onto the fantasy that the other gender will make them feel complete, will restore a fantasized fusion with the mother that subject formation does not allow.

The Lacanian law of subject formation posits that those who do not submit to the law become psychotic, and the law assumes only two possible gender positions, masculinity and femininity. As it establishes the rule of subject formation, the law creates not only the oedipal but the preoedipal, that is, the form that gender and desire take on before the oedipal moment. Thus, Butler argues convincingly, we cannot look to the preoedipal as a site of resistance to oedipal law, as a space outside the law. She further argues that the Lacanian law, like all laws, derives its power by assuming the necessity for its existence, when in fact it should be called upon to prove its necessity: the Lacanian law tells you you must obey or you will become psychotic. Obeying the law creates two genders, each of which yearns for the opposite gender. It is therefore a law that guarantees the continuation of compulsory heterosexuality and a law that limits to two the variety of genders and desires possible. The Lacanian law, Butler argues, claims to exist prior to the subjects it forms, another way that it takes itself out of history and another way that it attains its power.

Butler is increasingly critical of the Lacanian law. Her notion of performativity speaks not of law but of the constrained repetition of norms (in fact, she at first talks about citation of the norm and later increasingly talks about citation of norms). A sex and a gender are not assumed because of a previously existing law; rather, norms gain power with each citation of them. The norms of compulsory heterosexuality—that you are not to desire someone of the same sex and not to want to be like the one you are supposed to desire (that identification and desire are mutually exclusive)—compel citings that shore up those very norms. Thus Butler wants to replace the Lacanian idea that one assumes a sex in accordance with a previously existing law with the performative idea that one must repeatedly cite norms for them to continue to function as law (although Butler never makes it clear how norms become norms in the first place). If norms have to be cited to maintain their status as law, then there is always the threat that they will be cited differently from what is expected. And so Butler, via deconstruction, creates a space for resistant and transgressive citings. What motivates such transgressive citings is not terribly clear, perhaps the fact that no one ever incarnates the norm. Whatever the motivation, in *Gender Trouble* she argues that what is truly transgressive is that which challenges a one-norm logic, that which allows the variety of subjects, genders, desires to flourish. But in *Bodies that Matter* she begins to argue that gender performances are in fact not simple performatives, and her expanded idea of performativity resonates with decidedly non-Lacanian sources, particularly with the British Cultural Studies theory of Stuart Hall.

PERFORMATIVITY, ACT 2

Let us recall that in his essay "Encoding, Decoding" (1980), Hall proposed a theory of popular culture and its reception that was a critique of the Frankfurt School view. Adorno and Horkheimer (1972) had written about a monolithic culture industry where capitalist producers invaded not only work space but leisure space, and prepared not only the body but the psyche for a life of passive consumption. Hall criticized the Frankfurt School's totalizing vision; in his theory, producers of popular culture can never assume that messages will be received by audiences in the way that producers wish because of the multiple and contradictory nature both of messages and of people. He argued that language takes on meaning because of its embeddedness in social and historical contexts, its relation to other instances of language, and thus meaning can never be reduced to authorial intention. Further, so many elements make up a person's identity, and these elements enter into such conflictual and various configurations, that one could never predict what position a person might take in relation to a given instance of popular culture. Hall noted three possible positions subjects or groups of subjects might take: the dominant-hegemonic position, which reads the message approximately as it was intended (and thus, presumably, shores up a capitalist status quo); the negotiated position, which accepts the dominant-hegemonic but with exceptions to the rule based on situational conditions; and the oppositional position, which refuses the dominant-hegemonic and reads the message according to alternative interests and strategies.

As I read it, Hall's theory is similar to the version of performativity Butler (1993) puts forth in *Bodies that Matter*. In the essay "Gender is Burning," Butler adopts Lacan's idea that subjects misrecognize themselves in the law that endows them with fictive unity (a process that Althusser [1971] referred to as "interpellation"), but she contests the notion that the law compels citation in any one way. She then expands upon ways that subjects resist citing norms in the way norms expect to be cited—and she depathologizes these resistant performances. In the following passage, we can see how Butler alters her definition of performativity so that there is a space within it for agency, for the creation of something that has not always already been:

> The law might not only be refused, but it might also be ruptured, forced into a rearticulation that calls into question the monotheistic force of its own unilateral operation. Where the uniformity of the subject is expected, where the behavioral conformity of the subject is commanded, there might be produced the refusal of the law in the form of the parodic inhabiting of conformity that subtly calls into question the legitimacy of the command, a repetition of the law into hyperbole, a rearticulation of the law against the authority of the one who delivers it. Here the performative, the call by the law which seeks to produce a lawful subject, produces a set of consequences that exceed and confound what appears to be the disciplining intention motivating the law. Interpellation thus loses its status as a simple performative, an act of discourse with the power to create that to which it refers, and creates more than it ever meant to, signifying in excess of any intended referent. [p. 122]

Note the way that agency in Butler's writing gets shifted from subjects to laws and norms: norms expect to be cited in certain ways, norms are threatened because they are really contingent, laws produce subjects, and laws have intentions. Hall invests these agentic behaviors in subjects and collectivities.

Unlike Hall, Butler is not just talking about how someone reads a cultural text, but about how someone becomes this or that kind of subject. She goes on to suggest that the law becomes both violating and enabling, that while we cannot escape being constructed by norms, we have the possibility of opposing them from within them. Here, the subject is figured as always more than just a fictive ego, and Butler's description of rupture, refusal, and hyperbole echoes Hall's positions and endows subjects with agency.

Once gender identity is no longer figured as a simple performative, Butler's theory begins to require a motivational theory: Why do some cite norms in the preferred mode, others refuse to cite them, and still others negotiate the many possible options between resistance and compliance? The answer, I would think, entails a relational theory missing in Butler's work, one that speaks to the way people come into contact with norms, in what kinds of authorities, love objects, or enemies norms are conveyed and how they are negotiated intersubjectively. How does one make sense of conflicting gender norms conveyed by male and female parents (see Goldner 1991)? Might compliance with gender norms ever facilitate change? (Butler always seems to assume that compliance is oppressive.) Butler's work would be enriched by recognition of the multiplicity of norms that circulate in the culture and the way that dominant and non-dominant norms exist in people's lives. In any culture, there are competing gender norms at work, and instances of gender are always also instances of race, class, religion, and so forth.[6] There are also competing gender norms in the psyche. Butler tends not to take into account the conflict that occurs in political life, in every academic discipline, and in every psyche between hegemonic discursive positions that pretend to a seamless identity and counter-hegemonic discursive positions. (Even within psychoanalytic theory, we can identify counter-hegemonic and more hegemonic positions on subjectivity, or, perhaps more accurately, each theory contains more or less of the tendency to impose coherence on multiplicity.) Citing norms becomes a much more complicated affair when the multiplicity of internalized and external norms is taken into account (see Weir 1995). In Butler's defense, however, it must be emphasized that the norm she most contests, the division of people into male and female, has just about no cultural opposition.

PERFORMATIVITY, ACT 3

Hollway (1984) argues that people often select from competing gender norms (or, in her terms, discursive positions) in order to dis-

---

[6]Butler pays lip-service to such multiplicity, but it is interesting to compare her (1993) analysis of "Paris is Burning" to that of bell hooks (1992). Where Butler sees a lesbian filmmaker, hooks sees a white filmmaker; neither sees a white lesbian.

avow feelings they do not want to feel. She cites as example a male locating himself in the discourse of male lust as a way to deny longings for intimacy. In an essay mindful of deconstruction, relational psychoanalysis, and family systems theory, Goldner (1991) argues that taking on a male or female gender identity, which occurs in a complex relational matrix, is a strategy for not dealing with loss and thus a narcissistic strategy. Both of these positions anticipate Butler's latest reworking of the performative.

In this recent work (1995a), Butler again expands the realm of performativity, and this time she brings the expanded version into connection with her belief that gender is a construct infused with melancholy. While, to my knowledge, she has never formally retracted her claim in *Gender Trouble* that gender identity does not have the ontological status of an internalized set of relations, the fact that she starts the essay by accepting Freud's (1917) theory of identification in "Mourning and Melancholia" and ends it with a claim that gender performances are symptomatic products of splitting suggests that the latest version of performativity is a construct more consonant with certain feminist object relational and intersubjective positions. For example, Benjamin and Chodorow, as I mentioned at the beginning, have long argued that stereotypical femininity and masculinity are symptomatic expressions of ungrieved losses of those attributes and capacities, such as dependency needs or agentic strivings, that were repudiated as other in the process of attaining a gender identity.

Butler examines Freud's theory that the identifications that build the ego are constructed from losses of forbidden love objects and connects that theory with his developmental model, in which reaching the Oedipus requires passing beyond the negative Oedipus, the stage of same-sex love. Like Irigaray (1985) in "The Blind Spot of an Old Dream of Symmetry," Butler accepts Freud's developmental model as normative, then looks at what the norm hides, proscribes, at the way it naturalizes itself. In this case, Butler wants to show how the heterosexual presumptions of the Oedipus and the gender identities it assumes are built on a prior taboo of homosexual love. Here, she focuses on the way the ungrieved loss of same-sex love invests normative femininity and masculinity with melancholy, because these structures are built not only on repudiations of each other but on repudiations of homosexuality. In other words, normative femininity has split off not only masculinity but also same-sex love. As Butler puts it, "If one is a girl to the extent that one does not want a girl, then wanting a girl will bring being a girl into question; within this matrix, homosexual desire thus panics gender" (p. 169). Normative femininity and masculinity are heterosexual constructs; the more stereotypical they appear, she argues, the greater the degree of refusal to grieve the same-sex lost love object.

In this essay, Butler again returns to performativity and to drag. She is now aware that drag is not only subversive of gender but is also a performance of melancholy gender. The performative is reinterpreted as symptomatic, concealing what is barred from performance as well as revealing what is not. With this move, the performance becomes an expression of an internal conflict around gender and sexuality, one that Butler feels is instigated by norms that compel certain kinds of losses. Butler seems to have changed her view of the nature of subjectivity, now acknowledging a conflicted internal world of identifications and disidentifications that are exteriorized in complicated ways:

> It would not be enough to say that gender is only performed or that the meaning of gender can be derived from its performance, whether or not one wants to rethink performance as a compulsory social ritual. For there clearly are workings of gender that do not "show" in what is performed as gender, and the reduction of the psychic workings of gender to the literal performance of gender would be a mistake. Psychoanalysis insists that the opacity of the unconscious sets limits to the exteriorization of the psyche. It also argues, rightly I think, that what is exteriorized or performed can be understood only through reference to what is barred from the performance, what cannot or will not be performed. [1995a, p. 175]

She now says that her previous conception of drag "did not address the question of how it is that certain forms of disavowal and repudiation come to organize the performance of gender" (p. 176). She is for the first time struck by the longing for femininity in drag, a longing based in an ungrieved loss. Performance, she says, "understood as 'acting out,' is essentially related to the problem of unacknowledged loss" (p. 176). She seems no longer to reduce gender identity to one of the many guises of the coherent ego, although even in this essay her view of ego identifications is stuck in the Lacanian reduction.

And other problems remain that are equally significant. While showing some of the blind spots of Freud's theory, Butler ignores others, such as the way that Freud's most relational theoretical moments still reduce the intersubjective to the intrapsychic and deny the way that ongoing relations with others structure the psyche (see Benjamin 1988). One has to buy Freud's theory of identification and his theory of development to buy Butler's reworking of it—for example, the assumption that the motor of identification is loss. And Butler assumes that melancholia is inherent in gender identity within a heterosexist culture, even though she admits that melancholia is most clearly present in highly stereotyped versions of masculinity and femininity (another way that she blurs pathogenic and healthy development). Gender is marked by melancholia but also by internalized relationships that do not necessarily conform to dominant norms. The privileging of melancholia meshes not so much with Freud's (1930) social theory in *Civilization and its Discontents* as with Lacan's, where narcissism, the disease of unmourned losses, is at the core of identity development (that is, the Lacanian ego is a structure built on the refusal to mourn losses). Finally, Butler's concern with the oppressive nature of dominant norms perhaps keeps her from seeing the complexities that mark the internalization of competing norms within relational matrices.

Despite these problems, I would like to conclude this section by extrapolating from Butler's argument about melancholy gender to discuss the ways that melancholy might invest the citing of dominant gender norms and other dominant norms as well. Butler's essay helped me make a connection between the citing of dominant norms and the dysthymia that characterizes so many of my clients. Yet, as the following case vignettes demonstrate, something more than Butler's frame is necessary to make sense of this connection,

and I believe that what is necessary is a more complicated understanding of how norms compete for place in the psyche and how
they are embedded in relationship. What is missing from Butler's
account, even in its most psychoanalytic form, is an understanding
of what motivates people's relation to norms. Indeed, one reason why
it is so difficult to grasp what Butler means by agency is that her
system has no place for the mediating power of relationships, for
longings for love, approval, and recognition.

When getting love and approval seems contingent upon being
the kind of child significant figures in your life need you to be, connections to loved ones can be maintained only at high cost. Unable
or unwilling to mourn the losses caused by narcissistic injury, one
may "choose" to maintain connection through the sado-masochistic
bonds that characterize dysthymia. Such a choice often eventuates
in just the kind of self-reduction that Lacan takes as inevitable: alienation in the desire of the other. Dysthymics tend to deny the fluidity of self, to enact a self-blaming reification of self. Those afflicted
with dysthymia feel hopeless about changing what they perceive as
their flawed core. They are the depressed alter egos of the bourgeois
subjects who fancy themselves in control of all their attributes and
actions, for they are convinced that they are primarily to blame for
whatever is wrong with them.

DYSTHYMIA AS A PERFORMANCE
OF MELANCHOLY GENDER

This first set of examples shows dysthymia as an affective outcome of the citing of the dominant norms of femininity. At a recent conference, a panel entitled "Author Meets Critics: Robert
Connell's *Masculinities*" (1996) brought together two commentators,
a woman and a man. The woman began by apologizing for her presumption that a woman could critique a book about men. She repeated her apology more than once. Part of her discussion focused
on the challenge the book posed to her, as a researcher on women,
to look at the practices of femininity, what Connell (1995) might
call "doing femininity." Next the male commentator spoke, and he

began by remarking on the woman's apology; he said that men have talked about women for hundreds of years without apologizing. It immediately occured to me that the woman's self-effacing apology was a perfect example of the symptomatic nature of "doing femininity." The self that apologizes for putting itself forth enacts the dysthymic moment of the formation and continued performance of hegemonic femininity. (I am reminded of the many gender theorists who have tried to make sense of the observation [Mahler et al. 1975] that girls seem to exit from rapprochement depressed [see, for example, Benjamin 1988].)

My clinical examples show what Butler's theory does not address: the relational roots of the losses that hegemonic cultural positions require and the obstacles to grieving those losses. Ms. A. entered treatment when she was thinking of leaving her husband. She reported that when she got married she stopped dressing in the sexy, funky style she had created from her very artistic sensibility and toned herself down at Talbots, a conservative dress shop. On first telling, she said that she thought that the Talbots style was the way married women were supposed to dress. This seemed to me to exemplify what Butler called a simple performative, a faithful citation of the norm of married femininity that in fact keeps that norm dominant (the norm: married femininity is incompatible with sexy femininity). Later material revealed, however, that from the beginning of their courtship her husband subtly and not so subtly kept her from interacting with any other men, at times expressing bursts of jealousy when she was merely talking for a long time to a man. What the first norm hides is the patriarchal norm that structures it: that married and sexy are mutually exclusive because marriage makes a woman the possession of her husband.[7] Ms. A.'s change in clothes

---

[7]A note is necessary on the nature of the norm: a norm of patriarchal culture is that women are the possession of their husbands. This norm can be enacted through a variety of behaviors, some of which are contradictory. For example, Ms. A.'s husband may have required her to dress in a sexy way; compliance would still enact the norm of possession. Further, this norm is currently contested in our culture because of inroads made by feminism, and the contested nature of the norm allows Ms. A. and her therapist to envision other options besides continuing to cite it.

style was the beginning of self alterations enacted to keep her husband happy, to keep him from harrassing her or, worse, leaving her.

This vignette shows that the motivation for citing cultural norms often lies in a wish to preserve whatever connection one has with love objects. When love objects are incapable of recognizing the singularity and separateness of their children or partners, when they insist on conformity to whatever may be their own set of norms or values, the price exacted for compliance is depression. Dysthymic clients have neither grieved the disappointments in parents incapable of giving recognition, nor have they grieved the other, preferred ways of being that they are unable fully to claim as their own. Over time, Ms. A.'s small everyday yieldings led to full-blown depression, and she used treatment to reacquaint herself with all the things she had liked to do and ways she had liked to be before she slowly gave each and every one up to please the conventional man who enforced her parents' view of how she ought to be.

What makes someone more prone to yield than another might be? In Ms. A.'s case, her parents divorced when she was very young and she witnessed her mother crying constantly and worrying that she could not make it without a man. As a child she was also quite neglected, and the jealous love of her partner at first seemed like the real love she missed. Most important, the hurt about the love she missed was never fully acknowledged or worked through. In citing the gender norm, she showed a preference for a melancholy that preserves an early relational pattern, one that constricts possibilities both for different versions of self and different versions of relationships. Melancholia protects what meager bond there is with her husband and parents against the alternative, which is getting in touch with the rage and disappointment that would threaten the bond. This is too risky when there is no other kind of bond to take its place.

As this vignette demonstrates, the compulsion to cite gender norms draws its psychic power from relationships. Now Butler might argue that Ms. A.'s style of dress when she was single was no more her own than her married style, that one has no choice but to cite norms. Ms. A. felt that the style she had created was her own, and while she may have constructed that style from something available in another subculture, she was drawn to this subculture through some mix of artistic sensibility and the recognition she received there for her nonconventionality. When she cited the norms of this subculture, she was not depressed. However, being "artsy" made her anxious because it brought her into opposition with a norm of capitalist culture conveyed by her parents, who always discouraged her from being an artist because "it is not practical."

Although any moves in the direction of "artsy" caused Ms. A. the anxiety of anticipated loss of love from intimates, such moves were experienced as her own and not as the masquerade her parents wanted her to perform. Butler's theory of performance and masquerade is partially compatible with Winnicott's (1965b) false self, but, in Butler, there is nothing behind masquerade but more masquerade, only melancholia and no mourning in her vision of the self, only a false self and not a true one. The "true self" is a problematic concept, one that suggests precultural static essences. But, within the confines of Butler's theory, a clinician could not make sense of the differences between Ms. A.'s affective states and their relation to competing sets of norms: when she cites one set of norms she is depressed; when she cites another set, she feels anxious but "herself," whatever that may be.

Ms. A. tried to contest both the norms of patriarchy and the norms that dictate which activities are productive in a capitalist society and which are not. I have treated many artistic clients, and nearly all of them have been discouraged by either parents or the culture from doing art. (When are you going to grow up and get a real job? is the usual refrain.) It is striking how frequently therapists are called upon to treat the wounds wrought by a sexist, racist, homophobic, and capitalist culture. Clinically, I found that referring to Ms. A. as an artist, discussing with her the unequal cultural valuations of art and commerce, and pointing out how the gender assumptions behind her different versions of dress and femininity were linked to her husband's possessiveness and her wish for love, helped her legitimate her nonconventional leanings. These interventions may seem partisan, more in line with a feminist or anti-capitalist agenda than an analytic one, but they were in fact steps along the way to establishing a different kind of bond than that offered by her parents and culture, one based in recognition rather than condemnation of her choices, one that did not presume a one-norm logic of femininity or agency.

The dysthymic men I see in treatment often say that they do not feel masculine; one, in fact, told me that he had read *Women Who Love Too Much* (Norwood 1985) and thought it applied very much to him. This same man, Mr. B., has in fact split off aggression and assertiveness; he worries about foisting his needs on others and, like most of the women I see who are dysthymic, he is highly invested in being "nice." But, unlike them, he also feels terrible shame about having needs for others and rarely initiates with me discussions about relationships, focusing mainly on struggles with work. A frequent pattern in the treatment is that he begins by talking about his low mood, finds a hundred reasons for it in all the things he should be doing but isn't doing, and only in the last minutes of the session does he mention, as an aside, that he's had a hurtful rebuff by a woman he is interested in, which turns out to be the primary reason he feels low. Until I finally caught onto the pattern—the minimizing of the effects of love relationships—I would engage in what we have come to see as a reenactment of his relationship with his mother. Like his mother, I would try to help him understand what was getting in the way of doing each of the things he wanted to be doing: taking a course, traveling, finding a new job, and the like. In many sessions that took this form, as I got more aggressive about questioning him or coming up with ideas, he would eventually "take the wind out of my sails" by informing me that he had in fact been doing some of the things he had complained he had not been doing, that he wasn't quite as big a slouch as he had been claiming to be. This dynamic replicated a pattern with his father: when he got excited about things or showed some initiative, his father would "take the wind out of [his] sails."

Eventually, we recognized that he used to find comfort in telling his mother his complaints and hearing her suggestions for what he might do to get out of his funk. But these suggestions implicitly proferred a certain version of masculinity. His mother did and does compare him with successful, high earning corporate men as a way of suggesting what he ought to be doing. She believes strongly that he has the capacity for the achievements she covets, and he experiences her comparisons with others as both critical and supportive. She wants him to be an aggressive go-getter like her father, and not passive like her husband. Instead of motivating him, however, her comparisons and her wish that he not identify with his father deplete him, which makes him energyless and indecisive like his father, and all the more disdainful of himself. When he has me fully convinced he is slacking off, he realizes he has created in me the opposition he needs to be able to show his strength (the mother transference). Then he "takes the wind out of my sails" as his father did to him.

We found ourselves in an interesting stand-off: once I was aware of the pattern, I stopped colluding with his wish for me to find fault with him and took the stance that he is probably doing just fine. Sometimes he experiences this stance as a relief and feels less depressed, but at other times he interprets it as a sign that I have given up on the belief that he could be transformed into another, more aggressive person, the one his mother would *really* love. In some way, my giving up, too, might be comforting. For, if he were the aggressive man his mother would love, he would be rejected by his passive father, who, in not-so-passive moments, seems envious of Mr. B.'s attempt to take initiative.

In this case, Mr. B.'s dysthymia emerges from citing the appropriate gender norm, the norm of hegemonic masculinity incarnated in his mother's fantasies (and not incarnated by his father), but feeling that he always fails to cite it well enough. As Goldner (1991) has pointed out, gender must be seen in its full relational matrix, formed in a crucible of conflicting expectations. By engaging me in his gender performance, he recreates an old ambivalent bond with father and mother, stays depressed, and remains consciously unquestioning of and committed to the desired but unachieved gender norm of hegemonic masculinity.

This client has been very resistant to examining his parents' role in his depression. After a visit with his parents, he might spend a session talking about disappointments and anger with them. But by the next week's session, he is more than likely to say he cannot remember what we talked about last week. He is quite comfortable blaming himself for all his ills, and, as I said, the form this blame takes is one that it is easy to collude with in therapy: helping him understand what blocks him from being more productive and aggressive. It has in fact taken many years for both of us to be able to entertain the possibility that he does not need to be more productive or aggressive, that in fact he is more energetic and prone to take initiative when he lets go of the struggle to be another kind of man (see Chapter 7).

In the next section, I want to look more closely at the way the inability to grieve relational losses in dysthymia connects with perpetual self-dissatisfaction and an isolated form of individualism.

DYSTHYMIA AS A PERFORMANCE OF THE ISOLATED INDIVIDUAL

Mr. B. does not feel "normal." He, like all the dysthymic clients I see, feels that he struggles more than anyone else. On the one hand, he yearns to be different; on the other, he is convinced he cannot be. His anxiety, like Ms. A.'s, is in part due to the fear that if he is not critical of his own desires, his own way of being a person, he will lose love. But his resistance to understanding the relational origins of this conflict is seen in his insistence that his woes are all his fault, all a product of his flawed character. This highly negative way of viewing the self is a staple of dysthymia. Maintaining such a negative view depends on keeping the troubled relationships that formed it hidden, which is consonant with a culture that thrives on decontextualizations of all kinds. Dysthymia, then, is one of the many vehicles that perpetuate not only gender norms but an individualism that hides the troubled connections between people and between self and culture.

Ms. C. is a dysthymic but very bright, engaging client who is wont to discuss herself in relation to well-thought-out social analyses, such as what it is like to be married and over 40 or the ways in which female friendships differ from relations with men. I find her analyses quite compelling and can often locate myself and my friends within them. But fortunately for her and me, I nearly always hear something in the analysis that does not ring true, that appears to limit options symptomatically, and this has made me question the function of these critiques in her life. (It has also impressed upon me that what is therapeutic often involves the recognition of a slight difference between clinician and client that allows either one to hear something as marked that would otherwise pass as unmarked. It is frightening to think how often a likeness in view or affective disposition between clinician and client might lead to overlooking the source of the client's pain and thus maintaining the status quo.) For example, Ms. C. once spoke about how she used to do a lot of things with friends but now she cannot because everyone has children and no one has time. This led to a terrific analysis of the harried state of contemporary life and how destructive it is of relationships. Ms. C. illustrates well the connections between performativity, melancholia, and maintenance of the psychic and social status quo: what she tends to do is to place herself in relation to something normative in the culture, and in so doing she explains why she cannot do anything but what she is currently doing, which keeps her depressed.

Now, I am aware of at least some people who, despite marriage and children, still get out to do things that are stimulating to them, although I am also aware that this is not easy to accomplish. But in Ms. C.'s case, citing dominant norms reflects simultaneouly a wish to fit in and a deep fear and pessimism about relationships. When Ms. C. gives up on community, she becomes one of the lonely crowd that makes the norm continue to exist and exert power. In her case, the norm involves an individualistic pessimism about the possibility of community, and rationalization is the defensive mode in which the norm is cited.

Why does Ms. C. fear relationships? Her father was a very nonconventional man and highly dissatisfied with his work life. He did not allow his children to make noise, complain, dramatize—in short, be children. He demanded a kind of conventionality of her: if you have nothing pleasing to say, be quiet. Mother was more empathic but usually yielded to father's prerogatives. Both parents were rather insular and did not participate in the kinds of community and school activities that Ms. C. saw other families enjoy. What may have begun as "if dad were different, we'd fit it" soon became "If I were different, I'd fit it." When in pain, and it seems she frequently was so because she was quiet, felt out of place in school, and got little sympathy at home, she would go to her room and find ways to soothe herself. She came to see herself as superior to her peers for not needing to assert herself or to be recognized for asserting herself, but she also felt inferior for not fitting in. She reports that she tried in various ways to be a part of things, but that she really thought that the activities that made people popular were juvenile and ridiculous. In this way, she was both loyal to and rebellious against her father's nonconventionality. She identified with her father's critique of dominant norms, but her anger at his inability to give her recognition is expressed in an idealization of those who seem to incarnate dominant norms. The psychic story is even more complex: insofar as dominant norms for women include being quiet and nice, Ms. C's parents put her in a double bind vis-à-vis getting approval for conventionality and nonconventionality. She oscillates between trying to fall in line with dominant norms and rebelling against them; in each position she hopes but fails to find love. And she has become increasingly aware that what she'd *like* to do is *neither* fit in to dominant norms *nor* be alone (the price of her father's version of nonconventionality); she'd like acceptance of the way she is.

Ms. C. cannot find community because, like Ms. A. and Mr. B., she has not yet been able to work through her disappointments with her family. Trusting enough in relationships to find community, giving up her sense that she is the one who is aberrant, would threaten the existent sado-masochistic tie to her family. She, like Ms. A. and Mr. B., feels nonconventional in relation to social norms but seeks love and approval in appearing as though she does not rock the boat. Ms. C.'s sado-masochistic bond with her parents, which is created anew and naturalized each time she criticizes but nonetheless cites the norm, leaves her feeling alone and unable to make connections, just as she had felt as a child.

Although conventional wisdom has it that one feels alienated and depressed when out of step with dominant norms, the foregoing implies that dysthymia and depression are often the affective products of those performances that are tightly bound to dominant norms. Ungrieved loss keeps one in a particular kind of relation to dominant norms: norms are either cited faithfully or rebelled against in a way that brings no relief and actually strengthens the power of the norm. In this way, as Butler argues with respect to gender, "normality" and adaptation bear the traces of melancholia. The motivating force behind such adaptive performances, as object relations theory tells us, is an inability to mourn disappointments with love objects, disappointments that leave one convinced that relationships are so tenuous that boats ought not be rocked (a hypothesis that should make cultural feminists rethink their praise of women's so-called relational superiority).[8] What strikes me about this hypothesis is that it suggests that dysthymia serves to maintain the status quo, that it is essentially conservative—and thus that it may be normative (think of all those people on Prozac). I am not arguing, as Freud (1930) did in "Civilization and its Discontents" that dysthymia is the price one pays for being part of culture. Rather, I am arguing that dysthymia is produced by narcissistic intergenerational relationships that do not tolerate difference and that thus uphold, as Butler might argue, one-norm logics that guarantee the replication of the status quo. Difference that does not reduce to sameness (see Irigaray 1985) is produced only in relationships where self and other are both subjects, in relationships of mutual recognition (Benjamin 1988). In this mode of relating, identifications

---

[8]An interesting article by Elisabeth Young-Bruehl (1994) criticizes psychoanalytic feminism for idealizing women and devaluing men. She notes that in phallocentric gender theory, men project their castration anxiety onto women and find them lacking. In feminist gender theories, she argues, women claim a relational facility that men do not have. Had she proceeded with her analogy of two narcissisms, she might have said that just as men project onto women their fears of not being potent enough, so do women project onto men their fears of not being relational enough, their conflicts about being relational that in part come about from conflicts with autonomy.

are not forged solely from a refusal to mourn, the ego is not a substrate of such identifications, and performances of gender or anything else need not violate self or other.

In her earliest work, Butler had no theory of an inner world. In her most recent redefinition of performativity, she has opened a door onto object relations theory but it is a version of object relations theory that, like Freud's, is a one-person theory in need of the kind of revision offered by Benjamin (1988). Nonetheless, Butler's recent theorization of performance as symptomatically citing and reproducing norms provides crucial links between individual psychology, the cultural level of subject formation, and the production and reproduction of culture. While Butler is not always cognizant of the multiplicity of competing norms, the facilitative aspect of norms, and the relational roots of norms, her focus on the symptomatic character of "normalcy" contributes to a therapy that might link the individual and the social in a non-reductive way. In uncovering the symptomatic aspect of the citing of norms, the therapy relationship encourages both participants to reflect upon cultural norms and to reflect upon the origins of the compulsion to cite them. Understood in their relational contexts, norms become open to question in a way that they had not been—and competing options become available.

In Butler's theory, the people with whom we interact disappear behind laws and norms. In most psychoanalytic theory, the cultural laws and norms that form subjects and inform the interactions between them disappear. What we need as clinicians charged not only with discovering a client's subjectivity but determining in some measure what counts as a legitimate subject is a way to keep the individual, the intersubjective, and the cultural in mind. Only a therapy mindful of intrapsychic dynamics, family dynamics, and the way these link up to cultural norms can contribute to creating postconventional subjects.

Afterword

Whenever I prepare to reread my own work, I always hold my breath a little bit. I'm always anxious that I'll find something I now realize is much more complex than I thought at the time, something I said that is racist or sexist, homophobic or classist, something gratuitously judgmental, something that time has rendered irrelevant or just plain wrong, something I self-righteously believed at the time but no longer do ("Ohhhhh—never mind," as *Saturday Night Live*'s Emily Litella might have said). So it was with some trepidation that I reread, from start to finish, *Who's That Girl? Who's That Boy?* and I'd like to say a few words here about what I like about it, what I don't like, and where my thoughts and work have traveled since I completed the book in 1997.

I remain committed to the gender theory proposed in chapter two and applied throughout. That chapter summarizes many other people's theories, but what is original, I think, is the idea that genders are lived as particular, historically influenced versions of attachment and agency and particular relations between the two. During the period of industrialization and urbanization in the West, capitalism and patriarchy developed together in a way that split the public and private spheres, relegating men to the former and women to the latter. Capacities for agency and attachment became split and gendered; and, because these two sets of human capacities were split, each was severely compromised, forming, on one hand, a kind of autonomy that defends against dependency and, on the other, a kind of attachment that defends against self-assertion. Indeed, I claimed that the dominant patterns of attachment and agency for men and for women are two different forms of narcissistic character. But an individual psyche is never exhausted by the demands of the dominant culture. Gender, I argued, is an ongoing negotiation between competing patterns of attachment and agency, each emerging from different kinds of relating, some narcissistic and some grounded in mutuality.

Most of the essays that make up the book were written at a time when gender oppression was considered to be paradigmatic, if not the source, of other kinds of cultural oppressions. Many feminists thought that class oppression and cultural hierarchies, for example, were built from gender oppression and that the battle for liberation in the public sphere had to be fought first in the private sphere. If gender inequality in (heterosexual) couples were challenged, the theory goes, children would be raised differently, which would affect all kinds of other forms of inequality. In the 90s, I became acquainted with the work of feminists of color, queer theorists, and others who argued that oppressions ought not be ranked and, more important, that genders are always already classed, raced, and sexed—for example, a working-class white woman lives her gender differently from the way a middle-class black woman lives hers. While I knew this theoretically when writing the book, I did not sufficiently account for such intersectionality in my clinical examples, partly because I did not theorize such categories as whiteness or class status, the categories that go unmarked, even unsymbolized, because it serves the status quo to keep them so. For example, upper class interests are served and preserved by the fantasy shared by many in America that this is a classless society (or that we're all middle class). I did not sufficiently study the way my patients' whiteness or class status intertwined with the way they lived their gender. And I did not examine the unconscious processes that collude with dominant ideologies to keep certain categories unsymbolized.

One's way of conceptualizing and creating categories alters with time, because categories and the meanings of cultural artifacts are always open to contestation; their meanings continuously change as they are inserted into new, alternate, and even radically opposite ideological contexts. Springsteen's "Born in the U.S.A.," once it is in the public domain, could be used by Reaganite flag wavers, despite the fact that this use of his work nearly sent Bruce into anaphylactic shock. I once wrote a piece about the way that heavy metal music lyrics of the late 80s and early 90s centered on the abjection and abuse of young boys by parents and other establishment agents. One of my representative texts was Metallica's "The Unforgiven," another Pearl Jam's "Jeremy," which I considered to be heavy metal because Pearl Jam's songs regularly appeared on MTV's Headbanger's Ball under the heavy metal category. But within a couple of years, during which time Seattle became the center of all things alternative, Pearl Jam was "reclassified" as alternative, as grunge; and, indeed, they did have more in common musically with Nirvana than with Metallica (actually, they may have more in common with Bruce Springsteen than with any of the others!). When I wrote this book, I knew very little about the categories of "transsexual" and "transgender," categories that continue to be elaborated and contested in relation to straight, gay, queer, bisexual (on bisexuality, see Layton, 2000). I wish I had known more about the way these categories are being lived and fought about; it would have made my discussion of gender more complicated and rich.

In retrospect, too, I wish I had been more careful about distinguishing postmodernism and poststructuralism in this book. As I was finishing the book, it was starting to become clearer to me that, although the terms were often used interchangeably (and still are), what I didn't like were those things more aptly described as postmodern and what I did like were those ways of thinking more aptly described as poststructuralist. Nonetheless, even in *Bringing the Plague. Toward a Postmodern Psychoanalysis* (Fairfield, Layton, and Stack, 2002) my coeditors and I decided to use "postmodern" as our preferred term to describe what really is poststructuralist, only because we knew most of our readers in the clinical world thought of the things we described and endorsed in the book as postmodern.

There are two ways of thinking about this kind of category confusion; each belongs to a different conception of how ideology works. One way suggests that the categories are discrete and unrelated and that they are confused because of sloppy thinking. In this scenario, we just need to differentiate better and more carefully define the two so that confusion can cease. In this view, too, the categories are taken out of historical context (which is why they are seen as unrelated), and they are understood to have clear, if different, referents. One referent is ideology, the other truth. But another way of thinking about it relates to my Springsteen example and is, well, more poststructuralist: categories emerge from specific historical circumstances and never have a fixed referent; once in circulation, they can be taken out of one ideological context ("disarticulated") and "rearticulated" into other existent ideologies (see Hall, 1982; Laclau and Mouffe, 1985). Each ideology serves different power constituencies and has a very different intent. In this scenario, you can begin to discover meanings of terms only by investigating their use in living cultures or subcultures.

So, for example, both postmodernism and poststructuralism place a high value on respecting difference and on the fluidity of identity, because they are responding to some of the same cultural and historical dilemmas. Yet these common values have been articulated into very different ideological positions that serve very different political purposes. One version of postmodernism has been articulated into a liberal, multicultural ideology in which power differentials are ignored and all differences are celebrated as though they were politically of equal value. This postmodernism makes people feel that they are sharing in power when they are not and so, in fact, constrains movements for equality. In chapter five of *Who's That Girl?* I describe a version of academic postmodernism that celebrates fragmentation, glorifies schizophrenia, and prizes the transgression of norms, often just for the sake of transgression. Some culture critics have suggested that this postmodernism provides idelogical legitimation for a Western, late capitalist, global economy (Jameson, 1983; Harvey, 1989). Poststructuralism, on the other hand, has been articulated into a radical ideology that recognizes that difference and identity are currently lived within unequal power hierarchies that value some identities highly and devalue others, indeed, that define one identity only in relation to what the other is not (see Fraser, 1997, for a cogent differentiation of the contrasting articulations and their political consequences). I wish I had historicized postmodernism more in my text and that I had been better able to see the connections between its different uses.

I continue to feel that the theories of Nancy Chodorow (1978) and Jessica Benjamin (1988) are central to understanding dominant heterosexual white gender ideologies, and, since writing *Who's That Girl?* I have been investigating recent changes in the psychic structures they wrote about. As Benjamin suggested in *The Bonds of Love*, I have found that, given the right historical circumstances, the psychic gender positions offered as desirable by the dominant white culture—defensive autonomy and submissive relationality—are reversible. In recent work (Layton, in press-a, b), I have identified what appears to be a trend toward defensive autonomy in middle-class white heterosexual women—that is, a trend toward the kind of autonomy formerly held by white middle-class men, an autonomy marked by the devaluation and repudiation of such traditionally "feminine" attributes as dependency, nurturance, and emotionality. The entry of women into the workforce, with no modification either of workplace conditions or of the assumption that women do most of the work in the domestic sphere, put pressure on middle-class white women to value work at the expense of valuing relationships and care, and it pressured them and their families to hire other, lower class and non-white women to do the work of caring that still needs to be done (see Ehrenreich and Hochschild, 2002). In my more recent work, I have tried to reintegrate class, race, and other identity categories with gender. But it is clear that dominant white middle-class gender ideals still offer only two split, narcissistic alternatives and no real way of integrating our relational needs and capacities with our agentic needs and capacities. Only structural changes in work and the prerequisite value changes in culture would make such an integration possible, and it serves neither contemporary capitalism nor patriarchy to make that happen.

I continue to write mostly about the white middle class because that is largely where my clients come from. But many of these same clients began life as working class, and, even within the middle class, there are many different ways of living a gendered life. When I say this, I'm not referring to Chodorow's (1995) important insight that all people have an individual way of creating their gender. I agree with Chodorow, but, since I am more interested in cultural gender

trends than in individual idiosyncratic gender solutions, what I refer
to here is that classes contain many different fractions (Bourdieu,
1984). The white middle class, for example, contains some people
who were born working class and made a lot of money (e.g., construction workers who became developers), some whose primary form
of capital derives from education and status and not from money (e.g.,
academics and social service workers), and many who were born
wealthy and remain so (but who vary in education and social status).
When these class fraction differences are taken into consideration,
we can better account for the multiple ways that gender is lived. For
example, some of my middle-class heterosexual white female patients
have created a gender identity based in defensive autonomy, while
others have careers but show very little interest in them. They still
primarily feel that they are failed females if they cannot find a man,
and they still expect men to pay for them and take care of them
(Layton, 2002). I think that some of the sources of such differences
have to do with their parents' relation to different forms of capital
(education, money, social status). Bourdieu's (1984) work on class
fractions and on the way people build identities around what, to them,
signifies distinction (that is, what distinguishes them from those from
whom they want to distance themselves) has been very generative for
my own psychoanalytic thinking (Layton, in press-c).

Since writing *Who's That Girl?* I have been trying to elaborate
my own sense of the way that ideologies, politics, and unconscious
processes may be linked, for I continue to be primarily interested, as
I was in this book, in the ways that the most radical academic theories available today connect with the clinical world and can help clinicians in their work. Putting social class back into my theorizing
about gender, race, and sexual orientation has been one important
move in this direction—my earliest work (Layton, 1986) was about
capitalism and narcissistic character. Yet sometime in the late 80s and
90s the capitalism part got lost, and gender, racial, and sexual inequalities came to stand for all things wrong with American life. I suppose
the events of the past few years—the decline of the economy, increasing public awareness of the horrifying and inhuman effects of global
capitalism, the Republican yearning for empire and devotion to the

cause of welfare for the rich—have brought class squarely back into my consciousness and that of many others.

It is clear that class began to reappear in Left theory in the academy toward the latter part of the 90s. The time is right to return to theorizing the relation between narcissistic character and capitalism, now enriched by what we have learned about gender, race, and sexual orientation. Ideology, I believe, is largely lived as narcissistic character, a point brought home to me in a family dinner conversation not long ago. A 20-something relative was talking about a very successful colleague in the finance industry who "doesn't believe in any ideology." Indeed, he went on to argue, this man *uses* ideological arguments to rationalize his success, but what he actually believes is that he's better than anyone else and deserves what he has because he's better. That example shows that the most insidious form ideology takes is as character. As my relative's statements suggest, most of us are unconscious of the way ideology is lived as social character (Fromm, 1941), so like "human nature" or "personality" does it appear to us.

Finally, most of the work I have done since this book was first published has focused on what I have called normative unconscious processes—another potential link between the individual psyche, the familial context, and the wider sociohistorical context, with its dominant and competing ideologies. Taking off from this book's discussion about the way that splitting processes inform dominant gender constructs, I have suggested (2002, 2004d) that what is split off and either repressed or dissociated as we attempt to take on coherent and culturally approved identities (which we do in order to get love) "proliferates," as Freud (1915) said of the effects of repression, "in the dark" (p. 149). Character and culture intersect in unconscious enactments and repetition compulsions that both contest those splits and shore them up—and the identities they produce. I chose the term normative unconscious processes to characterize what, within us, works unconsciously to sustain the splits that preserve a hierarchical status quo, the very splits that cause us pain; and I have suggested that blind spots for difference are more often than not motivated by unconscious conflicts rather than by mere ignorance of otherness. Clinicians, as we all know, have unconscious conflicts, too, and my sense is that many of these culturally induced identity conflicts, such as, for example, the development of defensive autonomy in middle-class white women, might in fact be shared between clinician and patient. When this is the case, we clinicians are likely to collude in particular kinds of enactments that involve mutual unconscious attempts to maintain the status quo. This is contrary to the clinical ideal, which is to explore those attempts, to make them part of the clinical conversation.

It is exciting to me that many clinicians are currently questioning the field's ideological assumptions and are thinking about the way that politics, in all its many guises, enters the clinical encounter. I hope that *Who's That Girl?* continues to contribute to much-needed dialogue between academics and clinicians and that it also renders clinically useful political insights derived from academia and from everyday life.

References

Benjamin, J. (1988), *The Bonds of Love*. New York: Pantheon.

Bourdieu, P. (1984), *Distinction*, trans., R. Nice. Cambridge, MA: Harvard University Press.

Chodorow, N. J. (1978), *The Reproduction of Mothering*. Berkeley: University of California Press.

——— (1995), Gender as a personal and cultural construction. *Signs*, 20:516–544.

Ehrenreich, B. & Hochschild, A. R., eds. (2002), *Global Woman*. New York: Metropolitan Books.

Fairfield, S., Layton, L. Stack, C., eds. (2002), *Bringing the Plague: Toward a Postmodern Psychoanalysis*. New York: Other Press.

Fraser, N. (1997), *Justice Interruptus*. New York: Routledge.

Freud, S. (1915), Repression. *Standard Edition*, 14:143–158. London: Hogarth Press, 1964.

Fromm, E. (1941), *Escape from Freedom*. New York: Holt, Rinehart & Winston.

Hall, S. (1982), The rediscovery of ideology: Return of the repressed in media studies. In: *Culture, Society and the Media*, ed. M. Gurevitch et al. New York: Methuen, pp. 56–90.

Harvey, D. (1989), *The Condition of Postmodernity*. Oxford: Basil Blackwell.

Jameson, F. (1983), Postmodernism and consumer society. In: *The Anti-Aesthetic*, ed. H. Foster. Seattle, WA: Bay Press, pp. 111–125.

Laclau, E. & Mouffe, C. (1985), *Hegemony and Socialist Strategy*. London: Verso.

Layton, L. (1986), Narcissism and history: Flaubert's *Sentimental Education*. In: *Narcissism and the Text: Studies in Literature and the Psychology of Self*, ed. L. Layton & B. A. Schapiro. New York: New York University Press, pp. 170–191.

———— (2000), The psychopolitics of bisexuality. *Studies in Gender and Sexuality*, 1:41–60.

———— (2002), Cultural hierarchies, splitting, and the heterosexist unconscious. In: *Bringing the Plague: Toward a Postmodern Psychoanalysis*, ed. S. Fairfield, L. Layton & C. Stack. New York: Other Press, pp. 195–223.

———— (in press-a), Relational no more. Defensive autonomy in middle-class women. In: *Annual of Psychoanalysis. Vol. 32. Psychoanalysis and Women*, ed. J. A. Winer & J. W. Anderson. Hillsdale, NJ: The Analytic Press

———— (in press-b), Working nine to nine: The new women of prime-time. *Studies in Gender and Sexuality*.

———— (in press-c), That place gives me the heebie jeebies. *International Journal of Critical Psychology*.

———— (in press-d), A fork in the royal road: on "defining" the unconscious and its stakes for social theory. *Psychoanalysis, Culture & Society*.

References

Abel, E. (1990). Race, class, and psychoanalysis? Opening questions. In *Conflicts in Feminism*, ed. M. Hirsch and E. F. Keller, pp. 184–204. New York and London: Routledge.

Abelin, E. (1971). The role of the father in the separation-individuation process. In *Separation-Individuation*, ed. J. B. McDevitt and C. F. Settlage, pp. 229–252. New York: International Universities Press.

———— (1980). Triangulation, the role of the father, and the origins of core gender identity during the rapprochement subphase. In *Rapprochement: The Critical Subphase of Separation-Individuation*, ed. R. F. Lax, S. Bach, and J. A. Burland, pp. 151–169. New York: Jason Aronson.

Acker, K. (1978). *Blood and Guts in High School*. New York: Grove.

Adams, P. (1988). Per os(cillation). *Camera Obscura* 17:7–29.

Adelson, L. (1993). *Making Bodies, Making History*. Lincoln: University of Nebraska Press.

Adorno, T., and Horkheimer, M. (1972). *Dialectic of Enlightenment*. New York: Herder and Herder.

Aiosa-Karpas, C. J., Karpas, R., Pelcovits, D., and Kaplan, S. (1991). Gender identification and sex role attribution in sexually abused adolescent females. *Journal of the American Academy of Child and Adolescent Psychiatry* 30:266–271.

Alarcon, N. (1990). The theoretical subject(s) of *This Bridge Called My Back* and Anglo-American feminism. In *Making Face, Making Soul. Haciendo Caras*, ed. G. Anzaldúa, pp. 356–369. San Francisco: Aunt Lute.

Althusser, L. (1971). Ideology and ideological state apparatuses (notes towards an investigation). In *Lenin and Philosophy and Other Essays*, trans. B. Brewster, pp. 127–186. New York and London: Monthly Review Press.

American Psychiatric Association (1994). *Diagnostic and Statistical Manual of Mental Disorders, Fourth Edition (DSM-IV)*. Washington, DC: American Psychiatric Association.

Andersen, C. (1991). *Madonna Unauthorized*. New York: Simon & Schuster.

Anderson, A. (1992). Cryptonormativism and double gestures: the politics of post-structuralism. *Cultural Critique* 21:63–95.

Ansen, D. (1986). Stranger than paradise: Lynch's nightmare tour of homespun America. *Newsweek*, September 15, p. 69.

Anzaldúa, G. (1987). *Borderlands/La Frontera*. San Francisco: Spinsters/Aunt Lute.

Apramian, L., dir. (1995). *Not Bad for a Girl*. Film. Spitshine Productions.

Aron, L. (1990). One-person and two-person psychologies and the method of psychoanalysis. *Psychoanalytic Psychology* 7:475–485.

———— (1991). The patient's experience of the analyst's subjectivity. *Psychoanalytic Dialogues* 1:29–51.

———— (1992). Interpretation as expression of the analyst's subjectivity. *Psychoanalytic Dialogues* 2:475–507.

Assiter, A. (1988). Romance fiction. Porn for women? In *Perspectives on Pornography: Sexuality in Film and Literature*, ed. C. Bloom and G. Day, pp. 101–109. New York: St. Martin's.

Author Meets Critics: Robert Connell's *Masculinities* (1996). Panel presented at the meeting of the American Sociological Association, New York, August.

Barratt, B. (1993). *Psychoanalysis and the Postmodern Impulse*. Baltimore, MD: Johns Hopkins University Press.

Barthes, R. (1972). *Mythologies*, trans. A. Lavers. New York: Hill and Wang.

Bay, M., dir. (1996). *The Rock*. Film. Hollywood Pictures.

Beatty, W., dir. (1990). *Dick Tracy*. Film. Touchstone.

Belenky, M., Clichy, B., Goldberger, N., and Tarule, J. (1987). *Women's Ways of Knowing*. New York: Basic Books.

Benhabib, S. (1995). Feminism and postmodernism: an uneasy alliance. In *Feminist Contentions*, ed. S. Benhabib, J. Butler, D. Cornell, and N. Fraser, pp. 17–34. New York: Routledge.

Benjamin, J. (1988). *The Bonds of Love*. New York: Pantheon.

———— (1991). Father and daughter: identification with difference—a contribution to gender heterodoxy. *Psychoanalytic Dialogues* 1:277–299.

———— (1992). Reply to Schwartz. *Psychoanalytic Dialogues* 2:417–424.

———— (1994a). The omnipotent mother: a psychoanalytic study of fantasy and reality. In *Representations of Motherhood*, ed. D. Bassin, M. Honey, and M. Kaplan, pp. 129–146. New Haven, CT: Yale University Press.

———— (1994b). The shadow of the other (subject). *Constellations* 1:231–254.

———— (1995). *Like Subjects. Love Objects. Essays on Recognition and Sexual Difference*. New Haven, CT: Yale University Press.

———— (1996). In defense of gender ambiguity. *Gender and Psychoanalysis* 1:27–43.

Berry, B. (1988). Forever, in my dreams: generic conventions and the subversive imagination in *Blue Velvet*. *Literature/Film Quarterly* 16:82–90.

Bersani, L. (1995). *Homos*. Cambridge, MA: Harvard University Press.

Bertens, H. (1995). *The Idea of the Postmodern. A History*. New York and London: Routledge.

Bhabha, H. K. (1990). The third space. Interview with Homi Bhabha. In *Identity. Community, Culture, Difference*, ed. J. Rutherford, pp. 207-221. London: Lawrence and Wishart.

————— (1994). *The Location of Culture*. London and New York: Routledge.

Biga, T. (1987). *Blue Velvet. Film Quarterly* 41:44-49.

Bordo, S. (1993). Reading the male body. *Michigan Quarterly Review* 32:696-737.

Bradshaw, J. (1988). *Bradshaw On: The Family. A Revolutionary Way of Self-Discovery*. Deerfield Beach, FL: Health Communications.

Brenkman, J. (1993). *Straight Male Modern. A Cultural Critique of Psychoanalysis*. New York and London: Routledge.

Brennan, T. (1989). Introduction. In *Between Feminism and Psychoanalysis*, ed. T. Brennan, pp. 1-23. New York and London: Routledge.

Breslau, N., Davis, G. C., Andreski, P., and Peterson, E. (1991). Traumatic events and posttraumatic stress disorder in an urban population of young adults. *Archives of General Psychiatry* 48:216-222.

Bromberg, P. M. (1996). Standing in the spaces: the multiplicity of self and the psychoanalytic relationship. *Contemporary Psychoanalysis* 32:509-536.

Brown, L. S. (1991). Not outside the range: one feminist perspective on psychic trauma. *American Imago* 48:119-133.

Brest, M., dir. (1988). *Midnight Run*. Film. Universal Pictures.

Bundtzen, L. K. (1988). "Don't look at me!": woman's body, woman's voice in *Blue Velvet*. *Western Humanities Review* 42:187-203.

Butler, J. (1990a). *Gender Trouble. Feminism and the Subversion of Identity*. New York and London: Routledge.

————— (1990b). Performative acts and gender constitution: an essay in phenomenology and feminist theory. In *Performing Feminisms. Feminist Critical Theory and Theatre*, ed. S.-E. Case, pp. 270-282. Baltimore, MD: Johns Hopkins University Press.

————— (1990c). Gender trouble, feminist theory, and psychoanalytic discourse. In *Feminism/Postmodernism*, ed. L. J. Nicholson, pp. 324-340. New York and London: Routledge.

————— (1991). Imitation and gender insubordination. In *inside/out. Lesbian Theories, Gay Theories*, ed. D. Fuss, pp. 13-31. New York and London: Routledge.

————— (1992). Contingent foundations. Feminism and the question of "postmodernism." In *Feminists Theorize the Political*, ed. J. Butler and J. W. Scott, pp. 3-21. New York and London: Routledge.

———— (1993). *Bodies that Matter.* New York and London: Routledge.

———— (1994). Against proper objects. *differences* 6:1–26.

———— (1995a). Melancholy gender—refused identification. *Psychoanalytic Dialogues* 5:165–180.

———— (1995b). Contingent foundations. In *Feminist Contentions,* ed. S. Benhabib, J. Butler, D. Cornell, and N. Fraser, pp. 35–57. New York and London: Routledge.

———— (1995c). For a careful reading. In *Feminist Contentions,* ed. S. Benhabib, J. Butler, D. Cornell, and N. Fraser, pp. 127–143. New York and London: Routledge.

Chandler, R. (1953). *The Long Goodbye.* New York: Random House, 1988.

Chase, C. (1987). The material girl and how she grew. *Cosmopolitan,* July, pp. 130–133, 193.

Chasseguet-Smirgel, J. (1986). *Sexuality and Mind: The Role of the Father and the Mother in the Psyche.* New York: New York University Press.

Chodorow, N. J. (1978). *The Reproduction of Mothering.* Berkeley: University of California Press.

———— (1989). *Feminism and Psychoanalytic Theory.* New Haven, CT: Yale University Press.

———— (1994). *Femininities, Masculinities, Sexualities: Freud and Beyond.* Lexington: University Press of Kentucky.

———— (1995). Gender as a personal and cultural construction. *Signs* 20:516–544.

Christgau, R. (1991). Madonnathinking madonnabout madonnamusic. In *Desperately Seeking Madonna,* ed. A. Sexton, pp. 201–207. New York: Dell, 1993.

Cisneros, S. (1992). Woman hollering creek. In *Woman Hollering Creek and Other Stories,* pp. 43–56. New York: Random House.

Cocks, J. (1990). Madonna draws a line. *Time,* December 17, pp. 74–75.

Collins, P. H. (1990). *Black Feminist Thought: Knowledge, Consciousness and the Politics of Empowerment.* Boston: Unwin Hyman.

———— (1994). Shifting the center: race, class, and feminist theorizing about motherhood. In *Representations of Motherhood,* ed. D. Bassin, M. Honey, and M. Kaplan, pp. 56–74. New Haven, CT: Yale University Press.

Connell, R. W. (1987). *Gender and Power: Society, the Person and Sexual Politics.* Stanford, CA: Stanford University Press.

———— (1995). *Masculinities.* Berkeley, CA: University of California Press.

Cronenberg, D., dir. (1993). M. *Butterfly.* Film. Geffen Pictures.

Cushman, P. (1990). Why the self is empty: toward a historically situated psychology. *American Psychologist* 45:599–611.

———— (1991). Ideology obscured: political uses of the self in Daniel Stern's infant. *American Psychologist* 46:206–219.

Dahl, J., dir. (1994). *The Last Seduction*. Film. ITC Entertainment Group.

David, M. (1989). Postmodern girl. *Manhattan, Inc.*, August, pp. 98–99.

Dean, T. (1993). Transsexual identification, gender performance theory, and the politics of the real. *Literature and Psychology* 39:1–27.

Deevoy, A. (1991). "If you're going to reveal yourself, reveal yourself!" *Us*, June 13, pp. 16–24.

de Lauretis, T. (1984). *Alice Doesn't*. Bloomington: University of Indiana Press.

———— (1986). Feminist studies/critical studies: issues, terms, and contexts. In *Feminist Studies/Critical Studies*, ed. T. de Lauretis, pp. 1–19. Bloomington: University of Indiana Press.

———— (1987). *Technologies of Gender*. Bloomington: University of Indiana Press.

———— (1991). Queer theory: lesbian and gay sexualities: an introduction. *differences* 3:3–18.

———— (1994). *The Practice of Love: Lesbian Sexuality and Perverse Desire*. Bloomington: Indiana University Press.

Deleuze, G., and Guattari, F. (1983). *Anti-Oedipus: Capitalism and Schizophrenia*, trans. R. Hurley, M. Seem, and H. R. Lane. Minneapolis: University of Minnesota Press.

de Marneffe, D. (1997). Bodies and words: a study of young children's genital and gender knowledge. *Gender and Psychoanalysis* 2(1):3–33.

De Palma, B., dir. (1996). *Mission Impossible*. Film. Paramount.

Derrida, J. (1976). *Of Grammatology*, trans. G. Spivak. Baltimore, MD: Johns Hopkins University Press.

———— (1978). *Writing and Difference*, trans. A. Bass. Chicago: University of Chicago Press.

Dews, P. (1987). *Logics of Disintegration*. London and New York: Verso.

Dimen, M. (1991). Deconstructing difference: gender, splitting, and transitional space. *Psychoanalytic Dialogues* 1:335–352.

Dinnerstein, D. (1976). *The Mermaid and the Minotaur*. New York: Harper & Row.

DiPiero, T. (1991). The patriarch is not (just) a man. *Camera Obscura* 25–26:101–124.

Doane, J., and Hodges, D. (1992). *From Klein to Kristeva. Psychoanalytic Feminism and the Search for the "Good Enough" Mother*. Ann Arbor: University of Michigan Press.

Doane, M. A. (1987). *The Desire to Desire: The Woman's Film of the 1940s*. Bloomington: Indiana University Press.

Donner, R., dir. (1987). *Lethal Weapon*. Film. Warner Brothers.

Dor, J. (1997a). *Introduction to the Reading of Lacan*, ed. J. F. Gurewich with S. Fairfield. Northvale, NJ: Jason Aronson.

———— (1997b). *The Clinical Lacan*, ed. J. F. Gurewich with S. Fairfield. Northvale, NJ: Jason Aronson.

Dyer, R. (1991). Charisma. In *Stardom. Industry of Desire*, ed. C. Gledhill, pp. 57–59. London and New York: Routledge.

Ebert, T. L. (1992–1993). Ludic feminism, the body, performance, and labor: bringing materialism back into feminist cultural studies. *Cultural Critique* 23:5–50.

Edel, U., dir. (1993). *Body of Evidence*. Film. De Laurentis.

Emmerich, R., dir. (1996). *Independence Day*. Film. Twentieth Century Fox.

Erikson, E. H. (1950). *Childhood and Society*, 2nd ed. New York: Norton, 1963.

———— (1968). *Identity: Youth and Crisis*. New York: Norton.

Evans, D. (1996). *An Introductory Dictionary of Lacanian Psychoanalysis*. New York and London: Routledge.

Evans, S. (1979). *Personal Politics*. New York: Vintage.

Fairbairn, W. R. D. (1954). *An Object-Relations Theory of the Personality*. New York: Basic Books.

Fairfield, S. (1996). On deconstruction, psychoanalysis, and the master self. Unpublished manuscript.

Faludi, S. (1991). *Backlash*. New York: Crown.

Fanon, F. (1967). *Black Skin, White Masks*. New York: Grove.

Fast, I. (1984). *Gender Identity. A Differentiation Model*. Hillsdale, NJ: Analytic Press.

———— (1995). *Female separation-individuation: beyond the nurturing bond*. Paper presented at the meeting of Division 39, American Psychological Association, Santa Monica, CA, April.

Ferrara, A., dir. (1993). *Dangerous Game*. Film. Maverick Picture Company.

Finlay, M. (1989). Post-modernizing psychoanalysis/psychoanalysing postmodernity. *Free Associations* 16:43–80.

Fiske, J. (1989). Madonna. In *Reading the Popular*, pp. 95–113. Boston: Unwin Hyman.

Flax, J. (1987). Re-membering the selves: Is the repressed gendered? *Michigan Quarterly Review* 26:92–110. ·

———— (1990). *Thinking Fragments. Psychoanalysis, Feminism, and Postmodernism in the Contemporary West*. Berkeley: University of California Press.

———— (1996). Taking multiplicity seriously. Some implications for psychoanalytic theorizing and practice. *Contemporary Psychoanalysis* 32:577–593.

Foley, J., dir. (1987). *Who's that Girl?* Film. Warner Brothers.

Foucault, M. (1973). *Madness and Civilization: A History of Insanity in the Age of Reason*, trans. R. Howard. New York: Vintage.

———— (1979). *Discipline and Punish: The Birth of the Prison*, trans. A. Sheridan. New York: Vintage.

———— (1980). *The History of Sexuality, Vol. 1*, trans. R. Hurley. New York: Vintage.

———— (1982). The subject and power. *Critical Inquiry* 8:777–795.

Frankenberg, R. (1993). *White Women. Race Matters. The Social Construction of Whiteness*. Minneapolis: University of Minnesota Press.

Fraser, N. (1995). False antitheses: a response to Seyla Benhabib and Judith Butler. In *Feminist Contentions*, ed. S. Benhabib, J. Butler, D. Cornell, and N. Fraser, pp. 59–74. New York: Routledge.

Freccero, C. (1992). Our lady of MTV: Madonna's "Like a prayer." *boundary 2* 19:163–183.

Freud, S. (1914). On narcissism: an introduction. *Standard Edition* 14:69–102.

———— (1916). Introductory lecture 26. Libido theory and narcissism. *Standard Edition* 16:412–430.

———— (1917). Mourning and melancholia. *Standard Edition* 14:239–258.

———— (1920). Beyond the pleasure principle. *Standard Edition* 18:3–64.

———— (1925). Some psychical consequences of the anatomical distinction between the sexes. *Standard Edition* 21:243–258.

———— (1930). Civilization and its discontents. *Standard Edition* 21:59–145.

———— (1931). Female sexuality. *Standard Edition* 21:221–243.

———— (1933). Femininity. *Standard Edition* 22:112–135.

Friedman, E. G. (1993). Where are the missing contents? (Post)modernism, gender, and the canon. *PMLA* 108:240–252.

Frosh, S. (1994). *Sexual Difference. Masculinity and Psychoanalysis*. New York and London: Routledge.

Garber, M. (1992). *Vested Interests: Cross-Dressing and Cultural Anxiety*. New York: HarperPerennial.

Gates, D. (1993). White male paranoia. *Newsweek*, March 29, pp. 46–54.

Gates, H. L. (1988). *The Signifying Monkey*. New York: Oxford University Press.

———— (1996). White like me. *New Yorker*, June 17, pp. 66–81.

Ghent, E. (1992). Process and paradox. *Psychoanalytic Dialogues* 2:135–160.

Gilday, K., dir. (1990). *The Famine Within*. Film. Panorama Entertainment.

Gilligan, C. (1982). *In a Different Voice. Psychological Theory and Women's Development*. Cambridge, MA: Harvard University Press.

Gilmore, M. (1987). The Madonna mystique. *Rolling Stone*, September 10, pp. 37–38, 87–88.

Glass, J. M. (1993). *Shattered Selves: Multiple Personality in a Postmodern World*. Ithaca: Cornell University Press.

Glassgold, J. M., and Iasenza, S. (1995). *Lesbians and Psychoanalysis*. New York: Free Press.

Godard, B. (1989). Sleuthing: feminists re/writing the detective novel. *Signature* 1:45–70.

Goldberg, A. (1978). *The Psychology of the Self. A Casebook*. New York: International Universities Press.

Goldin, C. (1995). Career and family: college women look to the past. Working Paper No. 5188. Cambridge, MA: *National Bureau of Economic Research*.

Goldner, V. (1991). Toward a critical relational theory of gender. *Psychoanalytic Dialogues* 1:249–272.

Goodman, E. (1990). Another image in the Madonna rolodex. *Boston Globe*, December 6, p. 13.

Grafton, S. (1986). *B is for Burglar*. New York: Bantam.

Gramsci, A. (1971). *Selections from the Prison Notebooks*, ed. Q. Hoare and G. N. Smith. New York: International Publishers.

Greenson, R. (1968). Dis-identifying from mother: its special importance for the boy. *International Journal of Psycho-Analysis* 45:220–226.

Greifinger, J. (1995). Therapeutic discourse as moral conversation: psychoanalysis, modernity, and the ideal of authenticity. *Communication Review* 1:53–81.

Grosz, E. (1990). *Jacques Lacan. A Feminist Introduction*. New York: Routledge.

——— (1994). Experimental desire: rethinking queer subjectivity. In *Supposing the Subject*, ed. J. Copjec, pp. 133–157. London and New York: Verso.

Guntrip, H. (1961). *Personality Structure and Human Interaction*. New York: International Universities Press.

——— (1971). *Psychoanalytic Theory, Therapy, and the Self*. New York: Basic Books.

Hacking, I. (1986). Making up people. In *Reconstructing Individualism: Autonomy, Individuality and the Self in Western Thought*, ed. T. C. Heller, M. Sosna, and D. Willberry, pp. 222–236. Stanford, CA: Stanford University Press.

Hall, S. (1980). Encoding/decoding. In *Culture, Media, Language. Working Papers in Cultural Studies, 1972-79*, ed. S. Hall, D. Hobson, A. Lowe, and P. Willis, pp. 128–138. London: Hutchinson.

——— (1987). Minimal selves. In *Black British Cultural Studies. A Reader*, ed. H. A. Baker, Jr., M. Diawara, and R. H. Lindeborg, pp. 114–119. Chicago: University of Chicago Press, 1996.

Haraway, D. (1985). A manifesto for cyborgs: science, technology, and socialist feminism in the 1980s. *Socialist Review* 15:65–107.

Harris, A. (1995). *Animated conversations: embodying and engendering analytic discourse*. Paper presented at the meeting of Division 39, American Psychological Association, Santa Monica, CA, April.

Harris, D. (1992). Make my rainy day. *The Nation*, June 8, pp. 790–793.

Hartmann, H. (1950). Comments on the psychoanalytic theory of the ego.

In *Essays on Ego Psychology*, pp. 113–141. New York: International Universities Press, 1964.

Harvey, D. (1989). *The Condition of Postmodernity*. Oxford and Cambridge, MA: Basil Blackwell.

Harvey, P. J. (1992). *Dry*. CD. Island Records.

Hennessy, R. (1995). Queer visibility in commodity culture. In *Social Postmodernism. Beyond Identity Politics*, ed. L. Nicholson and S. Seidman, pp. 142–183. Cambridge: Cambridge University Press.

Henriques, J., Hollway, W., Urwin, C., et al. (1984). *Changing the Subject. Psychology, Social Regulation, and Subjectivity*. London and New York: Methuen.

Herman, J. L. (1992). *Trauma and Recovery*. New York: Basic Books.

Herman, J. L., Perry, J. C., and van der Kolk, B. A. (1989). Childhood trauma in borderline personality disorder. *American Journal of Psychiatry* 146:490–495.

Higginbotham, E. B. (1992). African-American women's history and the metalanguage of race. *Signs* 17:251–274.

Hill, W., dir. (1982). *48 Hrs*. Film. Paramount.

Hirschberg, L. (1991). The misfit. *Vanity Fair*, April, pp. 160–168, 196–202.

Hoffman, I. Z. (1983). The patient as interpreter of the analyst's experience. *Contemporary Psychoanalysis* 19:389–422.

——— (1987). The value of uncertainty in psychoanalytic practice. *Contemporary Psychoanalysis* 23:205–215.

Hole (1994). *Live Through This*. CD. Geffen Records.

Hollway, W. (1984). Gender difference and the production of subjectivity. In *Changing the Subject. Psychology, Social Regulation, and Subjectivity*, ed. J. Henriques, W. Hollway, C. Urwin, et al., pp. 227–263. London and New York: Methuen.

hooks, b. (1981). *Ain't I a Woman. Black Women and Feminism*. Boston: South End Press.

——— (1990). *Yearning. Race, Gender, and Cultural Politics*. Boston: South End Press.

——— (1992). *Black Looks. Race and Representation*. Boston: South End Press.

Horney, K. (1924). On the genesis of the castration complex in women. *International Journal of Psycho-Analysis* 5:50–65.

——— (1926). The flight from womanhood. *International Journal of Psycho-Analysis* 7:324–339.

Irigaray, L. (1985). The blind spot of an old dream of symmetry. In *Speculum of the Other Woman*, trans. G. Gill, pp. 13–129. Ithaca, NY: Cornell University Press.

Jaehne, K. (1987). *Blue Velvet*. *Cineaste* 15:38–41.

James, D. (1991). *Madonna.* Lincolnwood, IL: Publications International.

Jameson, F. (1983). Postmodernism and consumer society. In *The Anti-Aesthetic,* ed. H. Foster, pp. 111–125. Seattle, WA: Bay Press.

———— (1989). Nostalgia for the present. *South Atlantic Quarterly* 88:517–537.

Jones, A. R. (1986). Mills & Boon meets feminism. In *The Progress of Romance,* ed. J. Radford, pp. 195–218. New York: Routledge.

Jordan, J. V. (1984). Empathy and self boundaries. In *Work in Progress.* Wellesley, MA: Wellesley College, Stone Center for Developmental Services and Studies.

Jordan, N., dir. (1992). *The Crying Game.* Film. Channel Four Films/Nippon Film Development and Finance/Palace.

Juhasz, S. (1988). Texts to grow on: reading women's romance fiction. *Tulsa Studies in Women's Literature* 7:239–259.

Kaftal, E. (1991). On intimacy between men. *Psychoanalytic Dialogues* 1:305–328.

Kaleta, K. C. (1993). *David Lynch.* New York: Twayne.

Kaplan, E. A. (1983). Is the gaze male? In *Powers of Desire: The Politics of Sexuality,* ed. A. Snitow, C. Stansell, and S. Thompson, pp. 309–327. New York: Monthly Review Press.

———— (1987). *Rocking Around the Clock: Music Television, Postmodernism, and Counterculture.* New York: Routledge.

———— (1993). Madonna politics: Perversion, repression, or subversion? or masks and/as master-y. In *The Madonna Connection,* ed. C. Schwichtenberg, pp. 149–165. Boulder, CO: Westview.

Kellner, D., ed. (1989). *Jean Baudrillard: From Marxism to Postmodernism and Beyond.* London: Polity.

Kernberg, O. (1975). *Borderline Conditions and Pathological Narcissism.* New York: Jason Aronson.

———— (1976). *Object Relations Theory and Clinical Psychoanalysis.* New York: Jason Aronson.

———— (1980). *Internal World and External Reality: Object Relations Theory Applied.* New York: Jason Aronson.

Keshishian, A., dir. (1991). *Truth or Dare: On the Road, Behind the Scenes, and in Bed with Madonna.* Film. Miramax.

Kestenberg, J. (1968). Outside and inside, male and female. *Journal of the American Psychoanalytic Association* 16:457–520.

King, N. (1991). *Madonna. The Book.* New York: William Morrow.

Kingston, M. H. (1990). Tripmaster monkey in the land of women. *Speaking Race, Sexuality, Feminism* Conference, April 26, Cambridge, MA.

Kohut, H. (1971). *The Analysis of the Self. A Systematic Approach to the Psychoanalytic Treatment of Narcissistic Personality Disorder.* New York: International Universities Press.

——— (1977). *The Restoration of the Self.* New York: International Universities Press.

——— (1984). *How Does Analysis Cure?* Chicago and London: University of Chicago Press.

Kohut, H., and Wolf, E. S. (1978). The disorders of the self and their treatment: an outline. *International Journal of Psycho-Analysis* 59:413–425.

Kubrick, S., dir. (1971). *A Clockwork Orange.* Film. Warner Brothers.

Kvale, S., ed. (1992). *Psychology and Postmodernism.* London: Sage.

Lacan, J. (1977). *Ecrits. A Selection.* London: Tavistock.

——— (1985). *Feminine Sexuality,* ed. J. Mitchell and J. Rose. New York: Norton.

Lamb, C. (1992). *The Threat of Love.* Don Mills, Ontario: Harlequin Presents.

Lasch, C. (1979). *The Culture of Narcissism.* New York: Norton.

Layton, L. (1988). *An empirical analysis of the self and object love: a test of Kohut's conception of the self.* Dissertation. Ann Arbor, MI: UMI.

——— (1990a). A deconstruction of Kohut's concept of the self. *Contemporary Psychoanalysis* 26(3):420–429.

——— (1990b). What's behind the Madonna bashing? *Boston Globe,* December 16, p. A15.

——— (1992). The self you seek is the self you find. *Psychiatry* 55:147–159.

——— (1993). Like a virgin: Madonna's version of the feminine. In *Desperately Seeking Madonna,* ed. A. Sexton, pp. 170–194. New York: Dell.

——— (1994a). Blue velvet: a parable of male development. *Screen* 35(4): 374–393.

——— (1994b). Who's that girl? A case study of Madonna. In *Women Creating Lives: Identities, Resilience, and Resistance,* ed. C. E. Franz and A. J. Stewart, pp. 143–156. Boulder, CO: Westview.

——— (1995). Trauma, gender identity and sexuality: discourses of fragmentation. *American Imago* 52(1):107–125.

——— (1997). The doer behind the deed: tensions and intersections between Butler's vision of performativity and relational psychoanalysis. *Gender and Psychoanalysis* 2(2):131–155.

Layton, L., and Schapiro, B., eds. (1986). *Narcissism and the Text: Studies in Literature and the Psychology of Self.* New York: New York University Press.

Levenson, R. (1984). Intimacy, autonomy and gender: developmental differences and their reflection in adult relationships. *Journal of the American Academy of Psychoanalysis* 12:529–544.

Leverenz, D. (1991). The last real man in America: from Natty Bumppo to Batman. *American Literary History* 3:753–781.

Levinson, B., dir. (1994). *Disclosure.* Film. Warner Brothers.

Liem, J. (1992). *Need for power in women sexually abused as children.* Paper presented at conference on Trauma and its Sociocultural Context, Boston, MA, December.

Light, A. (1984). Returning to Manderley—romance fiction, female sexuality and class. *Feminist Review* 16:7–25.

Lisak, D. (1991). Sexual aggression, masculinity, and fathers. *Signs* 16:238–262.

————— (1992). *Gender development and sexual abuse in the lives of men.* Paper presented at conference on Trauma and its Sociocultural Context, Boston, MA, December.

Livingston, J., dir. (1991). *Paris is Burning.* Film. Off-White Productions.

Loewald, H. (1980). *Papers in Psychoanalysis.* New Haven, CT: Yale University Press.

Lusted, D. (1991). The glut of the personality. In *Stardom. Industry of Desire*, ed. C. Gledhill, pp. 251–258. London and New York: Routledge.

Lynch, D., dir. (1970). *The Grandmother.* Film.

————— (1977). *Eraserhead.* Film. Columbia Pictures.

————— (1980). *The Elephant Man.* Film. Paramount.

————— (1986). *Blue Velvet.* Film. De Laurentis.

————— (1990). *Wild at Heart.* Film. Samuel Goldwyn.

————— (1992). *Twin Peaks: Fire Walk With Me.* Film. New Line Cinema.

Lyne, A., dir. (1987). *Fatal Attraction.* Film. Paramount.

Lyons-Ruth, K. (1991). Rapprochement or approchement: Mahler's theory reconsidered from the vantage point of recent research on early attachment relationships. *Psychoanalytic Psychology* 8:1–23.

Lyotard, J.-F. (1984). *The Postmodern Condition: A Report on Knowledge.* Minneapolis: University of Minnesota Press.

Madonna (1983a). *Madonna.* CD. Sire.

————— (1983b). *Burning Up*, dir. S. Barron. Video.

————— (1984a). *Lucky Star*, dir. A. Pierson. Video. On *The Immaculate Collection*, Warner Reprise, 1990.

————— (1984b). *Like a Virgin*, dir. M. Lambert. Video. On *The Immaculate Collection*, Warner Reprise, 1990.

————— (1984c). *Like a Virgin.* CD. Sire.

————— (1985). *Material Girl*, dir. M. Lambert. Video. On *The Immaculate Collection*, Warner Reprise, 1990.

————— (1986a). *Open Your Heart*, dir. J.-B. Mondino. Video. On *The Immaculate Collection*, Warner Reprise, 1990.

————— (1986b). *Papa Don't Preach*, dir. J. Foley. Video. On *The Immaculate Collection*, Warner Reprise, 1990.

————— (1989a). *Like a Prayer*, dir. M. Lambert. Video. On *The Immaculate Collection*, Warner Reprise, 1990.

————— (1989b). *Like a Prayer.* CD. Sire.

———— (1989c). Oh Father, dir. D. Fincher. Video. On The Immaculate Collection, Warner Reprise, 1990.

———— (1990a). Justify My Love, dir. J.-B. Mondino. Video. Warner Reprise.

———— (1990b). I'm Breathless: Music from and Inspired by Dick Tracy. CD. Sire.

———— (1992a). Erotica, dir. F. Barron. Video. Maverick/Sire/Warner Brothers Records.

———— (1992b). Sex. New York: Warner Books.

Madonna, and Bray, S. (1989). Express Yourself. Single. Sire.

Mahler, M., Pine, F., and Bergman, A. (1975). The Psychological Birth of the Human Infant. New York: Basic Books.

Marsh, D. (1985). Girls can't do what the guys do: Madonna's physical attraction. In The First Rock & Roll Confidential Report, ed. D. Marsh, pp. 159–167. New York: Pantheon.

Martin, B. (1994). Sexualities without genders and other queer utopias. Diacritics 24:104–121.

———— (1996). Femininity Played Straight. The Significance of Being Lesbian. New York and London: Routledge, 1996.

Martin, B., and Mohanty, C. (1986). Feminist politics: What's home got to do with it? In Feminist Studies/Critical Studies, ed. T. de Lauretis, pp. 191–212. Bloomington: Indiana University Press.

Maxfield, J. F. (1989). "Now it's dark": the child's dream in David Lynch's Blue Velvet. Post Script 8:2–17.

May, E. T. (1988). Homeward Bound. American Families in the Cold War Era. New York: Basic Books.

May, R. (1986). Concerning a psychoanalytic view of maleness. Psychoanalytic Review 73(4):175–193.

Mayer, E. L. (1985). "Everybody must be just like me": observations on female castration anxiety. International Journal of Psycho-Analysis 66:331–347.

———— (1995). The phallic castration complex and primary femininity: paired developmental lines toward female gender identity. Journal of the American Psychoanalytic Association 43:17–38.

McClary, S. (1990). Living to tell: Madonna's resurrection of the fleshly. Genders 7:1–21.

McDougall, J. (1980). A Plea for a Measure of Abnormality. New York: International Universities Press.

McNay, L. (1992). Foucault and Feminism: Power, Gender and the Self. Cambridge: Polity.

Miller, J. B., Jordan, J., Kaplan, A., et al. (1991). Women's Growth in Connection. New York: Guilford.

Miller, N. K. (1986). Changing the subject: authorship, writing, and the reader. In *Feminist Studies/Critical Studies*, ed. T. de Lauretis, pp. 102–120. Bloomington: Indiana University Press.

Mitchell, J., and Rose, J. (1985). Introductions I and II. In J. Lacan, *Feminine Sexuality*, ed. J. Mitchell and J. Rose, pp. 1–57. New York: Norton.

Mitchell, S. A. (1988). *Relational Concepts in Psychoanalysis*. Boston: Harvard University Press.

———— (1993). *Hope and Dread in Psychoanalysis*. New York: Basic Books.

Modleski, T. (1982). *Loving with a Vengeance: Mass-Produced Fantasies for Women*. New York: Routledge, 1990.

———— (1986a). Feminism and the power of interpretation. In *Feminist Studies/Critical Studies*, ed. T. de Lauretis, pp. 121–138. Bloomington: Indiana University Press.

———— (1986b). Introduction. In *Studies in Entertainment*, ed. T. Modleski, pp. ix–xix. Bloomington and Indianapolis: Indiana University Press.

———— (1991). *Feminism without Women*. New York and London: Routledge.

Moraga, C. (1986). From a long line of vendidas: chicanas and feminism. In *Feminist Studies/Critical Studies*, ed. T. de Lauretis, pp. 173–190. Bloomington: Indiana University Press.

Moraga, C., and Anzaldúa, G., eds. (1983). *This Bridge Called My Back: Writings by Radical Women of Color*. New York: Kitchen Table Press.

Morley, D. (1980). Texts, readers, subjects. In *Culture, Media, Language: Working Papers in Cultural Studies, 1972–9*, ed. S. Hall, D. Hobson, A. Lowe, and P. Willis, pp. 163–173. London: Hutchinson.

Morrison, T. (1987). *Beloved*. New York: Knopf.

Mulvey, L. (1975). Visual pleasure and narrative cinema. *Screen* 16:6–18.

Musto, M. (1990). Interview. In *Madonna: Behind the American Dream*, dir. N. Haggar. BBC Omnibus Series, first broadcast in Great Britain, December 7.

Naylor, G., and Morrison, T. (1985). A conversation. *Southern Review* 21:567–593.

Neale, S. (1983). Masculinity as spectacle. *Screen* 24:2–16.

Nicholson, L. J., ed. (1990). *Feminism/Postmodernism*. New York and London: Routledge.

———— (1992). Feminism and the politics of postmodernism. *Boundary 2* 19:53–69.

Norris, C. (1987). *Derrida*. Cambridge, MA: Harvard University Press.

Norwood, R. (1985). *Women Who Love Too Much*. Los Angeles: J. B. Tarcher.

O'Connor, N., and Ryan, R. (1993). *Wild Desires and Mistaken Identities. Lesbianism and Psychoanalysis*. London: Virago.

Olsen, T. (1978). *Silences*. New York: Delacorte.

Orbison, R. (1963). *In Dreams*. Song. Milwaukee, WI: Hal Leonard.

Ou, T. Y. (1996). *Are abusive men different? And can we predict their behavior?* Honors thesis. Harvard-Radcliffe College, Cambridge, MA.

Pareles, J. (1990). On the edge of the permissible: Madonna's evolving persona. *New York Times,* June 11, pp. C11–C12.

Paretsky, S. (1982). *Indemnity Only.* New York: Ballantine.

——— (1987). *Bitter Medicine.* New York: Ballantine.

——— (1988). *Blood Shot.* New York: Dell.

Parker, R. B. (1980). *Looking for Rachel Wallace.* New York: Dell.

——— (1982). *A Savage Place.* New York: Dell.

Patton, C. (1993). Embodying subaltern memory: kinesthesia and the problematics of gender and race. In *The Madonna Connection,* ed. C. Schwichtenberg, pp. 81–105. Boulder: Westview.

Pellow, C. K. (1990). *Blue Velvet* once more. *Literature Film Quarterly* 18:173–178.

Penley, C. (1992). Feminism, psychoanalysis, and the study of popular culture. In *Cultural Studies,* ed. L. Grossberg, C. Nelson, and P. Treichler, pp. 479–500. New York and London: Routledge.

Penley, C., and Willis, S. (1988). Editorial: male trouble. *Camera Obscura* 17:4–5.

Person, E., and Ovesey, L. (1978). Transvestism: new perspectives. *Journal of the American Academy of Psychoanalysis* 6:301–323.

Pfeil, F. (1995). *White Guys. Studies in Postmodern Domination and Difference.* London: Verso.

Phillips, A. (1993). *On Kissing, Tickling, and Being Bored.* Cambridge, MA: Harvard University Press.

Pizer, S. (1992). The negotiation of paradox in the analytic patient. *Psychoanalytic Dialogues* 2:215–240.

Pollack, W. S. (1995a). No man is an island: toward a new psychoanalytic psychology of men. In *A New Psychology of Men,* ed. R. F. Levant and W. S. Pollack, pp. 33–67. New York: Basic Books.

——— (1995b). Deconstructing dis-identification: rethinking psychoanalytic concepts of male development. *Psychoanalysis and Psychotherapy* 12:30–45.

Powers, J. (1987). Bleak chic. *American Film* 12:46–51.

Pratt, M. B. (1984). Identity: skin blood heart. In *Yours in Struggle: Three Feminist Perspectives on Anti-Semitism and Racism,* ed. E. Bulkin, M. B. Pratt, and B. Smith, pp. 11–63. Brooklyn, NY: Long Haul.

Rabine, L. W. (1988). A feminist politics of non-identity. *Feminist Studies* 14:11–31.

Radway, J. (1984). *Reading the Romance. Women, Patriarchy, and Popular Culture.* Chapel Hill and London: University of North Carolina Press.

Ragland-Sullivan, E. (1987). *Jacques Lacan and the Philosophy of Psychoanalysis.* Urbana and Chicago: University of Illinois Press.

Raphael, A. (1996). *Grrrls. Viva Rock Divas.* New York: St. Martin's Griffin.

Reddy, M. T. (1988). *Sisters in Crime: Feminism and the Mystery Novel.* New York: Continuum.

Rivera, M. (1989). Linking the psychological and the social: feminism, poststructuralism, and multiple personality. *Dissociation* 2:24–31.

Rose, J. (1986). *Sexuality in the Field of Vision.* London: Verso.

Ross, J. M. (1994). *What Men Want.* Cambridge, MA: Harvard University Press.

Russell, C., dir. (1996). *Eraser.* Film. Warner Brothers.

Rutherford, J. (1988). Who's that man? In *Male Order. Unwrapping Masculinity*, ed. R. Chapman and J. Rutherford, pp. 21–67. London: Lawrence and Wishart.

Sandoval, C. (1991). U.S. third world feminism: the theory and method of oppositional consciousness in the postmodern world. *Genders* 10:1–24.

Sante, L. (1990). Unlike a virgin. *New Republic*, August, pp. 25–29.

Sarup, M. (1993). *An Introductory Guide to Post-Structuralism and Postmodernism*, 2nd ed. Athens, GA: University of Georgia Press.

Schifrin, M. (1990). A brain for sin and a bod for business. *Forbes*, October 1, pp. 162–166.

Schlesinger, J., dir. (1969). *Midnight Cowboy.* Film. United Artists.

Schwartz, D. (1992). Commentary on Jessica Benjamin's "Father and daughter: identification with difference—a contribution to gender heterodoxy." *Psychoanalytic Dialogues* 2:411–416.

Schwichtenberg, C., ed. (1993a). *The Madonna Connection.* Boulder, CO: Westview.

———— (1993b). Madonna's postmodern feminism: bringing the margins to the center. In *The Madonna Connection*, ed. C. Schwichtenberg, pp. 129–145. Boulder, CO: Westview.

Scott, R., dir. (1991). *Thelma and Louise.* Film. United International Pictures/MGM/Pathe Entertainment.

Scott, R. B. (1993). Images of race and religion in Madonna's video *Like a Prayer*: prayer and praise. In *The Madonna Connection*, ed. C. Schwichtenberg, pp. 57–77. Boulder, CO: Westview.

Segal, L. (1990). *Slow Motion.* London: Virago.

Seidelman, S., dir. (1985). *Desperately Seeking Susan.* Orion.

Seidler, V. J. (1994). *Unreasonable Men. Masculinity and Social Theory.* New York and London: Routledge.

Sessums, K. (1990). White heat. *Vanity Fair*, April, pp. 142–148, 208–214.

Sexton, A., ed. (1993). *Desperately Seeking Madonna.* New York: Dell.

Shattuc, J. (1992). Postmodern misogyny in *Blue Velvet*. *Genders* 13:73–89.

Silverman, K. (1980). Masochism and subjectivity. *Framework* 12:2–9.

———— (1988). Masochism and male subjectivity. *Camera Obscura* 17:31–66.

———— (1992). *Male Subjectivity at the Margins*. New York: Routledge.

———— (1996). *The Threshold of the Visible World*. New York and London: Routledge.

Simon, J. (1986). Neat trick. *National Review*, November 7, pp. 54,56.

Skow, J. (1985). Madonna rocks the land. *Time*, May 27, pp. 74–77.

Smith, B., ed. (1984). *Home Girls: A Black Feminist Anthology*. New York: Kitchen Table.

Smith, P. (1988a). *Discerning the Subject*. Minneapolis: University of Minnesota Press.

———— (1988b). Vas. *Camera Obscura* 17:89–111.

Snitow, A. B. (1979). Mass market romance: pornography for women is different. *Radical History Review* 20:141–163.

Spelman, E. V. (1988). *Inessential Woman. Problems of Exclusion in Feminist Thought*. Boston: Beacon.

Sprengnether, M. (1990). *The Spectral Mother*. Ithaca: Cornell University Press.

———— (1995). Reading Freud's life. *American Imago* 52:9–54.

Stacey, J. (1989). Desperately seeking difference. In *The Female Gaze*, ed. L. Gamman and M. Marshment, pp. 112–129. Seattle, WA: Real Comet.

Stern, D. N. (1985). *The Interpersonal World of the Infant*. New York: Basic Books.

Stoller, R. (1964). A contribution to the study of gender identity. *International Journal of Psycho-Analysis* 45:220–226.

———— (1965). The sense of maleness. *Psychoanalytic Quarterly* 34:207–218.

———— (1968). *Sex and Gender: On the Development of Masculinity and Femininity.* New York: Science House.

———— (1975). *Perversion—The Erotic Form of Hatred*. New York: Pantheon.

———— (1976a). *Sex and Gender. Vol. 2: The Transsexual Experiment*. New York: Jason Aronson.

———— (1976b). Primary femininity. In *Female Psychology*, ed. H. P. Blum, pp. 59–78. New York: International Universities Press.

———— (1985). *Presentations of Gender*. New Haven, CT: Yale University Press.

Studlar, G. (1985). Masochism and the perverse pleasures of the cinema. In *Movies and Methods*, Vol. 2, ed. B. Nichols, pp. 602–621. Berkeley: University of California Press.

Surrey, J. (1985). Self-in-relation: a theory of women's development. *Work in Progress*. Wellesley, MA: Wellesley College, Stone Center for Developmental Services and Studies.

Sweetnam, A. (1996). The changing contexts of gender: between fixed and fluid experience. *Psychoanalytic Dialogues* 6:437–459.

Tannen, D. (1990). *You Just Don't Understand. Women and Men in Conversation*. New York: Morrow.

Thompson, C. L. (1995). Self-definition by opposition: a consequence of minority status. *Psychoanalytic Psychology* 12:533–545.

Thurston, C. (1987). *The Romance Revolution. Erotic Novels for Women and the Quest for a New Sexual Identity.* Urbana and Chicago: University of Illinois Press.

Tompkins, J. (1992). *West of Everything: The Inner Life of Westerns.* New York: Oxford University Press.

Tyson, P. (1982). A developmental line of gender identity, gender role, and choice of love object. *Journal of the American Psychoanalytic Association* 30:61–86.

Verhoeven, P., dir. (1992). *Basic Instinct.* Film. CarolCo.

Veruca Salt (1994). *American Thighs.* CD. Geffen Records.

Walkerdine, V. (1986). Video replay: families, films, and fantasy. In *Formations of Fantasy*, ed. V. Burgin, J. Donald, and C. Kaplan, pp. 167–199. London: Methuen.

Walser, R. (1993). *Running with the Devil: Power, Gender, and Madness in Heavy Metal Music.* Middletown, CT: Wesleyan University Press.

Walters, S. D. (1996). From here to queer: radical feminism, postmodernism, and the lesbian menace (or, why can't a woman be more like a fag?). *Signs* 21:830–869.

Ward, T. (1985). Opaque object of desire. *Village Voice*, January 8, p. 55.

Waugh, P. (1989). *Feminine Fictions: Revisiting the Postmodern.* New York and London: Routledge.

Wayne, B., and Morris, L. (1963). *Blue Velvet.* Song. Los Angeles: Polygram Music.

Weir, A. (1995). Toward a model of self-identity: Habermas and Kristeva. In *Feminists Read Habermas*, ed. J. Meehan, pp. 263–282. New York and London: Routledge.

——— (1996). *Sacrificial Logics.* New York and London: Routledge.

Whitebook, J. (1992). Reflections on the autonomous individual and the decentered subject. *American Imago* 49:97–116.

——— (1995). *Perversion and Utopia. A Study in Psychoanalysis and Critical Theory.* Cambridge, MA and London: M.I.T. Press.

Williams, P. (1991). *The Alchemy of Race and Rights.* Cambridge, MA: Harvard University Press.

——— (1995). *The Rooster's Egg. On the Persistence of Prejudice.* Cambridge, MA: Harvard University Press.

Williamson, J. (1985). The making of a material girl. *New Socialist*, October, pp. 46–47.

——— (1986). Woman is an island. Femininity and colonization. In *Studies in Entertainment: Critical Approaches to Mass Culture*, ed. T. Modleski, pp. 99–118. Bloomington: Indiana University Press.

Winnicott, D. W. (1965a). The capacity to be alone. In *The Maturational Processes and the Facilitating Environment*, pp. 29–36. Madison, CT: International Universities Press.

——— (1965b). Ego distortion in terms of true and false self. In *The Maturational Processes and the Facilitating Environment*, pp. 140–152. Madison, CT: International Universities Press.

——— (1971). The use of an object and relating through identifications. In *Playing and Reality*. London: Tavistock, 1974.

——— (1974). *Playing and Reality*. London: Tavistock.

Wolf, E. S. (1980). On the developmental line of selfobject relations. In *Advances in Self Psychology*, ed. A. Goldberg, pp. 117–130. New York: International Universities Press.

Woodiwiss, K. E. (1972). *The Flame and the Flower*. New York: Avon.

Wyatt, J. (1995). On not being La Malinche: border negotiations of gender in Sandra Cisneros's "Never Marry a Mexican" and "Woman Hollering Creek." *Tulsa Studies in Women's Literature* 14:243–271.

Young-Bruehl, E. (1994). What theories women want. *American Imago* 51:373–396.

Index

ABOUT THE AUTHOR

Lynne Layton has a Ph.D. in Comparative Literature from Washington University and a Ph.D. in Clinical Psychology from Boston University. She is Assistant Clinical Professor of Psychology at Harvard Medical School and supervises residents at Beth Israel Deaconess Medical Center. She teaches popular culture and psychoanalysis and culture for the Committee on Degrees in Social Studies at Harvard University and also is on the faculty at the Massachusetts Institute for Psychoanalysis. With Barbara Schapiro, she is the coeditor of *Narcissism and the Text: Studies in Literature and the Psychology of Self*; and, with Susan Fairfield and Carolyn Stack, she is coeditor of *Bringing the Plague: Toward a Postmodern Psychoanalysis*. Dr. Layton is editor of the journal *Psychoanalysis, Culture & Society* and practices psychoanalysis and psychotherapy in Brookline, Massachusetts.